Contracting for Public Value

Contracting for Public Value

New Thinking for More Effective, Accountable, and Sustainable Public Service Contracts

CAROLYN J. HEINRICH

DEANNA MALATESTA

ELEANOR CARTER

MICHAEL GIBSON

NIGEL BALL

OXFORD
UNIVERSITY PRESS

OXFORD
UNIVERSITY PRESS

Oxford University Press is a department of the University of Oxford.
It furthers the University's objective of excellence in research, scholarship,
and education by publishing worldwide. Oxford is a registered trade mark of
Oxford University Press in the UK and in certain other countries.

Published in the United States of America by Oxford University Press
198 Madison Avenue, New York, NY 10016, United States of America.

Library of Congress Cataloging-in-Publication Data
Names: Heinrich, Carolyn J. author | Malatesta, Deanna author |
Carter, Eleanor, Dr. author | Gibson, Michael (Of Blavatnik School of
Government) author | Ball, Nigel (Of University of the Arts London) author
Title: Contracting for public value : new thinking for more effective,
accountable, and sustainable public service contracts / Carolyn J.
Heinrich, Deanna Malatesta, Eleanor Carter, Michael Gibson, Nigel Ball.
Description: New York, NY : Oxford University Press, [2026] |
Includes bibliographical references. |
Identifiers: LCCN 2025049333 (print) | LCCN 2025049334 (ebook) |
ISBN 9780197763124 hardback | ISBN 9780197763148 epub |
ISBN 9780197763155 ebook other
Subjects: LCSH: Public-private sector cooperation | Public contracts
Classification: LCC HD3871 .H45 2026 (print) | LCC HD3871 (ebook) |
DDC 658/.046—dc23/eng/20260126
LC record available at https://lccn.loc.gov/2025049333
LC ebook record available at https://lccn.loc.gov/2025049334

DOI: 10.1093/9780197763155.001.0001

The manufacturer's authorized representative in the EU for product safety is
Oxford University Press España S.A. of Parque Empresarial San Fernando de Henares,
Avenida de Castilla, 2 – 28830 Madrid (www.oup.es/en or product.safety@oup.com).
OUP España S.A. also acts as importer into Spain of products made by the manufacturer.

CONTENTS

LIST OF FIGURES, TABLES AND BOXES

FIGURES

TABLES

BOXES

1

Crafting Public-Private Partnerships that Champion What is Good for and Valued by the Public

INTRODUCTION

Enthusiasm for partnerships among government, the private sector, and civil society actors—known as public-private partnerships (PPPs)—has been increasing for decades, and today, PPPs are key to public services delivery throughout the world. Fiscal constraints on government funding for public services have spurred political and public interest in PPPs as a means to leverage private sector finance and expertise, potentially expanding the reach, efficiency, and effectiveness of government services (Osborne 2000). Private sector leaders have likewise recognized the importance of business, government, and nonprofits working together "synergistically to create the most value for society" (Ashoka 2013). This has prompted critical attention to the structure, management, effectiveness, and accountability of PPPs in an expanding range of public service areas.

Although there is no single, international definition used to characterize the wide variety of PPPs, they typically consist of a long-term arrangement between public and private sector entities for providing

Contracting for Public Value. Carolyn J. Heinrich et al., Oxford University Press.
DOI: 10.1093/9780197763155.003.0001

a public product or service, where the partners share financial and operational risks and management responsibilities (World Bank Public-Private Partnership Legal Resource Center).[1] Scholars and practitioners also refer to these arrangements by various labels, including cross-sector partnerships, cross-sector alliances, and multisector alliances. Some form of contractual agreement for delivering public goods or services typically undergirds a PPP, while the relationships between the partners serve as scaffolding.[2] The academic and practice literatures on PPPs highlight the many opportunities they offer for improving public services delivery,[3] such as combining public and private sector capabilities to foster innovation and more efficient use of public resources. PPPs aim to promote long-term institutional cooperation through multisector partnerships, potentially enhancing civil society and community engagement as well (Hodge and Greve 2007). In fact, the services provided through PPPs frequently involve the users as co-producers (Thomas et al. 2015).

While nation-states implement a variety of welfare state models and structures to address the social service needs of their citizens in accordance with their public values, research suggests that integrating PPPs into social services delivery is compatible with, and complements, most existing welfare state frameworks (Chiapello and Knoll 2020). A prominent example is the convening by the World Health Organization (WHO) (in November 2002) that encouraged the adoption of PPPs for

1. https://ppp.worldbank.org/public-private-partnership/about-us/about-public-private-partnerships

2. Despite the widespread adoption of PPPs across all forms of government, they remain, to an extent, elusive (Hodge et al. 2010). Most notably, differentiating PPPs from other governance arrangements has been challenging. Indeed, there are numerous definitions of PPPs in public administration literature, none of which has become fully institutionalized with scholars. Given the nature of our analytical discussion below, we follow the Rybnicek et al. (2020) definition: "cooperative arrangements between public and private partners to share resources, risks, responsibilities, and rewards to mutually gain social, economic, or environmental objectives" (176). This definition highlights the broad nature of PPPs but also emphasizes that cooperation is foundational.

3. The large majority of what is produced by the public sector through PPPs—whether directly provided by governments, for-profit, or nonprofit organizations—consists of services rather than products (Thomas et al. 2015). We acknowledge, however, that some scholars use "products" as an umbrella term to include both goods and services (e.g., Brown et al. 2013, 7n2). In this book, we clarify the distinction when relevant.

improving the delivery of health and social welfare services to some of the world's poorest and most vulnerable populations. PPPs such as those funded by the Bill and Melinda Gates Foundation became a key conduit for the delivery of services and aid to those affected by HIV/AIDS, malaria, and tuberculosis, as well as others with a multitude of unmet health needs (Barr 2007). Social Impact Bonds (SIBs) have also emerged as a prevalent form of PPP (approximately 300 worldwide by the end of 2024),[4] involving innovative financing mechanisms in which private investors fund social programs with the expectation of returns contingent on achieving specific, predefined social outcomes.[5]

Yet headlines such as "History RePPPeated II: Why Public-Private Partnerships Are Not the Solution" and "From the Bench to the Bush: The Children's Vaccine Initiative and Troubled Public-Private Partnerships for Health" also convey how PPPs are fraught with challenges and failure (Blavot et al. 2022; Janik 2014). Research suggests that at least half of PPP alliances experience conflict, and they terminate prematurely or unexpectedly at a rate of somewhere between 30–50% (Ariño and de la Torre 1998; Das and Teng 2000; Bakker et al. 2016). The Children's Vaccine Initiative (CVI) was formed in 1990 among the WHO, the Rockefeller Foundation, the United Nations Children's Fund (UNICEF), the United Nations Development Program (UNDP), and the World Bank Group, with the goal of developing a "magic bullet" vaccine to eradicate childhood diseases through collaboration among industry and public health agency partners. The vaccine program was hindered, however, by conflict among the partners and early financial difficulties. As cooperation and communication dissipated, the PPP fell apart in 1999 without achieving its larger goals. An analysis of the PPP's downfall suggested that underfunding—a problem that PPPs are often created to resolve—constrained the program in developing the capacities and tools required to execute its mission, which in turn undercut donor confidence and led to a further rescinding of PPP resources (Janik 2014).

4. https://golab.bsg.ox.ac.uk/knowledge-bank/indigo/impact-bond-dataset-v2/

5. Distinguishing SIBs as a form of PPP underscores their role in innovative public financing and highlights the evolving landscape of how governments and private entities collaborate to address complex societal challenges (Cooper et al. 2016; Chiapello and Knoll 2020).

The high costs of PPP failure have contributed to calls for curtailing their use. Critics assert that PPPs are more likely to drain public resources than to augment them, often falling short in serving the public interest (Böll Stiftung 2018). They argue that PPPs redirect accountability from citizens to shareholders, undermining democratic governance while increasing the risks borne by the state (Blavot et al. 2022), the ultimate guarantor of public interest and fiscal responsibility (Jørgensen and Bozeman 2007; Warner 2013). Debate also persists over whether market-based accountability—premised on the notion that private providers will be more responsive to market financial signals and thereby promote fiscal discipline and efficiency in services delivery—has increased or obscured accountability to the public in PPPs (Hodge and Greve 2016). The public recognizes that when a PPP dissolves, the government retains responsibility for accountability to legislative bodies, taxpayers, and the individuals who rely on public services for their well-being (Heinrich and Choi 2006; Afzal and Considine 2014). In fact, research on public perceptions of PPPs indicates a growing awareness that these partnerships do not always align with the public interest (Boyer et al. 2016; Chen et al. 2013). Boyer et al. (2018) found that promoting interactive engagement is critical to ensuring that these projects align with public priorities, which also fosters trust essential to the long-term sustainability and legitimacy of PPPs.

CORE CONTRIBUTIONS OF THIS BOOK

This book takes on the urgent topic of how PPPs can be better designed and managed to produce more value for the public in social services delivery. PPPs are often formed in contexts where a consensus on what constitutes public value—that is, what is good for and valued by the public (Alford and O'Flynn 2009; Benington and Moore 2011; Williams and Shearer 2011; Bryson et al. 2014)—is evolving or incomplete. In fact, a large body of research deliberates the conceptualization of "public value," recognizing that it is elaborate and multifaceted and thereby invites alternative approaches to qualitatively discerning or empirically operationalizing it (Moore 1995, 2013; Bozeman 2007;

Bryson et al. 2015). Looking to the literature or to articulations of public value in the texts of constitutions, legislation, policy proposals, or contracts, dimensions of public value that are frequently centered in these documents include efficiency, effectiveness, equity, responsiveness, accountability, justice, fairness, and more. In many contexts, these values may be competing or in conflict, requiring the parties engaged in public services delivery to assign priority to the values (normatively) as they execute the work dynamically. We illustrate how this plays out in two major case studies of PPPs in this book, one that failed and one that is on a path toward success.

In particular, we focus on how public value is embedded in contractual provisions and relationships that form PPPs, and how their design, management, cultivation, and evolution can in turn contribute to the achievement of desired public outcomes. When PPPs fail to deliver or to facilitate the institutional collaboration required to stay centered on achieving public value, major, negative consequences for the public often ensue. At the outset, institutional cooperation and processes are needed to forge agreement on public values, where the public and private partners define the collectively valued outcomes, or the "public value," they intend to create. This typically begins with the formal contractual agreement that is at the core of every PPP and that specifies the goals, obligations, and terms and conditions of the public-private collaboration, including how the partners will manage the financial and operational risks between them throughout the life of the partnership. With outcomes-based contracts increasingly common in 21st-century social services delivery, the contracting parties also typically operationalize public value through the specification of performance measures, standards, and schedules (i.e., how outcomes will be assessed according to public value criteria).

We delve deeply into the formal contractual infrastructure in our two case study PPPs and examine rich data on their performance configurations, tools, and results in Chapters 2, 3, and 4. It has long been acknowledged that it is rarely possible to specify complete formal contractual arrangements among the parties to a PPP that clearly articulate the partner roles and responsibilities and how they will address future events and contingencies that affect PPP operations and outcomes (cost-sharing provisions, stipulations for renegotiation, etc.) (Hart and Moore 1988). This has led to a widening embrace of a new form of contractual arrangement known as the "formal-relational contract." The formal-relational contract, as described in depth by Frydlinger and colleagues (2021) and Frydlinger and Hart (2023) and further defined in Chapter 2, entails the specification of mutual goals and governance structures in the context of a legally enforceable contract, while also fostering trust and cooperation at the outset to provide a foundation for keeping the contracting parties' interests aligned over time. The emerging knowledge base on formal-relational contracts suggests that they may be better suited to the complex, multiparty, longer-term relationships that are characteristic of many PPPs. In contrast, time-limited, transactional relationships may be just as well-served by a traditional formal contract. With an eye on the central goal of increasing public value, we explore the potential of *formal-relational contracts* for improving the functioning, effectiveness, and sustainability of PPPs in the delivery of social services as a central question in this book.

In addition, performance management—setting performance goals for achieving public value, measuring performance, reporting the results to the public, and using the results to boost public outcomes—has been a key component of public sector reforms intended to promote and foster the creation of public value and to ensure accountability of PPPs. Kroll and Moynihan (2015, 191) point out that measuring performance alone can contribute to public value by generating normative pressures for public accountability, in which public value is "represented, recorded and communicated" to key stakeholders and the public. At the same time, they also argue that the most critical activity to increasing public value is the *purposeful* use of performance information in decision-making to improve public services and outcomes. In the context of PPPs and their broader roles for private actors, purposeful use of performance information requires commitment from top leaders and managers, organizational routines, forums (for data sharing), and other capacity supports, while it also benefits from goal clarity, prosocial motivations, and political and cultural support for constructive performance information use (Kroll and Moynihan 2015). We illuminate these public responsibilities and the challenges (and opportunities) that public and private managers face in upholding their obligations for accountability to the public by contrasting the formal performance regimes and use of performance information in our two case study PPPs in Chapter 5.

Recognizing the ubiquity of PPPs around the globe and their expanding roles in social services delivery, Chapter 6 brings together theory with our case evidence to offer recommendations to guide contracting for public value in future PPPs, where government is frequently a co-creator of public value and no longer the sole institution with public value obligations (Jørgensen and Bozeman 2007). We contemplate institutional mechanisms and systemic changes for improving the governance and outcomes of PPPs and for maintaining a focus on public value throughout the life of a PPP, including reliance on relational governance configurations and other forms of social capital that facilitate and sustain collaboration (Frydlinger et al. 2021). The concluding chapter also addresses the legal, financial, political, and administrative responsibilities that public managers attend to (in collaboration with their community and private sector partners) in serving the public interest and citizen needs through PPPs (Dubnick and Frederickson 2010; Bryson et al. 2014). We highlight how systemic changes such as increased recognition of the legal enforceability of relational infrastructure and greater transparency in performance management regimes could contribute to improved outcomes and value for the public.

Before outlining the case evidence at the center of our investigation and providing a more detailed overview of how this book unfolds, we first describe the state of knowledge in this field and how our work aims to build on and advance key contributions made in related scholarly works on contracting in multisector alliances.

STATE OF KNOWLEDGE ON CONTRACTING IN PPPs AND INTENDED ADVANCES

In conventional procurement approaches for large-scale projects or initiatives, scoping and negotiation processes frequently descend into prolonged exercises of power and authority, with the resulting compromises or contract specifications reflecting the relative influence of the negotiating parties. Oftentimes, the agreements that emerge are lengthy formal contracts tailored more for legal professionals than for the stakeholders who will assume responsibility for their implementation. In delineating roles and responsibilities, these contracts typically focus on pricing, risk mitigation, and contingency planning, and provisions framed in standardized, legal language frequently dominate the agreements. For instance, Gilo and Porat (2006) critiqued such boilerplate clauses and standardized contracts for disproportionately favoring the most experienced parties, at the expense of fostering more collaborative relationships aligned with public values. Similarly, Dannin (2011) identified concerning provisions in PPP contracts, such as clauses granting private contractors decision-making authority over public interest issues traditionally managed by public officials in systems of democratic accountability.

Regardless of the contract length and complexity, it is rarely feasible to comprehensively define the roles and responsibilities of partners or to fully specify the mechanisms for addressing future contingencies, such as cost-sharing arrangements or renegotiation provisions (Hart and Moore 1988). Within the bounds of limited information, finite time, and cognitive constraints on human decision-making (Simon 1957), contract drafters frequently rely on heuristics or decision-making shortcuts and underestimate the significance of perceived fairness in the arrangements that can lead to future conflicts or dissatisfaction. These difficulties are compounded by the intractable nature and inherent complexities of many of the multidimensional social services challenges that PPPs are formed to address, such as poverty, homelessness, and unemployment. These challenges necessitate longer-term strategies and adaptive approaches that can respond to shifting economic and social conditions and foster resilience and responsiveness among the partners and project stakeholders.

In this book, we build on the collective contributions of some key scholarly works that draw on theory to generate important insights, as well as provide valuable practical guidance for more effective PPP contracting in complex contexts. One of these works is Brown, Potoski, and Van Slyke's (2013) detailed case study on the United States (US)

Coast Guard's implementation of an innovative procurement system, in which they derive important propositions and distill practical lessons for navigating the intricacies of public-private collaboration. A number of scholars, including Frydlinger, Vitasek, Bergman, and Cummins (2021), draw on Nobel Laureate Oliver Hart's theories on incomplete contracting and residual decision rights to expand our understanding of how to structure contracts in ways that account for future uncertainties and promote sustainable and adaptive collaboration, such as by embedding relational norms into contract design. Below we provide a brief overview of key insights from these works and then summarize the ways we aim to extend their contributions.

Research by Brown, Potoski, and VanSlyke (2013) on *Complex Contracting* draws on the Prisoner's Dilemma (PD) framework to describe rules versus relationship-based approaches to contract design and management and the incentives they generate for "perfunctory" versus "consummate" behavior. As is well-established in the literature, complex contracts conventionally rely on a rules-based approach to overcome the problems of incomplete contracts by specifying a priori "exchange" type rules or the terms and stipulations necessary to reduce uncertainty, allocate authority for decision-making, and mediate conflicts. Alternatively, in a relationship-based approach, also elucidated by Frydlinger et al. (2021), the contracting parties regularly engage to keep interests aligned and identify opportunities for cooperation and mutually beneficial (versus short-sighted, self-interested) responses to emerging challenges. Brown et al. and Frydlinger et al. recognize the strengths and limitations of both approaches and theorize about how contract incentive structures can be designed to meld the best features of both and strike the right balance between the rigidity of formal approaches and the flexibility of relational ones (Frydlinger 2024).

Brown et al. (2013; 2018) explicate that the rules governing the exchange relationship should ideally be designed to promote and bolster cooperation between the contracting parties. This will be influenced by the nature of the exchange relationship between the parties and the extent to which they have a similar understanding of the rules and foster mutual trust through repeated interactions. Under the assumption that the intent is to form a longer-term exchange relationship, the idea is that the parties' desire to preserve their reputation and the reciprocal benefits of the partnership will discourage adversarial contract interactions. Brown et al. (2018) suggest three principles to guide the formulation of contract exchange and governance rules to support the success of PPPs: (1) promote the sharing of decision-making, risks, and rewards; (2) ensure clarity of responsibilities and lines of accountability, and (3) cultivate arenas for cooperation. They also point to the importance of transparency—making contract terms public—and ensuring that the contract rules and mechanisms for accountability are explicit, particularly given the powerful role of performance incentives and compensation in motivating the parties' behavior.

Similarly, the works of Vitasek (2010), Frydlinger et al. (2021), and Frydlinger (2024) have promoted a widening embrace of contracting processes that focus on shared goals and the cultivation of enduring relationships, for example, emphasizing the role of relational norms such as trust and reciprocity in aligning interests and incentives and fostering highly collaborative relationships. The importance of relational norms in sustaining relationships was argued by Macneil (1963), as well as by Dyer and Singh (1998a, 1998b), who advanced the "relational view," highlighting the importance of trust, shared goals, and complementary resources and the strategic value of fostering strong, collaborative partnerships. These insights continue to inform both academic research and practical strategies on organizational management and strategic alliances, including our own work on PPPs in this book.

Brown et al.'s applications of these theoretical advances have focused primarily on contracting for complex products or "mission-critical" goods in the public sector, and Frydlinger et al.'s (2021) work on formal-relational contracts has focused primarily on private sector (business-to-business) applications. Our work responds to the broadly recognized need for additional applications of this theorizing to better understand how complex, multiactor service contracts and relationships can be more effectively designed to generate public value in public services delivery, and how they unfold in practice over time and in varying contexts. For example, when is mutual understanding insufficient to ensure cooperative behavior, or in what circumstances is it unrealistic to expect a shared understanding or interpretation of the rules over the life of a PPP? When are the contracting parties more likely to forego self-interest and adapt to sustain cooperation, and to what extent does this depend on the reference points they start with (i.e., in regard to expected outcomes and points of comparison for the outcomes)? We also see room to improve our understanding of how politics and institutions (or the lack of institutional safeguards) can influence the contracting parties' intentions and decisions to sustain or exit from the collaboration. And how should the contracts incorporate relational norms in a way that increases the chances that they succeed, while simultaneously ensuring that they can still be legally enforced by the courts? We currently have a limited grasp of the legal enforceability of relational components of contracts and how their transparency and enforceability might be increased in PPPs.

In Box 1.1, we summarize how we build from these key prior works to advance our conceptual thinking and the practice of formal-relational contracting in the public sector, through the exposition and analysis of two contrasting PPP case studies (described below) that resulted in very different outcomes for the public.

Box 1.1

How This Book Builds on the Contributions of Prior Works

Contracting for Public Value aims to extend the contributions of key prior works in the following areas:

- **Focus on public value**
  - Prioritizing public value as a central outcome, expanding on the mutual benefit focus of the US Coast Guard Deepwater case (Brown et al. 2013), and emphasizing societal benefits such as equity, accountability, and public interest in PPP governance.

Continued

Continued

- Offering guidance on defining public value for a jurisdiction and identifying the most relevant contract features, clauses, and practices for increasing public value, while illuminating how common public value priorities are in PPPs.

- **Longitudinal analysis of contract relationships**
  - Responding to calls for a better understanding of the evolution of partnership dynamics over time by providing a temporal analysis that explores the development of partnership relationships and how perceptions of fairness influence contracting behaviors (Frydlinger et al. 2021; Frydlinger 2024) in the context of changes in political, economic, and organizational landscapes.

- **Relational governance focus**
  - Advancing the discussion of trust and cooperation by exploring how relational norms can be integrated into enforceable contracts (Frydlinger et al. 2021; Frydlinger and Hart 2023), specifically discussing how courts are defining and enforcing relational contracts and "good faith" provisions.

- **Tailoring for public-private partnerships**
  - Exploring the unique constraints of the public sector in achieving PPP success, including government institutions, procurement rules, political pressures, and public accountability.

- **Leveraging case study comparison**
  - Examining the generalizability of formal-relational contracts by providing a comparative analysis across two PPPs in distinct contexts and offering insights into varying

challenges, the social and political nuances of public services delivery, and public-sector constraints and accountability demands.

- Expounding on key ideas in prior works that lend themselves to comparison in our case studies, including alternative approaches to the distribution of decision-making authority, different levels of rigidity and flexibility in underlying formal agreements, and varying approaches to communication and performance management.
- Probing the relevance of specific governance and relationship rules proposed in prior studies to improve partner cooperation and sustain long-term relationships (Brown et al. 2013; Frydlinger et al. 2021) to evaluate the extent to which they are necessary or sufficient factors for PPP success in differing contexts.

CASE EVIDENCE IN THIS BOOK

In both conceptually illuminating how we can improve on contracting for public value in PPPs and practically understanding the challenges they reckon with as they evolve, we draw on case evidence from recent PPPs in the United States (US) and the United Kingdom (UK) that employed outcomes-based contracts in arranging for service provision to vulnerable populations. In the US, we focus in depth on a case study of a PPP that was formed between the State of Indiana, International Business Machines (IBM), and other partners to modernize Indiana's welfare system. In this PPP, an extensive formal agreement guided the PPP arrangements, yet the partners experienced intensive conflict and the collaboration and contractual relationship subsequently came to an acrimonious end. The PPP received considerable attention among politicians, news outlets, and academics, and the major partners ultimately entered the court system in a decade-long legal dispute. In the UK, we draw on case study data compiled by the Government Outcomes Lab

(GO Lab) of the University of Oxford on social outcomes contracts, including rich information about a PPP known as the Kirklees Better Outcomes Partnership (KBOP) and a longitudinal evaluation of the KBOP outcomes. In 2019, Kirklees Council in Yorkshire, UK revamped its approach to services delivery for homelessness prevention services in the form of a single five-year outcomes contract with the expectation of better achieving longer-term outcomes in the areas of well-being, accommodation, and education, training, and employment. Early outcome analyses have suggested that the PPP is performing above expectations, as defined in the PPP contract. These case studies (further detailed in Chapter 3) are significant in and of themselves because their failure or success has substantial effects on vulnerable populations that rely on the PPPs for essential services.

The case study data we utilize are rich and multilayered, including data from contractual documents, performance reports and other evaluation data, interviews with partners and stakeholders, correspondence internal to the PPPs, court filings and depositions, press accounts, and other information. Our analyses of these data are informed by multiple theoretical models that we introduce in Chapter 2 and apply in the case analyses in subsequent chapters, as we scrutinize both formal and informal aspects of the PPP relationships and explore the dynamics of the collaborations that influence decision-making among the partners and the PPP outcomes over time. We draw out evidence and insights for policymakers and public managers who deliberate the outsourcing of critical social services and craft complex multiparty PPPs, and we derive lessons on how public and private partners can make formal-relational contracts work in practice and sustain cooperation to achieve important public goals.

OVERVIEW OF THE BOOK

Chapter 2 of this book introduces the theories and conceptual distinctions among them that help to frame our thinking about how PPP contractual arrangements can be structured to create public value. We draw on theoretical developments concerning the governance of PPPs, including from New Public Management (NPM) and New Public Governance (NPG) theories, among others. We elicit insights from economic theories of contracting, such as transaction cost economics (TCE), and meld them with knowledge derived from game theory and behavioral psychology, which together inform our understanding about how formal and informal aspects of the contractual relationships can be configured or cultivated to support the effective functioning and durability of PPPs. We also consider legal theory and precedent that affect the interpretation and enforcement of contracts, which may depend on the courts' appraisal of a contract as transactional or relational. We importantly build on the seminal contributions of Frydlinger et al. (2019, 2021) and Frydlinger and Hart (2023) in this chapter, who describe the paradigm of a "formal-relational contract" and offer a set of guiding principles for developing the formal and informal structures that can scaffold and sustain the complex contractual relationships embodied in PPPs. We also describe how we selected the case studies and other case evidence presented in this book to illuminate both the theoretical discoveries and practical contributions of this work.

In Chapter 3, we present the key case studies that we feature in the book and describe who is collaborating in the PPPs and the short-term and longer-term goals defined by the partners. We elucidate the core relationships among the PPP actors and intermediaries, and how the primary work of the PPP is delegated, subcontracted, and shaped through the partnership structures (formal and informal). We consider overall where the contractual relationships lie on a spectrum from formal to relational, factoring in key aspects of their formal elements, such as delegation of authority, risk-sharing, and residual rights of control, as well as relational aspects such as trust, autonomy, and reciprocity that shape the partners' psychological engagement in the PPP. We also describe how the PPPs have defined the outcomes and impacts that reflect the goals of the PPP and the contractual infrastructure for performance evaluation (e.g., metrics, incentives, sanctions, and payout terms). In addition, we highlight important features of the case study settings—political, economic, social, and others—that motivate, facilitate, or constrain the evolution of the formal and informal relationships and outcomes of the PPPs over time.

The core of our theoretically-informed analysis that generates new insights and thinking about how to improve contracting for public value is expounded in Chapter 4. In this chapter, we illuminate the challenges and opportunities of the PPPs as we describe their progression and unfolding, drawing on the case study information and evidence introduced in Chapter 3. We examine in depth the formal contracts undergirding the PPPs, including their strengths and breaking points, as well as the relational structures that facilitate collaboration and mediate conflicts to sustain the PPPs. We also scrutinize the PPP performance and contract revisions and renegotiations over time, with attention to the PPP dynamics (formal and informal) that influence decisions to continue or exit the partnership. Our analysis also gives considerable attention to the contexts in which PPPs operate, including political, economic, and social factors and ethical issues that affect the risks and incentives the partners navigate in their interactions and efforts to achieve their collective goals.

Chapter 5 continues the in-depth analysis of PPPs with a focus on the outcomes (performance) of the PPPs we study, including how they relate to those of an "ideal" formal-relational contract as envisioned in recent conceptual thinking on this paradigm (e.g., Frydlinger and Hart's "guiding principles" for sustaining contractual relationships). In the case study of the US-based State of Indiana-IBM PPP, we investigate what led to the collapse of the PPP, drawing on the rich case study data and court proceedings that followed the demise of the partnership. Importantly, we assess the outcomes from the perspective of the Indiana citizens the PPP was intended to serve, and we consider whether this PPP could have been "saved" if it had been positioned differently on the formal to relational spectrum. In the UK case study of the Kirklees-KBOP PPP, we explore the status of this PPP in terms of its evolving social outcomes contract structures, relational dynamics, and challenges it continues to navigate, as well as the PPP outcomes to date for citizens.

In the final chapter of this book, we collate lessons drawn from both theory and practice (our cases) to highlight pivotal issues and challenges in contracting for public value. We organize the final discussion around four central themes and consider their implications for the future design and implementation of PPPs centered on public value. These include (1) championing public value in both *formal* and *informal* aspects of the PPP contract; (2) rethinking PPP governance and centering relationship building in the scaffolding of the PPP; (3) fortifying PPPs with effective institutional and accountability mechanisms; and (4) envisaging systems change for furthering long-term, public-private collaboration. We recognize that in reflecting on how future PPPs can be more effectively designed and managed to generate greater public value, we need to challenge the predominance of the traditional formal contract that has governed most PPPs and introduce new thinking about systems change to enhance the opportunities for and success of formal-relational contracting in PPPs. This might involve, for example, changing public procurement rules that constrain the formation of relational infrastructure at the outset of a PPP, or refining traditional approaches to ensuring legal enforceability of PPP contracts that can undermine a collaborative orientation and the cultivation of relational norms among the partners. Private partners may likewise need to come to the table with a willingness to concede changes in their conventions or expectations for contracting with the government, such as protections demanded for commercial sensitivity that limit transparency and accountability to the public. We conclude by offering recommendations that flow from the analysis and lessons discerned in the book for both practice and research on contracting for public value.

2

Contractual Pathways to Sustained Public-Private Partnership Collaboration and Success

"[C]ovenants without the sword are but words and of no strength to secure a man at all . . . [T]here must be some coercive power to compel men equally to the performance of their covenants . . ." (Hobbes 1651). Hobbes's philosophizing on covenants alleged that a contractual relationship without a strong-arm approach to compelling adherence to its terms could not be enforced nor deliver on its objectives. This line of reasoning is embedded in one of the key theories, transaction cost economics (TCE), that has long influenced thinking about the optimal design and governing principles of contracts, including in many public-private partnerships (PPPs) (Williamson 1979, 1981). The TCE logic, like principal-agent theory, begins with the assumption that contracting parties are guided by self-interest and that the parties will behave opportunistically when their goals or incentives do not align. TCE and principal-agent theory consider how different contract mechanisms, such as monitoring clauses, performance metrics, and penalties, can be employed to align incentives between the parties and achieve the desired efficiencies and outcomes (Sappington 1991).

Contracting for Public Value. Carolyn J. Heinrich et al., Oxford University Press. © Oxford University Press (2026).
DOI: 10.1093/9780197763155.003.0002

In addition to TCE and principal-agent theory, there are numerous other theories and intellectual perspectives that have influenced our contemporary understanding of PPPs (see brief synopses in Table 2.1). We begin by describing the formal aspects of a contract that configures a PPP, drawing on TCE, principal-agent theory, and other established bodies of theory that have guided the design and execution of formal contracting in PPPs. We next consider the informal or relational aspects of contracting and the public management theories that have influenced our thinking about how to incorporate relational norms, principles, and other informal structures into contract design and implementation to improve PPP functioning. We then bring the formal and relational together to discuss in greater depth the formal-relational contract and the theories and new lines of thinking that inform this model of contracting. This includes the dynamics of formal and relational elements in the contracting arrangements and how they might shape the progression of a PPP, its sustainability, and outcomes. Lastly, we also describe how our conceptual spectrum from formal to relational contracting informed our case study selection, and the contributions we intend to make in our case analysis of two high-profile PPPs, which differ in their contractual design and implementation along this spectrum.

THE FORMAL CONTRACT

A primary reason why parties choose to memorialize their understanding of the relationship in a **formal contract**—a written agreement that establishes the terms of the partnership and is enforceable under law—is so that they can access the legal system to adjudicate the relationship and remedy any harms in the event contract promises are not kept (see Box 2.1). The formal, legally enforceable contract that frequently scaffolds a PPP typically delineates the roles and responsibilities of the partners, the objectives and sequencing of the primary work, the financial terms and conditions of the partnership, and expectations for and measures of performance, and it also provides guidelines

Table 2.1 Theories that Influence our Contemporary Understanding of PPPs

Theory	Theory-Based Recommendations
Transaction Cost Economics	
TCE offers a framework for the "make or buy" decision, focusing on the costs of coordinating and managing economic exchanges. TCE suggests that the choice between in-house production and outsourcing hinges on a comparative analysis of transaction costs under different governance structures. Transaction costs encompass the costs associated with searching for, negotiating, and enforcing agreements between parties. TCE highlights the need to consider the allocation of responsibilities, risk-sharing mechanisms, and contractual arrangements to minimize transaction costs and ensure efficient outcomes.	The decision to enter into a PPP should be based on a thorough cost-benefit analysis, considering both the transaction costs (like monitoring and enforcement costs) and the expected benefits of the partnership. When specialized investments are necessary, the risk of opportunistic behavior in PPPs necessitates careful contract design with clear terms, responsibilities, and mechanisms for dispute resolution.

Principal-Agent Theory Principal-Agent theory explains why organizations enter into collaborative contracts, focusing on the dynamics and incentives between principals (organizations seeking specific services or outcomes) and agents (those tasked with executing these provisions). Contracts are expected to align the interests of both parties: principals define their expectations and performance standards, incentivizing agents to act in the principal's best interest. This approach addresses information asymmetry, as agents typically possess more task-specific knowledge. Contracts mitigate this by stipulating information sharing, reporting mechanisms, and performance monitoring, fostering transparency and enabling principals to effectively oversee the agents' actions.	Aligning the goals of the public and private sectors in PPPs can reduce agency costs. When both parties share common objectives, the likelihood of conflicts and the costs associated with resolving them decrease. Information asymmetry between the government and private entities can lead to agency problems in PPPs. The private entity may have more information about its actions and capabilities, which it might not fully disclose to the government. PPP contracts should include mechanisms for risk-sharing that align the interests of the principal and agent. This alignment ensures that both parties bear a portion of the risks and benefits, motivating the private entity to act in the best interest of the project.

Continued

Table 2.1 CONTINUED

Theory	Theory-Based Recommendations
Property Rights The study of property rights offers valuable perspectives for comprehending contracts and PPPs by analyzing the distribution and safeguarding of property rights. The property rights theory delves into the influence of property rights allocation and protection on economic behavior and outcomes. This theory aids in understanding the ownership and control of assets and resources involved in contracting and PPP arrangements. It addresses fundamental questions such as the holders of property rights, the process of assigning them, and their impact on decision-making, incentives, and the distribution of benefits and risks within contractual relationships.	Clearly defined ownership rights are crucial in PPPs. These rights determine who has the authority to make decisions in cases not specified in the contract. Granting residual control rights (rights to make decisions in unforeseen contingencies) to the party with the highest stake in performance leads to more efficient outcomes. In PPPs, this suggests that the party most affected by performance variations should have greater decision-making authority. The allocation of risks affects investment decisions. Parties are more likely to invest when they are protected from risks they cannot control. The allocation of asset ownership between public and private partners should align with who can manage the assets most effectively.

Game Theory Game theory, with its focus on strategic interactions among rational decision-makers, is a valuable tool for understanding PPPs. It offers insights into how parties with different interests can collaborate effectively. For instance, the Prisoner's Dilemma (PD) highlights the importance of cooperation and the risks of noncooperation, guiding the structuring of contracts and incentives. Coordination games emphasize the need for aligning strategies to achieve common objectives, crucial in PPPs. Public Goods Games shed light on the challenges of funding and contributing to public projects, central to PPP dynamics.	When one party has more or better information than the other (a common scenario in PPPs), it can lead to suboptimal outcomes, such as adverse selection or moral hazard. Contract mechanisms are needed to mitigate these risks. The Stag Hunt game implies that cooperation is more likely when parties anticipate future interactions. In the context of PPPs, fostering long-term relationships and/or signaling the potential for contract extensions can encourage partners to work collaboratively. The PD highlights the risk of parties acting in their self-interest to the detriment of the collective good. It's crucial to design contracts and incentives that align the interests of all parties. This might include performance-based rewards that are contingent on meeting agreed-upon objectives, ensuring that both parties are incentivized to work toward the common goal.

Continued

Table 2.1 CONTINUED

Theory	Theory-Based Recommendations
Social Exchange Theory (SET)	
Social exchange theory (SET) is a sociological and psychological framework that explains human behavior in social relationships, emphasizing the exchange of resources, rewards, and costs between individuals or groups. It focuses on the dynamics of reciprocal interactions and the balance of benefits and obligations in relationships. SET helps us understand how individuals and organizations engage in reciprocal exchanges in contract relationships and PPPs. The theory helps us understand how trust develops, is maintained, and influences the behavior and decision-making of the involved parties.	SET emphasizes the importance of reciprocity in relationships. In PPPs, this translates to creating a sense of mutual obligation and cooperation. Both public and private partners should feel that their contributions are valued and reciprocated, whether through resources, expertise, or other forms of support. SET acknowledges that power dynamics can influence exchanges. In PPPs, it's important to recognize and manage power imbalances, ensuring that one party does not dominate or exploit the other, which could lead to resentment and undermine the partnership. PPPs should be flexible and adaptable, allowing for adjustments in the partnership agreement as circumstances, goals, or capacities of the parties evolve.

Resource Dependence Theory Resource Dependence (RD) theory can significantly improve our understanding of contracts and PPPs by shedding light on the power dynamics and dependencies that exist between parties involved. RD emphasizes that organizations depend on external resources to fulfill their objectives. In contracts and PPPs, this theory helps identify the power dynamics and dependencies between the public and private sectors. It recognizes that parties may possess different resources, such as financial, technological, or regulatory, which can shape their bargaining power and influence their decision-making in the contractual relationship.	A justification for PPPs is the formation of strategic alliances to gain access to necessary resources and capabilities. PPPs should be structured such that neither party becomes overly dominant, ensuring a more equitable and sustainable partnership. Over-reliance on a single resource provider can lead to vulnerability. In PPPs, both public and private partners should seek to diversify their resource sources to reduce dependence and potential power imbalances.

Continued

Table 2.1 Continued

Theory	Theory-Based Recommendations
Contracts As Reference Points The theory of contract reference points extends traditional contract theory by integrating the concept of reference points into contractual relationships. Contracting parties use specific terms or conditions as reference points that shape their expectations and satisfaction with the contract. These reference points significantly influence their behavior and perception of the contractual relationship. The theory highlights that satisfaction depends not just on objective outcomes but also on how these compare with the expectations set by the reference points. It emphasizes the importance of adaptation mechanisms for unforeseen events, considering that contracts cannot cover every scenario. The theory also recognizes the crucial role of fairness perceptions and the nature of the relationship between contracting parties.	In PPPs, it's crucial to establish clear and realistic reference points within contracts. These reference points, which include key terms and conditions, serve as benchmarks for expectations and satisfaction. They should be mutually agreed upon and reflect a realistic understanding of the project's goals and constraints. PPPs should be designed to align expectations with achievable outcomes. This involves setting terms that are not only clear but also adaptable to changing circumstances, reducing the likelihood of disputes arising from unmet expectations. Reference points in PPPs will need to balance between specificity and ambiguity in contracts. While clarity is important, some level of ambiguity allows for adaptive responses to unexpected changes. Contracts should be perceived as fair by all parties. In PPPs, ensuring that the distribution of risks, responsibilities, and rewards is equitable can enhance satisfaction and commitment to the partnership.

for communication, coordination, and control in executing the work (Schilke and Lumineau 2018).

Box 2.1

The Impetus for an Enforceable Agreement

The inclination to rely on formal contracts in PPPs is understandable. Consider a situation in which the government hires a private supplier to deliver social services. Not unlike other PPPs, the service agreement would undoubtedly be complex. Government officials are likely to spend weeks, if not months, negotiating terms, including, among many other details, the specific tasks to be performed, how and under what conditions the supplier will be paid, how performance will be monitored and measured, the length of the agreement, and what penalties may be applied if the supplier does not meet performance expectations. The public would expect no less, as such a contract comes at a considerable cost to taxpayers. Furthermore, the supplier in this case could be a business corporation with considerable resources but also with obligations to shareholders. The supplier would likewise expect all the protections afforded by a clearly specified agreement, especially if the supplier makes costly upfront investments, for example, in computer hardware or staff training, to deliver the services. The supplier expects to make a profit and is also concerned with minimizing the risk of a loss. Thus, both government and the supplier view the formal contract as an instrument necessary to protect their respective interests, and both entities anticipate an agreement that is enforceable in court in the event contract promises are not kept. The public and private parties are also keen to mitigate the risks of adverse actions that will work against their own interests. Thus, the government anticipates how to ensure that the supplier meets performance expectations and contemplates what to do if service quality is lacking, while the supplier anticipates what to do if the government unfairly withholds payments.

At the outset of the partnership, the contracting parties will try to anticipate and account for the *totality of costs* associated with transacting (for all partners) in the contract terms. These include costs to acquire information and forecast future costs and benefits of the arrangement, negotiate contract terms and monitor compliance, manage disputes, and renegotiate or plan for how to terminate the contract if the partnership fails. Both TCE and the principal-agent theory also emphasize the costs associated with guarding against opportunistic behavior, which occurs largely because of the challenges of specifying a complete contract and monitoring the behavior of parties to the contract (and/or their subcontracted agents). Typical problems include adapting the arrangements ex post to unexpected contingencies or circumstances, addressing information asymmetry that arises when agents possess different levels of information and expertise, shirking on service quality, and shading behaviors such as free-riding or deliberate efforts (ex ante or ex post) to undermine cooperation and elevate one party's interest above the others (Williamson 1979; Hart et al. 1997; Hart and Moore 2008). In other words, it is assumed the mindset the parties bring to the exchange is one of mistrust; each expects the other to act in their own self-interest, compelling efforts to mitigate the risks that their own interests will be undercut in the collaboration.

Given the assumption of mistrust, principal-agent theory accordingly argues for more effort to align the interests of contracting parties at the start and to establish monitoring and control mechanisms to ensure that agents act responsibly and fulfill their obligations, which should reduce the risk of opportunistic behavior. In clarifying roles and expectations before launching the PPP, the contracting parties may also reduce transactional frictions and minimize the need for ongoing negotiation or renegotiation of the contract terms when situations arise and the parties' interpretations might otherwise diverge. Moreover, consistent with New Public Management (NPM) theory and its emphasis on market mechanisms and efficiency, principal-agent theory calls for contract incentives that provide clear expectations for behavior and performance and that help to clarify risk-sharing and mitigate risks associated with potential losses or adverse outcomes. Such contract incentives and reporting mechanisms are typically embedded in the contract structures and reinforced via the use of performance-based rewards or penalties that motivate agents to act in ways that advance the desired outcomes. For example, performance-based contracts might tie specific fractions of total contract payments to concrete, measurable goals, so that if outcomes fall short of the mutually agreed standards, the provider bears the loss. And importantly for public sector contracting, the stipulation of information sharing through performance reporting also fosters transparency and accountability, not only for the major parties to the contract who oversee its execution, but also to a broader range of public and private stakeholders to PPPs.

The reality, however, is that it is exceedingly rare in the context of PPPs that the partners will be able to establish a complete formal contract. This incompleteness necessitates consideration of the residual rights of control, that is, which party should retain authority or decision-making power for handling noncontracted contingencies (Hart et al. 1997). In public programs serving vulnerable populations, it is known to be particularly challenging to establish a clear and enforceable contract, as the primary work and performance are subject to the vagaries of political and economic cycles and other external forces (Sandfort 1999; Heinrich and Choi 2007). Brown and Potoski (2003) observe that such services also require more specialized investments to produce (asset specificity), and the outcomes or impact of these services is more difficult to assess (a lower level of service measurability), magnifying the challenges of writing an effective, complete formal contract.

In fact, TCE and property rights theorists identify asset specificity and uncertainty as two key factors associated with opportunistic behavior and increased transaction costs (Williamson 1979, 1981, 1985; Hart 1990). When investments are specialized (or for a specific transaction), they do not have market liquidity, implying that these resources cannot be readily redeployed for another contract. One party's upfront investment in or contribution of specialized knowledge or training is an example of an asset-specific investment. When transactions involve asset-specific investments, the party making the investment is more vulnerable to calculating behavior by the other party, which may use its leverage to extract benefits. For example, a contracting party might unilaterally raise prices, miss deadlines, or suddenly terminate the contract because it can. The literature describes this as "hold-up" and considers the conditions that contribute to hold-up and ways to guard against it (Williamson 1985).[1] A major motivation for parties to enter into formal contracts is to address the hold-up problem brought on by asset-specific investments and the dependent relationships they create (Hart and Holmström 1986).

The second factor associated with opportunistic behavior and higher transaction costs, uncertainty, arises in numerous ways, particularly in complex contracting arrangements like PPPs. Uncertainty increases the risk that costly changes in the contract will be induced. An example of an environmental uncertainty is a sharp increase in labor costs or technology that may prompt a supplier to cut corners to stay on budget; in fact, the chance that one party may change its behavior is another source of uncertainty. Moreover, if one party to a contract interprets a rule, provision, or the behavior of another party differently than the other sees it—described as "interpretative uncertainty" (Weber and Mayer 2014; Brown et al. 2018)—the risks that the parties will impugn or dissolve the relationship rise. This is why the parties to a PPP frequently attempt to reduce uncertainty by "investing in up-front specificity" (Brown et al. 2018, 743), such as in the form of contract clauses, schedules, and other terms that, in effect, make the formal contract more rigid. The contract might specify how the parties would share the unanticipated production or service costs and assess the quality of the product or services to substantiate that it is not degraded. Macaulay (1963) cautions, however, that attempting to address every uncertainty or hold-up can signal distrust in the relationship and undermine the agreement. Indeed, even some prominent TCE, principal-agent, and property rights theorists have acknowledged a role for relational mechanisms in resolving these inherent contracting challenges.

1. Notably, there are distinctions in the literature regarding the hold-up problem. For example, Klein et al. (1978) view hold-up as a principal rationale for entering into formal contracts, whereas Oliver Williamson (1993) contends that "adaptation is the central problem" (to which hold-up is a contributing factor, but only in conjunction with incomplete contracting and mainly in relation to the need to adapt to disturbances)" (40).

THE RELATIONAL CONTRACT

An alternative to layering on more rules, clauses, schedules, and stringency to a formal contract is to lay down the "sword" and cultivate a more collaborative approach to structuring and managing a contract. Regardless of the nature of a given relationship, an implicit or explicit understanding of what the parties expect in terms of the behavior of others will influence their interactions, and norms will guide their behavior. Social exchange theory (SET) is particularly illuminating in understanding the sociological and psychological aspects of behavior in social relationships, such as the reciprocal exchanges in contracting and PPPs that often involve the allocation of resources, rewards, penalties, costs, and more (both anticipated and unforeseen). SET asserts that trust is crucial for effective collaboration and cooperation, and it helps us to understand how trust is developed, maintained, and critical in shaping the behavior and decision-making of the parties. For example, SET highlights the reciprocal nature of trust building and how breaches of trust can damage relationship dynamics. This theory also points to the importance of perceptions of fairness and equity in relationships as parties strive to balance benefits and obligations in partnerships.

Specific to contracting, Macaulay (1963) likewise recognized the importance of relational norms and perceptions among the parties and is credited with being one of the first to observe and identify what is known in the literature as a *relational contract*. He envisioned contracts as broader than formal written agreements, arguing that courts should not rely solely on the written formal contract because "words do not have a fixed meaning that every speaker of the language will translate the same way" (45). The true meaning of the written language can only be understood by bringing "some measure of context, background assumptions, our experiences," and he also cautioned that meaning (or interpretation) is a function of any biases and ignorance that the parties bring to the relationship (45–46).

Macneil (1960) shared Macaulay's broader view of contracts and described relational norms as the internal contract framework that characterizes the exchange relationship among the parties. In *The New*

Social Contract (1980), Macneil elaborated on ten norms that he viewed as tools for analysis of contracts, that is, the relationships through which the parties gain the full advantages that exchange can offer them. These include (1) role integrity, (2) reciprocity (the principle of getting something back for something given), (3) implementation of planning, (4) effectuation of consent, (5) flexibility, (6) contractual solidarity, (7) restitution, reliance, and expectation interests (the "linking norms"), (8) creation and restraint of power (the "power norm"), (9) propriety of means, and (10) harmonization with the social matrix (Macneil 1980, 347). SET similarly recognizes the presence of power dynamics in relationships and how power differentials affect the exchange process, behavior, and decision-making of the parties. In the context of PPPs, this includes how power is negotiated over the course of a relationship, the exercise of influence, and the potential for exploitation versus cooperation in these relationships. In addition, Macneil extended the consideration of these norms to the complex but indelible connections between the contracting parties and society, as rendered in the formal contract. That is, the "contract is an edifice partly built by the parties but also partly built by society, by the law" (Macneil 1960, 177). A "contract without language is impossible; and contract without social structure is—quite literally—rationally unthinkable" (Macneil 1980, 1).

In-depth studies of PPPs and other complex contracting practices have substantiated SET tenets and Macneil and Macaulay's early thinking about the importance of relational norms for their success. Brown et al. (2018) argued that complex contracts (which they analyzed in the US military defense sector) will not bear fruit in the absence of a cooperative approach to the relationship that encourages the parties to forego their self-interest, particularly when opportunities arise to exploit the ambiguities and asymmetries inherent in complex, longer-term contracts. In the context of social outcomes contracts, Ball and Gibson (2022) suggest that most parties to a PPP will naturally work relationally to foster higher levels of trust and reduce the chances that the partnership falters or goes to court for arbitration. In fact, Macneil described situations where parties to a contract simply agreed on some terms and started performing; in other words, the contract was made incrementally as the work of the partnership rolled out. In cases such as these, the contract becomes more than what the parties agreed upon initially or what was committed to in writing at the start. The ensuing behaviors and interactions are guided by relational norms that fill in the gaps left by incomplete written contracts. Similarly, Macaulay (2003) warned courts not to "close their "eyes to real expectations" as writings labeled "contract" do not capture many, if not most, of the expectations of those who sign them" (43).

Together, the work of Macneil and Macaulay has inspired many of the foundational ideas associated with new approaches to contracting that are emerging in PPPs, particularly the process of embedding norms into written agreements to align the partners' interests and preserve the harmony as circumstances change (Frydlinger et al. 2019). Box 2.2 describes "The Vested Way," one approach to filling in the gaps of an incomplete contract by developing relational governance. In addition, it is clear from their philosophizing that government contracting engages society and should benefit society (Macneil 1969), that is, create public value. This line of thinking is also developed in the context of New Public Governance (NPG) theory, which centers the importance of creating public value (public services outcomes) in PPPs. Rather than assuming a competitive orientation (or self-interest and mistrust) among the partners (as in NPM), NPG focuses on the interorganizational or multisector relationships (the plural state[2]) that form the core governing structure of a PPP (Osborne 2006). Informed by organizational sociology and network theory, NPG envisages how cooperation, trust, and other relational aspects of the multisector collaboration emerge to improve public services. NPG also recognizes the value of pluralism and diverse perspectives in decision-making and the importance of adaptive, flexible management responses to changing needs. These principles collectively reflect a shift toward a more integrated, collaborative approach in public sector governance, tailored to the complexity of modern societal

2. In the plural state, multiple interdependent entities from the public and private sectors contribute to the delivery of public services.

challenges. As Albertson et al. (2020, 3) describe it, the NPG interpretation of how PPPs create value places "co-creation" between the users of services (society) and the parties delivering services "at the heart of public service management."

Box 2.2

The Vested Way Toward Relational Governance Structures

Kate Vitasek, David Frydlinger, and Oliver Hart (2019) set forth a well-grounded plan for developing relational governance structures that place relationships at the forefront for sustaining more successful PPPs. This structured 5-step approach, known as "The Vested Way," emphasizes the importance of building the right foundation for the relationship from the start to keep the parties aligned as circumstances inevitably change. First, it requires both parties to define a clear vision and objectives for the partnership, ensuring mutual alignment on the end goals. Next, the approach mandates a comprehensive assessment of existing processes, resources, and capabilities to understand the current situation. The third step involves crafting an agreement that clearly outlines the responsibilities, risks, and rewards for each party. The partnership then establishes a governance structure that promotes effective communication, decision-making, and conflict resolution. That is, the parties add a plan to the vision and objectives already agreed upon, establishing how they will ensure relational norms such as trust, integrity, honesty, autonomy, and reciprocity and "good faith" efforts. The plan requires investments at the outset that increase early stage-transaction costs. As disagreements and ambiguities arise, the parties stay on course with the plan to resolve disputes and clarify the way forward. The agreement, governance structures, and plan become part of the formal agreement and the basis for regular evaluations of the PPP's performance, which guide the entities in identifying growth opportunities and ensuring the partnership adapts to changing conditions. In turn, the parties realize dividends as the project is implemented, with fewer costs associated with navigating the challenges of implementation, including costs typically associated with renegotiation, amendments, and performance issues, not to mention the significant costs associated with litigation and switching partners when contracts fail.

Although Hart's (1995) research was largely centered in TCE and property rights theory, he also recognized that the sheer complexity of many contractual relationships necessitates the embrace of some relational elements in the contracting arrangements, particularly where adaptations are required amid uncertain and evolving circumstances. More recently with David Frydlinger (2023), they present a (TCE) theory-informed analysis of how to address the longstanding challenges of contractual incompleteness based on the assumption that the parties to the contract will generally adhere to widely accepted social norms and will act with integrity and fairness in their dealings, while also invoking standard economic assumptions that the contracting parties are self-interested and rational. They construct a model for contracting in which the social norms are incorporated formally into the written contract in the form of guiding principles and are applied when unanticipated contingencies arise. Frydlinger and Hart's work suggests a convergence of diverse theoretical perspectives on the importance of relational norms for guiding the intricate and dynamic work of PPPs, including game theory. Game-theoretic perspectives highlight how contracting parties reconcile differing interests and the potential payoffs of acting opportunistically with the importance of cooperating to align interests and achieve common objectives.

THE FORMAL-RELATIONAL CONTRACT

The discussion above brings us to the emergent concept of the formal-relational contract, first introduced in Chapter 1. The formal-relational contract recognizes that relational contracts are unlikely to ever supersede the formal contract as the overriding structure in PPP governance and execution, but also that even the most elaborate and firmly buttressed formal contract will be fragile in the absence of relational aspects to guide the parties' interactions. A formal-relational contract that is enforceable by the courts begins with an effort by the contracting parties to develop a foundation of trust and cooperation that guides the partners' work and aligns their goals and interests throughout the partnership, while also detailing the governance structures and written terms concerning provisions such as payments, risk-sharing, and other obligations among the contracting parties. In effect, the formal-relational contract is distinct in that it provides legal recourse for a breach of *both* the formal and relational terms of the contract (Frydlinger et al. 2021). This stands in contrast to a typical approach to contracting with a public sector partner, where emphasis is placed on the rules and regulations of procurement at the initial tendering and selection stages of the partnership, rather than on informal relationship building. This typical approach contributes to a more rigid contract design that may forego the opportunity for more collaboratively developed, flexible, and adaptable contract specifications.

Although the concept of the formal-relational contract has been gaining traction in theory and in practice in the private sector (Frydlinger et al. 2021),[3] the integration of relational contracting has been slower to take hold in the public sector. As Ball and Gibson (2022) discuss, there are some who see it as inappropriate for PPPs, specifically because one of the parties is a public body or government entity. They outline eight central concerns that have been raised about moving toward a relational approach to contracting with a public sector partner, most of which derive from the theories discussed above (see Box 2.3).

3. In describing this approach to contracting, we hyphenate "formal-relational," whereas the prior literature largely presents it as "formal relational" contracting. Our use of formal-relational is intentional to signal that this contracting approach necessarily involves *both* components and is distinctive as a whole from traditional formal and emergent relational approaches.

Box 2.3

Challenges to a Relational Approach to Public-Private Partnerships

1. Opportunism: the risk that one party may take advantage of loose contract terms for their own (unfair) benefit.
2. Scrutiny and corruption: close relationships and flexible contract terms can make scrutiny difficult and increase the risk of nefarious practice.
3. Restrictive procurement rules: highly rule-bound or open market procurement procedures tend to favor a transactional approach.
4. Misunderstanding: broadly scoped contract terms might increase the chance of misunderstanding, which could lead to conflict.
5. Unequal power dynamics: weakened legal protections can make the contract risky for the smaller party.
6. High upfront investment: when a large upfront investment is required of a provider in assets that cannot easily be repurposed, the protection of a more rigid contract may be essential.
7. Cost: building and maintaining a high-intensity relationship drives up costs on both sides (which may or may not be justified by the benefits).
8. Staff turnover: the personal relationships which drive trust may dissipate due to staff turnover or political change.

Ball, N. and Gibson, M. (2022). Partnerships with principles: putting relationships at the heart of public contracts for better social outcomes. Government Outcomes Lab, Blavatnik School of Government, University of Oxford.

First, they suggest that in the face of opportunistic behavior, the reliance on trust in relational contracting may be too optimistic. Assuming that it is possible to align the interests of all parties and sustain that alignment over the life of a PPP leaves public value exposed to opportunism. If competing goals or interests emerge among the parties to the PPP, as is more the norm than the exception, will trust be sufficient to protect the public interest? Where public managers hold the mantle for upholding public value, is it appropriate to trade enforceability for trust? The psychological concept of reference points bears on these concerns as well, in that the contracting parties will use specific terms or conditions as reference points (at the outset of the relationship) that will shape their expectations for and perceptions of the others' behavior and the contract outcomes. We contend that the role of reference points in the parties' interactions reinforces the case for relational mechanisms in PPP contracts, given the importance of candid communication and adaptation in the face of unforeseen circumstances that may surface occasions for opportunistic or self-serving behavior.

Second, relational contracting replaces rigid, legally motivated "guardrails" intended to shield the PPP from corruption and other unscrupulous behaviors with close relationships. Ball and Gibson (2022) argue that this could lead to collusion and undercut the formal protections for the public against corrupt behavior, particularly if the partners do not sustain their commitment to "shared principles" that they rely on to navigate uncertainties that arise across the course of a PPP. Resource dependency theory calls attention to the power dynamics and dependencies that exist between contracting parties, including the potential for power imbalances that can magnify the challenges imposed by differences in organizational capabilities for PPPs. If broad principles that are more open to varying interpretation replace carefully written specifications that clearly allocate authority and stipulate recourse, power imbalances may be exploited or exacerbated. Recognizing this, Ball and Gibson (2022) point to the protections provided in a formal contract through the legal system for the less powerful parties.

The legal enforceability of the shared governance principles in a formal-relational contract is a key issue for PPPs and is still the subject of some debate, particularly given varying legal traditions across countries and contexts (Ball and Gibson 2022). Legal intermediation is standard practice in the formation and execution of PPPs to ensure that the public and private parties are balancing the various stakeholder interests and centering public value in the primary work of the partnership. Legal governance, argues Pongsiri (2002), needs to be shrewdly designed and administered to both support public welfare and the advantages market forces bring to PPPs, such as by avoiding excessive or unrealistic controls (Savas 2000). He also acknowledges, however, the potential for PPPs to veer toward traditional forms of "command and control" legal governance when circumstances such as contract complexity, forfeiture of autonomy, and information asymmetry outweigh collaborative norms and values. Williamson (1975) asserts that legal frameworks serve to align the goals, interests, and incentives of the contracting parties, thereby reducing opportunistic behavior, resolving disputes, and providing a stable, trusted structure for maintaining a fair balance of interests and rights among the parties.

Our examination of pivotal (UK and US) court cases (see Box 2.4) suggests a judicial inclination to respect the relational principles embedded in a PPP and affirm the enforceability of "good faith" norms when they are integrated in explicit and precise language in formal contract arrangements. In these cases, the courts both acknowledged the challenges in fully defining good faith obligations but also recognized the value of good faith that is cultivated through relational elements in PPPs. The first court case highlights the drawbacks of overly strict and formal agreements in long-term, dynamic projects. More generally, existing legal review and precedence suggests that ensuring a shared understanding of the foundational norms, contract terms, and expectations in PPPs, as well as their legal viability, can help to mitigate the challenges that might otherwise arise with divergent interpretations of the principles or a partner's behavior in the course of a longer-term contract.

Box 2.4

Pivotal PPP Court Cases Referencing Relational Contracts and Good Faith Obligations

***Amey v. Birmingham City Council*, [2018] EWCA Civ 264.** The Court recognized relational contracts as a distinct legal category, often entailing an implied duty of good faith. It classified a contract as relational despite its complexity and length (over 5,000 pages), as evidenced by factors such as its status as a Private Finance Initiative (PFI), prolonged duration, and the need for significant mutual commitment and cooperation. It emphasized the importance of interpreting contracts based on their broader purpose, highlighting the drawbacks of overly strict and formal agreements in long-term, dynamic projects.

***Bates v. Post Office Ltd.*, [2019] EWHC 606.** The Court ruled that the contracts between the Post Office and subpostmasters were relational, incorporating duties of good faith that encompass honesty, fairness, transparency, and cooperation. The Court outlined nine characteristics typically defining a relational contract, including the absence of specific terms precluding good faith, long-term mutual intentions, integrity in execution, collaborative commitment, recognition of the contract's spirit, establishment of trust and confidence, high communication and cooperation levels, significant financial investment, and potential exclusivity of the relationship.

***Compound Photonics Group Ltd; Faulkner v Vollin Holdings Ltd.* (2022 EWCA Civ 1371).** The Court emphasized that good faith clauses must be interpreted based on the specific context of each case, rejecting the idea of a universal set of standards for the duty of good faith in contracts. It recognized that this duty fundamentally includes an obligation to act honestly, but breaches can occur through means other than dishonesty. The case underscores the importance of clearly defining the scope of an express duty of good faith in contracts.

***Centex Corp. v. United States*, 395 F.3d 1283 (Fed. Cir. 2005)**. The Federal Circuit ruled that the government breached the implied covenant of good faith and fair dealing by retroactively eliminating tax benefits it had promised as an incentive for acquiring failing thrifts. Although the contract did not explicitly guarantee the tax advantages, the court held that the government could not use its legislative power to undercut its commitments. This decision reinforces the principle that good faith in contracts requires both parties to honor their agreements and not act in ways that deprive the other party of expected benefits.

***Metcalf Constr. Co. v. United States*, 742 F.3d 984 (Fed. Cir. 2014)**. The Federal Circuit ruled that the government breached its duty of good faith duty by unreasonably refusing to acknowledge the differing site conditions and hindering Metcalf's performance. The court emphasized that a breach of this duty does not require a violation of an express contract provision; rather, it encompasses actions that undermine the contractor's reasonable expectations and the contract's intended benefits.

Other features of relational contracting that may create problems in their use for PPPs reflect some of the distinctive aspects of contracting with the public sector, such as public procurement rules that are intended to guard against misuse of public funds. A "byzantine tower of rules and regulations" (Brown et al. 2018, 740) is frequently embodied in legislation and policy directives that aim to promote transparency, fair and open competition, efficiency, and public value, while reducing the chances for corruption or collusion. Adhering strictly to these rules can also limit opportunities for cultivating a relational approach to the contract design and execution, including the negotiation of contract terms that would allow for norms and principles to be agreed on at the beginning of the process. In addition, the larger the initial investment of the government (or any party to the PPP), the keener that partner may be to protect their investment (and the public interest) by adhering strictly to the rules and other terms specified in a traditional, formal contract (Ball and Gibson 2022). Particularly in the area of social welfare, contracts with the public sector may be more vulnerable to political developments that bring about major changes in leadership and policy direction or to resource dependencies that contribute to financial instability, which can disrupt the trusted relationships of a relational contract undergirding a PPP.

These constraints to relational contracting continue to inspire new thinking about forms of public-private contracts that can leverage the advantages of *both* the formal and relational aspects of contracting in highly complex settings such as those of PPPs. In their work that presents "A New Approach to Contracts," David Frydlinger, Oliver Hart and Kate Vitasek (2019) lay out a set of shared principles that should form the core of a relational contract and facilitate a "partnership mentality" to the contracting process, where the parties become vested in a relationship that advances their collective interests (see Box 2.5). Their approach begins with a stronger focus on the values that will guide the partnership and how the partners will behave and interact with one another, positioning the legal and financial terms of the deal and the balance of power as second order. If the partners do come into dispute, or one objects to the behavior of another, the principles provide a framework through which to work out the grievances. By setting out the principles formally, they could also form the basis for judicial intervention in the case of a breach of partnership. In effect, the guiding principles become the foundation for a legally enforceable governance plan that recognizes what the partners bring to the collaboration, as well as a tool to navigate the complexities encountered in working toward their shared objectives.

In our case study analyses in this book involving PPPs engaged in complex social services delivery, we will consider how formal and relational elements are balanced in the context of contract enforcement and the legal responsibility to protect public value and ensure accountability to the public in PPPs. As discussed below, we also consider the dynamic nature of PPPs and the political, social, and economic contexts that they navigate as they collaborate to achieve their goals. Inevitably across the life of a longer-term PPP, how the partners balance formal and relational elements of the contract may evolve. As partners navigate a range of opportunities and challenges, they will need to weigh the costs of leaning more on tightly specified, formal provisions to address risks or prospects of hold-up with the perils and costs of investing time in fostering trust, cultivating good faith, and relying on principles and guidelines to sustain cooperation and progress toward the PPP end goals.

Box 2.5

Guiding Principles for a Formal-Relational Contract

1. **Reciprocity** recognizes the unique strengths and resources each partner contributes and obliges the partners to return fairness in kind.
2. **Autonomy** allows each partner to make autonomous decisions that align with the collective interest and obliges them to refrain from undue influence.
3. **Honesty** calls for the partners to be truthful, authentic, and transparent in disclosing their intentions, even in a position of vulnerability.
4. **Loyalty** asks the partners to value each other's interests equally and look out for the relationship first, including through times of adversity.
5. **Equity** compels the partners to share rewards in proportion to resources invested and risks taken by each, where fairness does not always imply equality.
6. **Integrity** obliges the parties to be consistent over time in words, decisions, and actions in a way that aligns with the collective interest.

See pages 193–199 in Frydlinger et al. (2021). *Contracting in the New Economy: Using Relational Contracts to Boost Trust and Collaboration in Strategic Business Relationships*. Palgrave Macmillan.

FORMAL AND RELATIONAL DYNAMICS IN PUBLIC-PRIVATE CONTRACTING

In bringing together a "transactional" lens and a "relational" lens on the complex contracting predicament, Oliver Williamson (1975) highlighted the strengths and limitations of each. Figure 2.1 offers an overview of alternative responses to contracting difficulties, flowing from our discussion above of formal, relational, and formal-relational approaches to contracting. For many person-facing social services and programs, our starting position is the vexed bottom left quadrant at "precarious contracting circumstances." Precarious contracting circumstances are brought on by the properties of these programs and the external context in which they operate. Person-facing social services, and particularly those supporting individuals with multiple and complex needs, are characterized by a complex and broad scope of work, with uncertainty over what will be effective for a given cohort and for each person (product complexity). These services also often embody asset specificity, requiring specific investments from the delivery organization that cannot be easily redeployed to other projects, such as

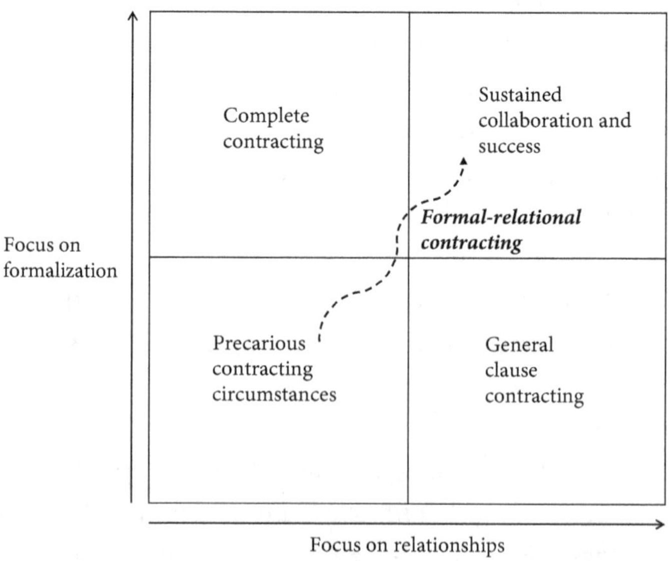

Figure 2.1 Navigating Away from Contracting Difficulties Toward Sustained Success

specialized staff training. Moreover, such services are more difficult to measure, particularly in terms of their quality.

In addition to these "internal" properties of the services, programs regularly reckon with external challenges. For example, there may be a limited number of providers (within a reasonable geography) capable of providing the required services, which constrains the potential for market efficiencies. Services are also frequently affected by environmental disruptions or unpredictable events, such as the challenges brought into sharp relief by the COVID-19 pandemic and its ensuing restrictions on social service routines for delivering interventions. Such dramatic shifts in context may demand an equally abrupt and extensive adaptation to service delivery.

To move beyond the problematic zone of precarious contracting circumstances, the typical approach is to formalize (as much as feasible) through tighter contract specifications, i.e., to write rules and to manage via specific and binding plans, to inject clear controls, and to specify monetizable obligations. These specifications, intended to defend from opportunism and pave the way out of uncertainty and risk, often also include "carrot-and-stick" incentives through features such as contract penalties, performance metrics, and/or outcome payments.

This approach that leans into complete (or comprehensive) contracting is, in theory, more amenable to *formal-transactional* contracts with a narrow or discrete scope of work, short duration, limited need for future cooperation, and high measurability (see Figure 2.2). This may apply, for example, to government contracts involving stationery orders or one-off purchases like property refurbishment, where the pursuit of greater specification in these cases may lead to better contract outcomes. However, in PPPs that exhibit broad scope, longer-term engagement, high complexity, and measurability challenges, even if it were possible to overcome bounded rationality by "working harder" in specifying the contract, the process will be extremely costly. Moreover, the resulting contract may be too rigid to adequately adapt and manage the inherent internal and external complexity the partners will encounter.

Informal to Formal

Formal-Transactional Narrow and straightforward scope, few partners Short contract duration, future cooperation not anticipated High levels of product/service measurability Complete binding plans Specific and monetizable obligations and outcomes Limited communication Arms-length relationship	**Formal-Relational** Defined scope, adaptable over time Longer term with specified process for future cooperation Measurement is adaptable Planning and risk-sharing continually negotiated Clear structures for ongoing communication Social norms articulated as contractual obligations
Informal-Transactional Autonomous partners with no interdependencies One-time (spot) transaction High product/service measurability Price is the authority Brief, direct communication	**Informal-Relational** Broad, complex scope with more partners Duration long or unknown, future cooperation is critical Low levels of product/service measurability Inability to fully plan ex ante, changeable, or nonspecific obligations Extensive communication needed Expectation of reciprocity and altruistic behavior

Transactional to Relational

Figure 2.2 Contracting Considerations on the Spectrum from Formal to Relational

The features of many social, person-facing public services point instead toward a form of *informal-relational* contracting known as general clause contracting. This domain hallows positive relationships between parties, undergirded by concepts of network governance, trust, and reciprocity. Acknowledging bounded rationality in the face of precarious contracting circumstances, the parties instead engage in practices that foster mutual understanding and reliance. Emphasis is placed on cultivating flexible and nonbinding relationships with one another, rather than achieving greater contract specification. This lays the foundation for addressing challenges as they arise, drawing on trust and cooperation to jointly address issues of scope, adaptation, and quality. At its most extreme, general clause contracting may simply specify that parties will work together to achieve the goals of the contract.

At the same time, general clause contracting may pose significant challenges to public accountability and the ability to center and deliver on public value. In PPPs, "enforceable contracts form the connective tissue between public and private actors" (Freeman 2000, 667). A lack of specificity in the contract gives providers leeway to pursue their interests to the detriment of quality and public value (Hart et al. 1997). Governments are not only responsible for the outcomes—or lack thereof—delivered by PPPs, but they also typically hold particular moral or legal duties to uphold the rights of vulnerable groups, creating an additional demand for extending clearly defined public duties through contracts that govern outsourced public programs (Freeman 2006, 106–107). This implies that no government could defensibly enter into anything approaching a general clause contract for these kinds of complex public service programs. The demands of public accountability instead call for formalization, pushing once again in the direction of specification of more rules rather than guidelines and good faith. How, then, can one reconcile this need for accountability to ensure public value with the responsiveness and flexibility needed to address the complexity of person-facing public services?

As we have argued in this chapter, neither the pursuit of formalism nor relationalism *alone* holds the solution for complex, social welfare–focused PPPs. We suggest that these types of multiactor, social service PPPs are better off striving for the best possible balance along the curved line toward "sustained collaboration," that is, adeptly combining and managing the formal *and* relational elements of the contract over time. We do not expect, however, that this route will necessarily be direct or linear. For example, the parties to the contract may learn over time about how and when they are leaning too heavily on the formal, prescriptive terms of the contract to the detriment of the trust that underpins its relational elements. At the same time, they will have to monitor their reliance on relational mechanisms to ensure that this does not come at the expense of public accountability. In other words, they will braid together the formal and relational (Gilson et al. 2010), drawing on the strengths of each in order to reach the overarching goals of sustained collaboration and success in delivering public value. Figure 2.1 demonstrates this route, weaving between greater formalization and greater relationality depending on time and circumstance.

In effect, contracting parties in a complex PPP will rarely find the most direct route from difficulty to sustained collaboration and success. There is no singular "right" path to follow, and partnerships will vary over time in the relative focus they place on formal specifications and relationship management. Indeed, there are likely to be features of either the service or context that, at a given time, will suggest a greater emphasis on one path versus another is more constructive. We suggest this can be conceived as a spectrum from formal to relational, as shown in Figure 2.3, where a given PPP may fall at different points along the spectrum at different times in its course.

THE SPECTRUM FROM FORMAL TO RELATIONAL AND OUR CASE STUDY SELECTION AND CONTRIBUTIONS

Increasingly by design and in practice, most PPPs are centered on contracts that lie somewhere on a spectrum between formal, strictly transactional to fully relational contracts, as shown in Figure 2.2. Macneil (1974) first articulated the idea that contracts could be characterized on a spectrum from more to less relational (transactional), according to factors such as the number of parties and the focus of the relationship (narrow or broad); the nature of communication; measurability of the product or service and the level of difficulty in monetization of the exchange; duration of the contract and sharpness of the expectation for its start and termination; the forms and "bindingness" of planning; and the degree of completeness and specificity. We elaborate on these dimensions in Table 2.2, illustrating the primary distinctions between formal-transactional, informal-transactional, formal-relational, and informal-relational contracting on each.

Specific contextual features and contractual imperatives may lead one approach to become more productive than another. For example, in a situation where future cooperation is required and where the incidence of benefits and burdens in the relationship are shifting over time, we also add to these dimensions the nature and extent of public regulation in procurement, the levels of and differences in upfront investment

Table 2.2 Comparison of Formal, Formal-Relational, and Relational Contracting Approaches

Dimension	Formal (transactional)	Formal-Relational	Relational
Focus and scope of work	Tightly defined with a clear boundary around the commercial transaction.	Quite broad and defined in a way that may be adapted. Strategic aims are articulated as a shared mission.	Broad and unspecified.
Duration and planning	Shorter and/or beginning and end of the contract are clearly defined. Initial planning is complete and specific and completed ex ante. Almost no cooperation is required after the start of the contract.	Longer term but with clear expectations and articulation of how future work will be developed and approached. Specifies a process for developing and adapting plans. Further collaboration is required, and the expectations for collaboration are set out in the contract.	Indefinite and/or with expectation for long-term cooperation. Only limited specific planning at the beginning. Success is entirely dependent on further cooperation.

Continued

Table 2.2 Continued

Dimension	Formal (transactional)	Formal-Relational	Relational
Exchange rules, control rights, and risk management	Everything is measured in monetary terms, and each particular benefit, burden, and risk is specifically assigned to a named party.	Risk management is an ongoing process. Efforts are made to allocate risk to the party most able to address it on an ongoing basis, based on circumstances. Efforts are made to protect asset-specific investments.	Many aspects of the service/product are difficult to measure in monetary/nonmonetary terms. There is ad hoc sharing of both benefits and burdens.
Governance and communication	Limited, formal communication. Problems (e.g., against performance measures) will be responded to via clear, specific rights. Everything is measured in monetary terms.	Establishes an approach for both formal and informal communications. Issues are navigated via established governance forums and at strategic/ operational levels, with a balanced, adaptable framework to continuously align interests.	Extensive, informal communication. The possibility of (unanticipated) risk or trouble is dealt with by ad hoc cooperation and adjustments.
Social norms/principles	Disconnected from social norms and obligations. Arm's length relationship.	Explicitly includes social norms as contractual obligations. Relationship with clearly articulated expectations.	Expectation of reciprocity and significant expectation of altruistic behavior.

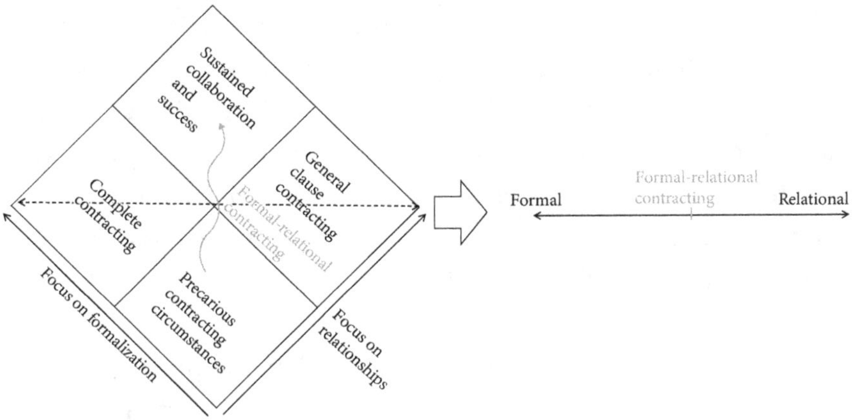

Figure 2.3 The Spectrum from Formal to Relational

the partners bring, the balance of power and authority among the partners, and the level of vulnerability of the PPP work to external political, economic, and social forces that may make a "formal-relational" contract more suitable than simply adopting greater relationality. Figure 2.3 depicts this expanded conceptualization of the spectrum from strictly formal to fully relational graphically, where the *formal-relational contract* would ostensibly fall somewhere along the spectrum, although where it lies may evolve over time.

In selecting the two major case studies for this book, we aimed to focus on PPPs that would situate in different places on the spectrum from strictly formal to fully relational during their execution, as we will further describe in Chapter 3. A second criterion was to choose one PPP that was considered a failed collaboration and another that is viewed as being on a path to success, while also ensuring that there were some similarities in their purpose or objectives, structures, service sectors, and exposure or vulnerability to external forces to allow for comparability as well as contrast in the case analyses. In addition, we sought cases that would allow for longitudinal study of the PPPs so that we could observe how the relationships among the partners and the PPP infrastructure evolved over time as well as their performance or public services outcomes. It was also important to select cases that were sufficiently high profile for the governments involved to generate publicly available data on the PPP relationships and outcomes for our analysis. Locating this study approach in Gerring's (2004) typologies of case study design, we are leveraging within-unit and cross-unit spatial variation and within-unit temporal variation—using primarily qualitative analysis—which characterizes our case analysis as a "comparative-historical" study.

Some of the questions we explore through our theory-informed, case study analyses include the following:

- How do partners integrate the formal-relational contracting approach alongside standard governmental contracting procedures?
- Can the concepts and approach that underpin formal-relational contracts work effectively when public services delivery involves a network of actors and organizations (versus a simpler bilateral agreement), as characteristic of PPPs and other NPG types of arrangements?
- What role can political or governance institutions play in fortifying the parties' incentives to cooperate?
- What role can political institutions and leadership play in mitigating against self-interested behaviors that may undermine long-term public-private sector relationships?
- What standard contract provisions and clauses could be modified to be more consistent with principles of reciprocity, integrity, autonomy, and equity?
- Are there additional norms of behavior that should be adopted as principles in PPP contracts?

3

Two High-Profile Public-Private Partnerships on the Spectrum from Formal to Relational

In this chapter, we present key information about the cases we use to elucidate our conceptual thinking about public-private partnership (PPP) governance and explore the role of formal-relational contracting in generating greater public value through PPPs. We draw on case evidence from both the US and UK, focusing on two primary cases: a PPP between the State of Indiana and International Business Machines (IBM), and a PPP between Kirklees Council and the Kirklees Better Outcomes Partnership (KBOP) in the north of England. The ultimate goal in undertaking a detailed dissection of these two PPPs is to ground the theoretical concepts introduced in the preceding chapters, explore their practical implications, and derive guidance for improving the design, functioning, and effectiveness of future PPPs.

The two primary cases explored in this book were studied by the authors independently of their theoretical framing around formal-relational contracting[1]. That said, over the course of these separate investigations, each case emerged as a valuable opportunity for

1. Heinrich and Malatesta independently became interested in the Indiana-IBM case and connected when Malatesta encountered Heinrich's deposition as an expert witness in the civil trial of this PPP. Ball, Carter, and Gibson are members of the Government Outcomes Lab (GO Lab), a research center and learning and evaluation partner to the UK government's Life Chances Fund, which was set up in 2016 to explore innovation in commissioning. The Kirklees-KBOP social impact bond is co-commissioned by the Life Chances Fund and has

Contracting for Public Value. Carolyn J. Heinrich et al., Oxford University Press. © Oxford University Press (2026).
DOI: 10.1093/9780197763155.003.0003

exploring larger questions around the practice and potential of formal-relational contracting in complex PPPs. As such, our case "selection" follows a nominal approach (Soss 2021). Instead of considering whether our selected cases are representative examples of complex PPPs, we instead consider "what can be learned by treating this phenomenon as a case" of a complex PPP? (ibid., 88).

In the following sections, we first begin with a discussion of methods used for case selection and in our case analysis. We then describe the *Indiana-IBM Welfare Modernization* contract and the *Kirklees-KBOP Integrated Support Service SIB* contract in turn, offering a brief overview of the context of these PPP arrangements. We apply the conceptual framework laid out in Chapter 2 to our cases, exploring the key formal and relational elements of each contract and considering where each sits on the spectrum from formal to relational. We summarize the commonalities and differences between these two cases and highlight key factors affecting the responses of these two PPPs to the contracting challenges they faced.

CASE SELECTION

In case-driven research, there is no single approach to ascertaining which cases should be used. Traditional approaches tend to focus on the selection of appropriate cases from a whole population of theoretically relevant potential cases. Realist case selection is accordingly concerned with the identification of cases that are representative of the population and offer a useful variation on the dimensions of theoretical interest to support the causal inference (Seawright and Gerring 2008). However, such formal sampling and selection approaches are not viable for the issues we explore in this book. Emerging theoretical developments on formal-relational contracting do not (yet) point to an easily operationalized indicator or set of indicators that would allow us to readily determine the relational character of a particular contract or partnership. Even if such indicators were available, there

been used as an in-depth case study site by the GO Lab to explore the use of social impact bonds as a commissioning tool.

are no comprehensive or standardized data assembled (even within a single jurisdiction or state) that comprise a substantial set of complex public-private contracts and their key features. In the absence of requisite data, we lack a ready approach to coherently map a population of complex, cross-sector contracts that serve social welfare objectives and, further, to assess the extent to which these contracts incorporate novel or intentionally relational elements in practice.

Importantly, the methodological value of comparative case analysis does not rest on perfect comparability between cases. As Flyvbjerg (2006, 241) argues, while large-N studies offer breadth, case studies provide depth, and "both approaches are necessary for a sound development of social science." Case studies can yield valuable theoretical insights even with significant differences between cases, provided they are properly contextualized (Flyvbjerg 2006). Mahoney and Goertz (2006) further demonstrate that valid causal inference does not require perfect comparability, emphasizing instead the importance of understanding contextual conditions and scope limitations. Indeed, George and Bennett (2005) suggest that case differences can enhance analytical leverage by illuminating how varying conditions potentially influence outcomes.

Acknowledging that case differences carry methodological implications, we address these through careful attention to process rather than scale, focusing particularly on the mechanisms, timing, and consequences of different approaches in each case. The distinctions between our cases enable robust comparisons of governance mechanisms, relationship dynamics, and adaptation patterns. Although we characterize our case analysis as primarily exploratory, the casing method and process-tracing approach we employ aligns with recent methodological work emphasizing the value of analyzing varying cases to develop middle-range theory about public management mechanisms and contexts (Barzelay 2007; Pollitt 2013).[2] Our most theoretically generative comparisons emerge from the analysis of relationship management and performance management strategies, which we elaborate in subsequent chapters.

2. Barzelay (2007) is a key methodological piece about learning from case studies, focusing on how to extract theoretical insights from varying cases. We apply these insights in the last chapter. Similarly, Pollitt (2013) provides framework for analyzing contextual differences.

CASING METHOD

Because traditional case selection techniques do not comport well with this study, we instead follow an approach that has been used to great effect in prior studies of complex public-private contracting arrangements (see Brown et al. 2013; Frydlinger et al. 2021). We employ a process of *casing*—a more reflexive method—to develop our understanding of a case and how it speaks to the broader issues of contracting for public value (Ragin 2009). It is this close engagement that enables us to evaluate the extent to which each PPP exhibits the features of formal-relational contracting and to understand the PPP dynamics that shape their outcomes.

As Ragin (2009) explains, this approach is characterized by iterative engagement with evidence, dynamic case boundaries, continuous theoretical dialogue, and reflexive interpretation that leads to evolving understanding. The reflexive nature of casing means that understanding of the case evolves throughout the research process. Initial case boundaries may shift as new aspects become relevant, understanding deepens, and theoretical implications emerge. This iterative process is particularly valuable in our PPP analysis, as it enables researchers to understand formal-relational features, identify dynamic patterns, recognize contextual factors, and discover causal mechanisms that might not be apparent in a more static approach. Through continuous cycles of theoretical framework application, evidence collection, reframing understanding, and theory refinement, we develop deeper insights into how the cases speak to broader theoretical issues—that is, in this context, how PPPs exhibit features of formal-relational contracting and how their dynamics shape outcomes.

PROCESS TRACING

One of the techniques we employ to leverage both theoretical and practical insights from the cases is process tracing—a research method that systematically examines diagnostic evidence, selected and analyzed in light of research questions and hypotheses posed by the investigator. In an in-depth case study, process tracing involves a detailed analysis of plausibly causal processes, with the aim to identify the intervening causal mechanisms between independent variables and outcomes (Bennett and Checkel 2015, 7). The method requires careful documentation of how events unfold over time, with particular attention to sequence, timing, and conjunction of different factors leading to observed outcomes. Unlike other case analysis methods, process tracing explicitly investigates the decision-making processes, focusing not just on what happened but how, when, and why it happened.

Process tracing is particularly valuable for analyzing "critical junctures," that is, key decision points where different paths become possible or probable (Mahoney, 2012, 571). To this end, we interviewed key program participants and decision-makers using open-ended questions. Following guidelines for process tracing from Beach and Pedersen (2013) and George and Bennett (2005), we supplemented interviews with other forms of evidence, including internal correspondence, court records, press releases, government reports, and archival records. The interview data, combined with other documentation of the case events, allowed us to reconstruct the sequences of events and decision points that led to particular outcomes. We identify and draw on this evidence in subsequent chapters.

As Beach and Pedersen (2019:1) explain, process tracing is inherently iterative, with preliminary observations leading to new questions and insights that require additional evidence collection and analysis. Given these guidelines, we started with initial observations on how actors in the two cases differed in their approaches and formed propositions that could be assessed via process-tracing tests. These tests, often referred to as Bayesian tests, help to identify the strength and relevance of evidence for potentially inferring causality. The four main types of tests are Straw in the Wind, Hoop, Smoking Gun, and Doubly Decisive. Each test type varies in terms of its ability to confirm or disconfirm a hypothesis and its diagnostic power. Using these tests systematically allows researchers to more rigorously assess evidence, differentiate between competing explanations, and construct a plausibly causal narrative. By combining these tests within a single case and across cases, researchers can enhance the validity and reliability of their findings. Table 3.1 summarizes the purpose and interpretation of each of the four tests, which we apply in subsequent chapters.

Table 3.1 Purpose and Interpretation of Process-Tracing Tests[A]

Test	Purpose	Interpretation
Straw in the Wind Test	Provide initial support for hypotheses. *Weakest test	Passing suggests possibility but does not confirm hypothesis.
Hoop Test	Eliminate hypotheses by testing necessary conditions; akin to jumping through a hoop, i.e., must pass through to stay in consideration.	Passing eliminates other hypotheses.
Smoking Gun Test	Confirm hypotheses through sufficient evidence; requires evidence that would be highly unlikely to exist unless the hypothesis is true, e.g., something that definitively "proves" the causal relationship. The metaphor is finding a smoking gun in a suspect's hand; while this doesn't prove they committed the murder (they could have picked it up after), it would be very unlikely to observe this evidence if they were innocent.	Passing strongly confirms hypothesis, but absence doesn't disprove hypothesis.
Doubly Decisive Test	Confirm hypothesis and eliminate alternatives. *Strongest test	Passing proves hypothesis as both necessary and sufficient.

[A]Table information is modified from Beach (2020), Bennett and Checkel (2016), and Collier (2011).

THE INDIANA-IBM CONTRACT

Governor Mitch Daniels entertained grand ambitions for Indiana when he took office in 2005. Long a champion of privatization, Governor Daniels set out to modernize and improve "America's worst welfare system," one that, in his words, was "broken" and "plagued by high error rates, fraud, wasted dollars, poor conditions for its employees, and very poor service to its clients." A project of this scope was novel and complex, yet the governor was not deterred, as he envisioned a role for the private sector as the key to turning the system around from its bottom-tier ranking among the states (Marion County Superior Court, Findings of Fact 2012, 3).

Toward that end, the State of Indiana established a $1.3 billion–dollar contract (Master Services Agreement) in 2006 with the International Business Machines (IBM) Corporation and a coalition of subcontracted partners. As the prime contractor, IBM oversaw twelve other companies that became known as the "Hoosier Coalition for Self Sufficiency." For the State's part, the governor appointed Mitch Roob as Secretary of the Indiana Family Social Service Administration (FSSA), the core agency involved in the day-to-day operations of welfare services delivery. The FSSA itself was large and departmentalized, with divisions for Family Resources, Aging, Disability, Medicaid, Early Childhood, and Mental Health, to name just some of the organization's service areas. Roob was a former vice president of Affiliated Computer Services (ACS), a Dallas-based firm with strong ties to the governor's inner circle that provided information technology services and business process outsourcing to businesses, government agencies, and not-for-profit organizations. Given the high political stakes associated with the contract, members of the governor's office were also hands-on from the project's inception and as it unfolded.

Governor Daniels showcased the project in his 2008 re-election campaign, and with presidential ambitions, avowed that privatizing the system's management would lead to the improvements in performance and efficiency that the State desired. The project correspondingly received considerable attention among politicians, news outlets, academics, and ultimately, the court system. The intent in designing the bilateral contract known as Master Services Agreement (MSA) was for it to govern the Indiana welfare system's management—in particular, decisions about welfare eligibility—for 10 years, yet the agreement was severed less than three years later. Ironically, in the words of the governor, "the project did not work because the concept itself was flawed."

The need for change in "America's Worst Welfare System"

Since 1991, the State of Indiana's welfare system has been overseen by the FSSA, which is broadly responsible for human services within the state, including its major public assistance programs: Medicaid, the Supplemental Nutrition Assistance Program (SNAP, formerly known as Food Stamps), and Temporary Assistance for Needy Families (TANF). The FSSA was initially formed by consolidating the state's departments of Mental Health, Public Welfare, and Human Services to better coordinate social services provision for citizens. The following years, however, brought about national welfare reform and a changing political context, alongside a range of challenges within the FSSA, and the agency was perceived to be unfit for purpose.

In 1996, the federal government passed the Personal Responsibility and Work Opportunity Act (PRWORA), which marked the most significant reform to the US welfare system since the New Deal. It significantly curtailed welfare provision, imposing new eligibility requirements and a conditionality regime (work requirements) on participants. In addition, it granted much broader autonomy over welfare programs to state governments (O'Connor 2001). These changes, in combination with rapid economic growth, resulted in a reduction in welfare caseloads across the US of 58%. In Indiana, however, caseloads declined by a mere 6.3% between 1996 and 2005, placing the state at 50th out of 50 states in terms of welfare caseload reductions and over 20 percentage points behind 49th-place Kansas. Internal reviews and an independent audit by KPMG identified a range of issues, including a lack of training and oversight, and internal silos that were exacerbated by limited coordination in contracting, accounting, and technology systems (Indiana Legislative Services Agency 2004).

Upon assuming office in January 2005, Governor Daniels oversaw a series of reforms aimed at addressing the FSSA's failings. Direct responsibility for child welfare was removed from the FSSA and transferred to the newly created Department of Child Services. This left the Division of Family Resources (DFR) within the FSSA to act as a gateway to the state's key welfare support programs—Food Stamps, TANF, Medicaid, and the Child Care and Development Fund (CCDF)—by determining whether clients were eligible for support.

Yet concerns persisted about the DFR's eligibility system. A 2006 report, *Eligibility Modernization: The Need for Change*, identified a series of problems with the existing system. These included inconsistencies in the application of rules and policies and extremely high caseloads for staff, which contributed to several knock-on effects. The three major welfare programs had case error rates between 12% and 35%, implying that taxpayer money was being paid to ineligible recipients. The system was also slow, with many cases not processed within federally mandated timelines and a backlog of more than 13,000 cases. At an individual level, 82% of clients required two or more face-to-face visits to become eligible for support, placing significant burdens on applicants, with 65% rating their satisfaction with the service as "below average" (ibid.).

Modernizing Indiana's welfare eligibility system

When Governor Daniels and his team sought to contract out Indiana's welfare eligibility system to the private sector, the "Hoosier Coalition for Self Sufficiency" responded to the Request for Information (RFI) calling for proposals to build and implement a new system. This precipitated complex and protracted contract negotiations, culminating in the 160-page MSA that included numerous exhibits and appendices, and 24 schedules clarifying the parties' responsibilities and detailing performance metrics and penalties for nonperformance (Goldsmith and Burke 2009, 99). The State's legal team brought extensive experience and political connections to the negotiating table, and IBM's lawyers were equally experienced and skilled at negotiating onerous contract terms (Overby 2012). FSSA officials, including Secretary Roob, had specific ideas on how the contract should be structured, and a key subcontractor organization, ACS, was also involved in the negotiations.

The parties recognized that a complete system overhaul was required, and they agreed that the contract should be long-term to account for IBM's significant upfront capital investment in information technology. IBM, along with ACS, assumed the major responsibilities for developing the technology and systems for receiving and processing applications for public assistance, including collecting and verifying data, document imaging and management, and in some counties, operating and managing Vendor Service Locations, or local service offices, directly. Approximately 99% of the state's government employees went to work with IBM or its subcontractors, with comparable pay, benefits, and pensions (email message to Dennis Ryerson, July 29, 2007 [FSSA1_07392708]).

To hold the Hoosier Coalition accountable to the public and improve performance as assessed federally, the MSA included numerous specific performance standards (MSA §3.8) and extensive reporting requirements (MSA §3.13.1). In the end, despite efforts to achieve some balance between rigidity and flexibility and to be "pragmatic" about how to define success (Dryer 2012, 15), the 10-year agreement between the State of Indiana and IBM (signed in December 2006) was a performance-based contract replete with clauses that sought to shift risk away from the State if the desired standards were not met.

While the State and the IBM-led Coalition established a joint vision for the Indiana welfare system and set milestones, under the MSA (Schedule 14), IBM was the sole point of contact for contractual matters and was solely responsible for obligations, services, and functions performed by the subcontractors (see Figure 3.1). Typically, this apex role is called a "prime contractor." With an IBM investment of $9.5 million in hardware and software to accommodate new workflows, the Hoosier Coalition embarked on a groundbreaking, high-tech privatization revolution to assist the state's most vulnerable citizens in a new and more financially responsible way. Nonetheless, IBM was required to provide evidence of the subcontractors' ability to perform their contracted functions, and the State reserved the right to replace subcontractors for performance concerns. In addition, IBM was required to

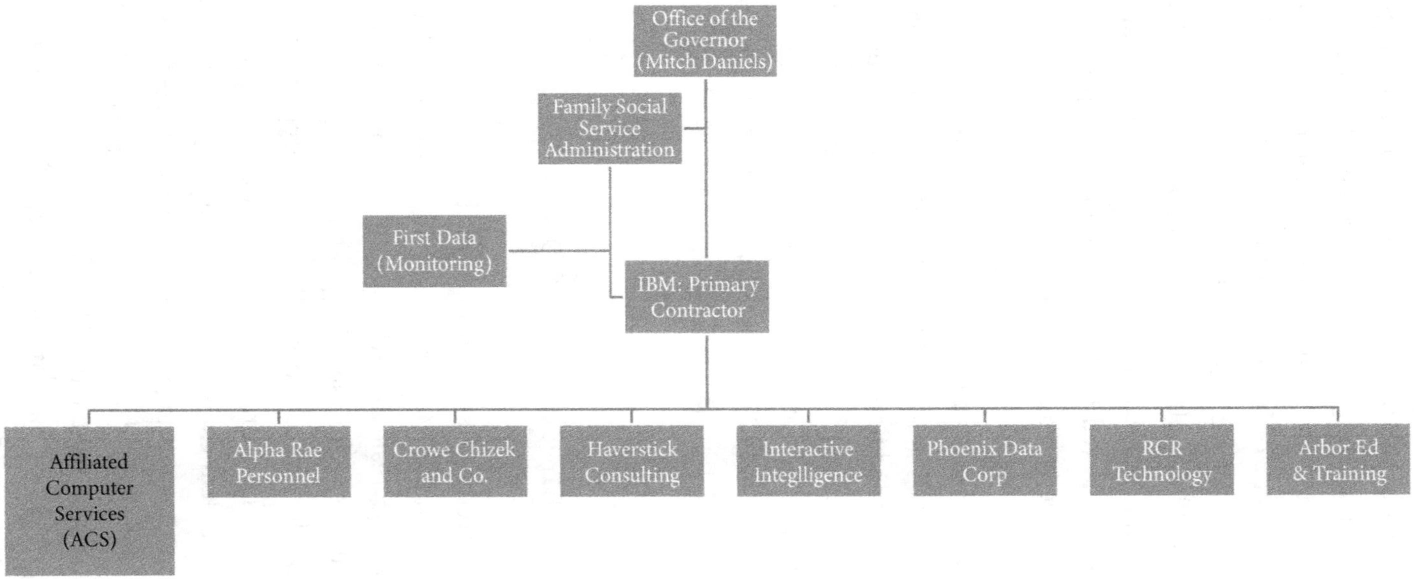

Figure 3.1 The Formal Structure of the Indiana-IBM PPP

include specific, mandatory provisions in its agreements with subcontractors. Consequently, the State retained tight control and oversight of services provision, including in areas where the MSA appeared to cede authority to IBM as the overarching prime contractor. These contractual features situate the State of Indiana-IBM PPP on the formal end of the spectrum shown in Figure 2.3 in Chapter 2.

The Hoosier Coalition rolled out the modernization project in three stages to 59 Indiana counties. Phase 1 of the project began in March 2007, and Phase 2 followed over seven months beginning in October 2007, initiating a twelve-county pilot representing about 10% of the state's caseload. Although the public record shows continuing client service complaints, high error rates, and backlogs in these early phases, progress was hampered in part by a severe (Indiana) recession in 2007 and a series of storms and floods. The State thus gave its authorization to move forward with the modernization plan, and the Coalition initiated Phase 3 involving an additional 27 counties in March 2008. It expanded to 20 more counties in May 2008 when the State gave the go-ahead again. The State gave IBM notice of termination of the MSA just 15 months later, in August 2009.

THE KIRKLEES COUNCIL–KBOP CONTRACT

Our second case study centers on an award-winning partnership arrangement led by Kirklees Metropolitan Council in Yorkshire, northern England. To support residents who are at risk of homelessness, the Kirklees Council has a longstanding set of contracts with a group of nonprofit provider organizations. This local support service has its origins in a £1.8 billion–grant from the national Supporting People program, which was launched in 2003. Supporting People aimed to improve funding and local integration for housing-related services such as tenancy management, drug and alcohol support, or employment support for vulnerable people (ODPM Committee 2004). Provision of accommodation was not part of the service offer, and it came to be known as Floating Support. The program's ambition articulated in 2001 still applies: to "enable people to remain in a more independent living situation, avoiding institutional care such as hospitals or, at the extreme, prison or a life on the streets. Equally it aims to help people in such institutional care to move to a more independent and stable home in the community" (Department for Environment, Transport and the Regions, Supporting People—Policy into Practice, January 2001; cited in Jarrett 2012, 6).

The services for adults facing social disadvantage in Kirklees have not always been award winning. Our research predates the introduction of the acclaimed Kirklees Council–KBOP contract. From 2003 to 2019, the service providers were contracted via a set of fee-for-service contracting arrangements. The Supporting People grant ended in 2010, when a new national government in the UK began an austerity program after the 2007–2008 global financial crisis. The Council endeavored to maintain the service itself but had to cut the budget. In dialogue with service providers, this reduction was achieved by shortening the duration of support, increasing the threshold of eligibility, and reducing staff numbers. In Kirklees in 2019, there were nine providers operating under 15 separate Council contracts with a total value of £3.4 million to support around 2,000 adults per year.

By 2019, a combination of repeated cuts to the funding and a lack of attention to the continued suitability of the contracts had led to persistently poor outcomes for the people accessing these services. The arrangements faced five significant challenges (Rosenbach and Carter 2021).

1. Neglect of the provider market

The Council team who managed the contracts was severely constrained, creating multiple issues. Limited resources were available for shaping services or for stewarding local delivery organizations to ensure a thriving market to buy from, and there were occasional difficulties in replacing poorly performing service providers. Several organizations were simultaneously delivering very similar contracts. Successive short-term contract arrangements reduced providers' ability to address long-term participant outcomes and diverted resources from helping service users to managing contract extensions.

2. Lack of understanding of demand and range of needs

There was limited information on the relative demand for, and performance of, services offered by different providers. This meant the Council could not easily estimate the overall demand for the service, nor the range of individual needs, and could not track service users re-entering the system (referred to as a "revolving door"). Because there was no central referral or allocation process, service users were put on multiple waiting lists with different providers. Council managers indicated that a key obstacle to better oversight was the failure to establish a central intelligence system. Yet an attempt to establish a unified case management computer system had failed due to austerity measures.

3. Limited performance management

Key performance indicators (KPIs) in the legacy contracts appeared to drive some perverse behaviors. Providers had to report a KPI based on how much their service was being used, giving them an incentive to recruit users to their own service, and leading them to compete with each other for referrals. The large number of contracts between the Council and service providers (which peaked at 27 in 2017–2018) meant the scarce contract management function of the Council was thinly spread. The approach focused on compliance with processes, leaving providers themselves to determine success. The Council lacked both granular, meaningful performance information, and the contractual levers to act on it.

4. Inflexible services

The type and amount of support to be offered was strictly specified in contracts. This meant service providers were not able to offer tailored, person-centered services. Support length and the frequency of interactions between frontline staff and service participants were fixed. This inflexibility made it especially hard to help people with the most acute needs.

5. Insufficient collaboration leading to user disengagement

Neither the providers nor the Council could access information on who was receiving support, or had done so in the past, unless that information happened to be held by the same, single provider organization. This meant providers were not able to access or consider service user histories or prior support experiences. This resulted in duplicated effort and reproduced support practices, even if inappropriate or unsuccessful. Service users receiving support from multiple providers had to tell their story multiple times. This lack of coordination between providers working with the same individuals discouraged people from continuing to engage with support.

In 2019, the Council launched a remodeled set of services operating under a single contract with the involvement of a new coordinating organization: the Kirklees Better Outcomes Partnership (KBOP). The ambition was for a partnership that would combine the expertise of each of the partnering organizations (Kirklees Better Outcomes Partnership 2020). Like the Hoosier Coalition, KBOP would be an overarching or "prime" contractor, meaning there would be a single contract with the Council and several subcontracts with multiple providers (see Figure 3.2). Working with these subcontracted providers, the Kirklees-KBOP PPP sought to improve accommodation, employment, stability, and well-being outcomes for vulnerable aults, some of whom might face multiple challenges, including homelessness or the immediate risk of becoming homeless, mental health or substance misuse issues, domestic violence, and offending.

The single contract between KBOP and Kirklees Council differed from the previous 15 provider contracts in three important ways. Rather than specifying the length and intensity of support to be provided (e.g., 4–8 hours of support from a case worker per week), it specified social outcomes to be achieved: sustained accommodation; education and qualifications; employment; volunteering; engagement with drug and alcohol services; and well-being. Rather than a monthly advance block payment calculated on week-by-week costs, payment was to be based on performance. And rather than performance being based on service utilization and a loosely interpreted "independent living" indicator, it would be regularly measured through standardized outcome metrics with predefined evidence requirements.

These three differences mark the Kirklees-KBOP contract as a so-called "social outcomes contract." The UK Government has been experimenting with performance-based contracting as a way to improve public services for many years (Carter et al. 2018; NAO 2015). When

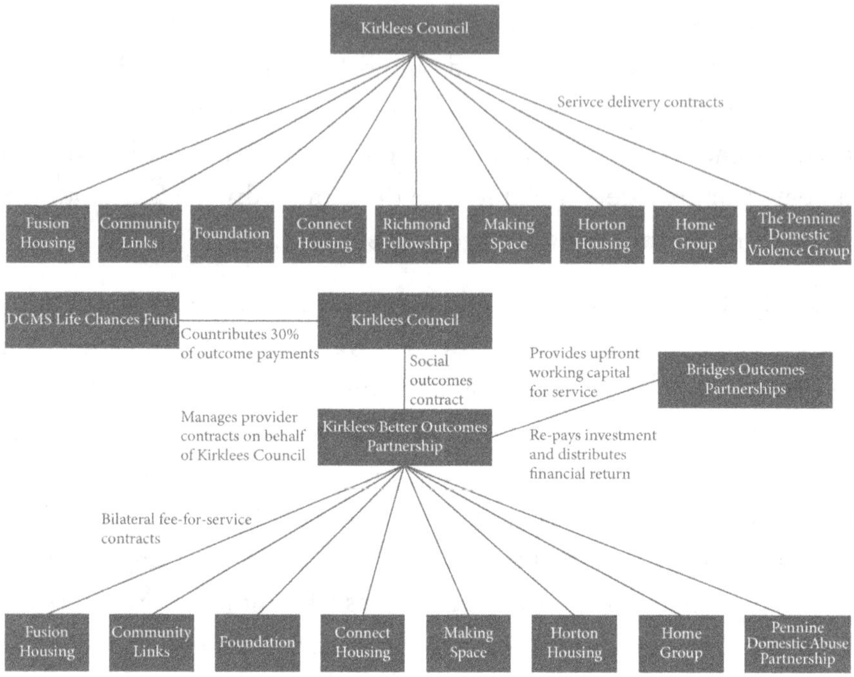

Figure 3.2 The Formal Structure of the Kirklees Council-KBOP PPP

large proportions of payment are backended and contingent on the achievement of outcomes, this creates a need for upfront working capital. In the case of Kirklees, this was provided by third-party intermediaries, Bridges Outcomes Partnerships, who brought in independent social investment funds that were used to set up KBOP, which they own. This combination of outcomes-based contract and upfront social investment marks the Kirklees-KBOP arrangement as an SIB, as introduced in Chapter 1.

As we further describe in the next chapter, the Kirklees Council–KBOP contract has other important features beyond being outcomes-based. It sets out expectations for strong collaboration, a clear joint governance structure, and processes for managing change. These features situate the Kirklees Council–KBOP PPP on the relational end of the spectrum shown in Figure 2.2 in Chapter 2.

In addition, there are two key ways in which the KBOP was expected to improve services and outcomes for participants. At the frontline, it was expected that the outcomes focus would bring greater flexibility to respond to service user needs so that support workers could focus on and be responsive to an individual's strengths. The single prime contractor, KBOP, was expected to facilitate coordination by shaping service pathways, supporting service providers, and providing collaborative infrastructure so that delivery organizations could work together toward the same goals. Unlike in the Hoosier Coalition, KBOP could manage the entry and exit of subcontracted service delivery organizations.

COMPARING THE CASES

Based on the Indiana-IBM and Kirklees-KBOP case overviews presented above, we first highlight some commonalities that make the cases valuable for comparison.

(i) **A failing system requiring intervention**. Indiana's welfare system, delivered fully via a single public agency (the FSSA), was manifestly failing, as described above. The State chose to outsource its welfare services delivery to multiple, private sector organizations. Kirklees had a mixed provision of multiple independent providers, but this arrangement was similarly failing to achieve satisfactory results, due to budgetary erosion and a failure to adapt accordingly. Thus, both cases start with a less-than-desirable performance record that can only be improved going forward. Such reference points offer a standard for expectations (Hart and Moore 2008).

(ii) **Political prominence.** In Indiana, the Republican Party Governor Mitch Daniels made state welfare reform a prominent part of his election campaign. This accorded the program greater political salience than it might otherwise have had. In addition, the governor's commitment to the project appeared guaranteed at least until he secured re-election in 2008. In Kirklees, the contracting reform was enabled by the Life Chances Fund, an £80-million fund announced by the newly elected Conservative government in 2016 to stimulate the use of SIBs by local authorities across England. Like in Indiana, this gave the initiative political salience, and both were oriented toward satisfying conservative interests and demonstrating the value of innovative public sector forms that leverage private sector expertise and resources.

(iii) **High strategic importance and thus high cost of failure.** Both projects were high stakes for their respective governments and the acting political figures in terms of accountability to the public. In both cases, failure would be extremely costly, and not just financially. Both pecuniary and nonpecuniary costs would be incurred by vulnerable populations in need of social services, citizens, taxpayers, politicians, and multiple contracted organizations.

(iv) **Novelty and complexity.** The Indiana-IBM and Kirklees-KBOP projects were innovative, bringing new approaches to long-standing delivery challenges in social welfare services. This complexity arises from the need to address diverse and interconnected issues such as healthcare, housing, or welfare support. Vulnerable populations often require services that are not one-size-fits-all, necessitating tailored approaches. Multistakeholder coordination ensures services are holistic and comprehensive, as no single provider can address all needs effectively.

(v) **Partnership structure.** Both cases involve the use of a prime contractor–subcontractor network. The prime contractor in the UK case is KBOP. In the Indiana-IBM case, IBM is the prime contractor. The prime in each case coordinates the subcontractors, ensuring compliance with standards and contract goals. Both included an intermediary between the public contracting authority and the rest of the market and in both cases, this manifested as a prime contractor managing multiple subcontractors. Indeed, complex governance arrangements are required to manage overlapping roles, distribute risks, and ensure accountability. In both cases, there was a clear need to ensure that an array of nongovernmental agencies were well coordinated and that each party had clearly delineated scope and duties, and ideally, alignment of end goals. In addition, both projects had to grapple with a complicated web of accountability demands operating at multiple levels and via multiple lines.

(vi) **Performance management.** Both cases employed complex performance management systems, essential for evaluating the success of PPPs. This includes tracking KPIs such as the number of individuals served, improved outcomes like employment rates, or cost-efficiency metrics. Performance management is particularly challenging with multiple stakeholders with potentially differing priorities.

(vii) **Disruptive external events.** Both projects were disrupted by external events that were not predicted at the outset when the contracts were negotiated and signed. In Indiana, the global financial crisis of 2007–2008 hit within the first two years, while the project was still being rolled out. In 2008, people across the state experienced widespread damage and personal loss from storms and floods. These two scenarios sharply escalated demand for social welfare services, as more people found themselves in material distress and applied for welfare. In Kirklees, the COVID-19 pandemic of 2020–2021 made delivery of support services much more challenging due to social distancing and "lockdown" restrictions. The fallout from the pandemic also disrupted cost and demand assumptions made when the contract had been negotiated and signed in the previous year (2019).

The commonalities across the cases are summarized in Table 3.2 below.

In addition, the case study PPPs have important differences as described below.

(i) **Scale and scope.** The Indiana case involves a much larger financial scale ($1.3 billion) compared to Kirklees (£22.3 million). Indiana-IBM's contract value, $1.3 billion at the time of signing in 2006, was more than fifty times larger than the Kirklees-KBOP contract at the time of signing in 2019

Table 3.2 CASE COMMONALITIES

A Failing System	• Began as a result of failing programs • Initiated PPPs to correct or improve failing programs
Political Prominence	• Involved political actors with key roles in approving the PPP approach • Included programs and outcomes requiring political support
High Importance and High Cost of Failure	• High stakes for vulnerable populations • Significant and multifaceted consequences for government revenue and fiscal sustainability
Novelty and Complexity	• Involved complex social services delivery • Targeted vulnerable populations • Required multistakeholder coordination • Operated through prime contractor models
Partnership Structure	• Used prime contractor-subcontractor network • Involved public-private collaboration • Required complex governance arrangements • Managed multiple service providers
Performance Management	• Used outcomes-based performance management for accountability • Required public value demonstration • Managed multiple stakeholders' interests
Disruptive External Events	• Faced major, unanticipated external disruptions • Required crisis adaptation • Managed demand fluctuations • Needed stakeholder coordination during crisis

(£ 22.3 million, equivalent to $22.4 million in 2006, the year that the Indiana-IBM contract was signed).[3] A US state is

3. Average exchange rate in 2019 was £1 = $1.2772; $1 in 2006 was worth $1.27 in 2019, https://www.exchangerates.org.uk/GBP-USD-spot-exchange-rates-history-2019.html; https://www.in2013dollars.com/us/inflation/2006?endYear=2019&amount=100.

considerably larger in terms of the population served and has considerably more autonomy than an English Council. These differences reflect distinct population sizes and geographic scopes, likely influencing the complexity and reach of the respective projects.

(ii) **Institutional context.** The institutional settings of the US and the UK bring inherent contrasts. The Indiana-IBM case operates at a statewide level, while Kirklees is a municipal case. The US and UK governance systems differ in their political structures, regulatory frameworks, and public service traditions. These distinctions shape how projects are planned, implemented, and monitored, with varying degrees of centralization and public accountability.

(iii) **Time period.** We present three timelines to illustrate the time periods of the two cases. Although the contract execution in these cases occurs in distinct time periods, the case timelines overlap because the Indiana-IBM PPP outcomes played out in two subsequent phases, initial legal proceedings (competing lawsuits) and a damages phase through 2020 (see Figure 3.3). Hence, although the contracts were initiated and the PPPs implemented in different economic contexts, levels of technological advancement, and political and social times (see Figures 3.4 and 3.5), the time period of our analysis overlaps in the Indiana-IBM and Kirklees-KBOP cases, spanning the years 2006–2024. We recognize that having been initiated at a later time (2017), the Kirklees-KBOP PPP may involve learning from earlier or parallel cases, especially as global knowledge–sharing has improved.

A summary of the basic case differences is presented in Table 3.3 below. In the next section, we describe the contrasting ways in which the PPP partners in each case handled challenges in executing their project work.

Figure 3.3 Indiana-IBM (Legal) Case Timeline

Table 3.3 CASE DIFFERENCES

Scale and Scope	• Indiana-IBM ($1.3B) vs. Kirklees-KBOP (£22.3M) • State-wide vs. municipal level • Different population sizes • Different geographic scope
Institutional Context	• US vs. UK governance systems • Different political structures • Different regulatory frameworks • Different public service traditions
Time Period	• Different economic contexts • Different technology available • Different social expectations • Indiana-IBM "hard" ending (contract termination) vs. Kirklees-KBOP "soft" ending (contract extension) • Learning from previous cases possible

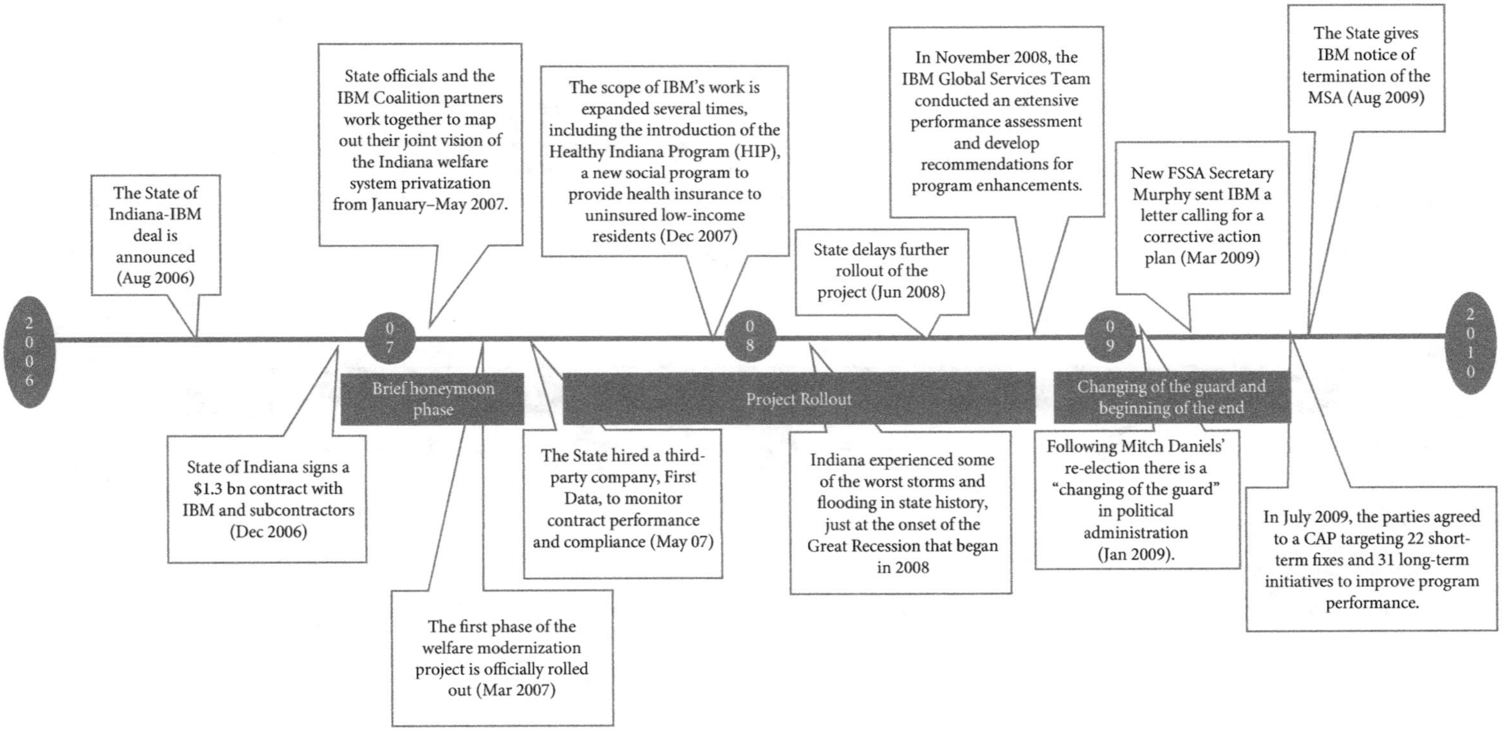

Figure 3.4 Indiana-IBM PPP Contract Execution Timeline

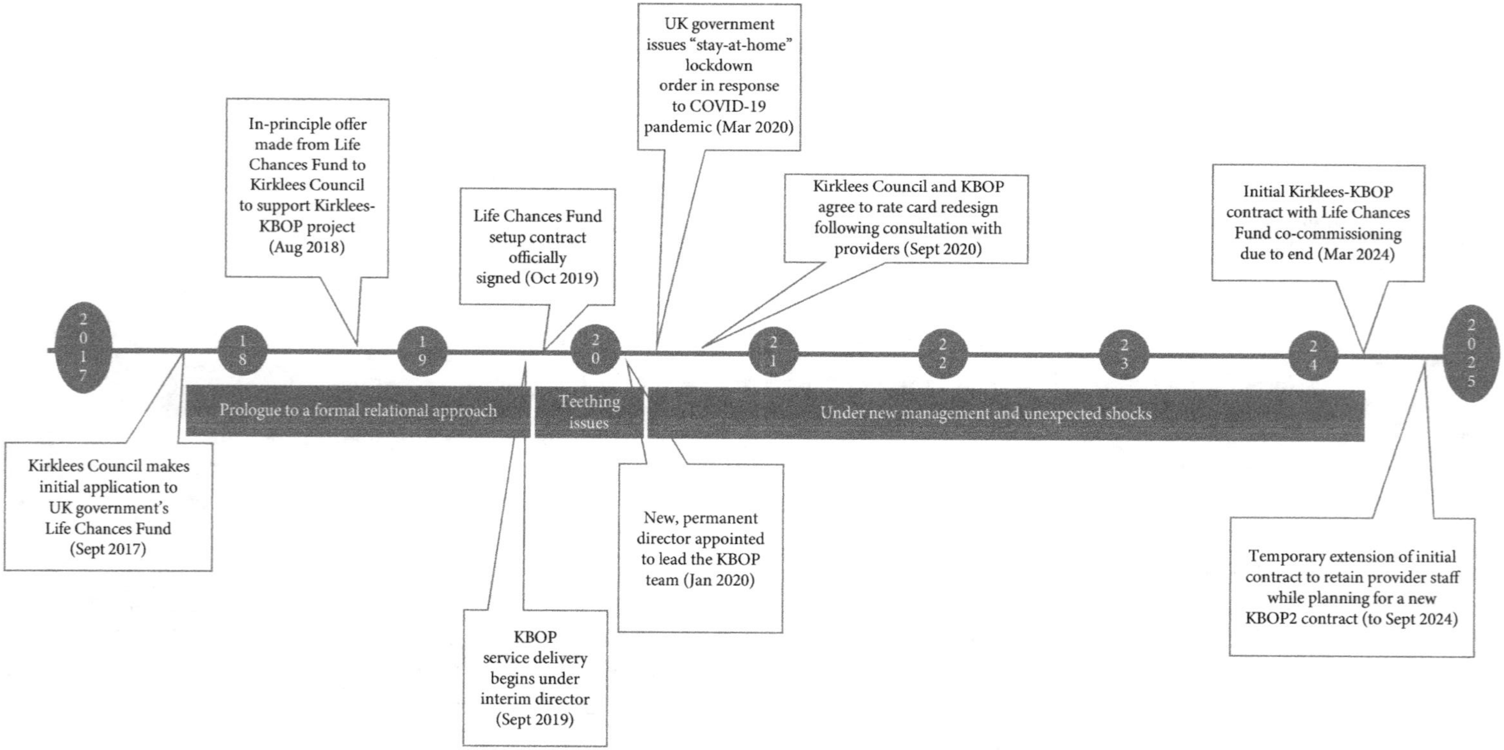

Figure 3.5 Kirklees Council-KBOP PPP Timeline

CONTRASTING APPROACHES TO PPP CHALLENGES: NORMS AND EXPECTATIONS

As we elaborate in Chapter 4, the Indiana-IBM and Kirklees-KBOP cases addressed the challenges they encountered in very different ways. In previewing these differences, we outline key factors affecting how the PPP parties responded to them (see Table 3.4), firstly in terms of how they are dealt with in the written contract, and secondly in how they manifest in the partnerships in practice.

1. Focus and scope of work

The two projects had contrasting approaches to how the work to be done was specified and how rigidly that specification was policed.

The Indiana-IBM contract emphasized compliance over cooperation. Paradoxically, the rigid contractual specifications for service delivery and KPIs did not prevent ambiguity and contrasting interpretations of scope, including what was and wasn't billable. The contract was subjected to four amendments in the first 16 months of delivery, but these focused on renegotiating minutiae of the contract rather than

Table 3.4 Key Factors Affecting the PPP Responses to Challenges

Dimension	The Written Contract	The Partnership in Practice
Focus and Scope of Work	Is the objective of the partnership tightly specified? Is this framed as a commercial transaction?	How do the parties understand the purpose of the partnership? Do they work toward a shared overarching goal?
Duration and Planning	What is the expected duration of the contracted partnership and is future cooperation anticipated?	How do the parties come together? Are there references to prior relationships or accommodations for time needed for relationships to be established and embedded?

Continued

Table 3.4 CONTINUED

Dimension	The Written Contract	The Partnership in Practice
Exchange Rules, Control Rights, and Risk Management	Are payment incentives tied to performance? How is this verified? How are risks allocated between parties? What formal rights does the contract confer on each party, and what remedies are available? Do contract terms apply throughout the chain of subcontractors? What right does each party have to initiate or execute contract changes or termination? Does the contract explicitly anticipate changing circumstances? If so, what allowances are made?	Do partners accept evidence of performance/underperformance? How do parties seek to protect their interests in practice? Are formal contract rights referred to or renegotiated during contract performance (delivery)? Are they relied upon in court? Does the contracting agency prioritize compliance over adaptation? Is ongoing learning welcomed or discouraged?
Governance and Communication	How should key decisions be made? Are formal processes described for this? Who is accountable to whom, and for what?	When unforeseen risks arise, how are they navigated? Are decisions made jointly through negotiations or unilaterally imposed? How does communication flow between the partners?
Social Norms and Principles	Does the contract describe expectations of behavior or social norms that each party must adhere to, such as fairness or equal treatment?	Do actors in each party behave pro-socially, or are negative "shading" behaviors exhibited? How does poor performance (or a perception of poor performance) affect behaviors?

directly addressing challenging operational and performance matters. This continual renegotiation failed to stop opportunistic behavior and shading. Nor did it lead on its own to an increase in trust among the parties.

The Kirklees-KBOP contract has considerably looser contract specifications, offering the prime contractor high flexibility in terms of service specifications, provider composition, and contract modifications. For example, it includes formal mechanisms to "flex" outcome measures as circumstances change. The need for review and adaptation is actively anticipated with scheduled review processes in the contract. There were uncertainties in the early stages around the evidence requirements for outcome achievement, but these had been resolved through dialogue between the Council and KBOP, alongside a major reworking of the rate card against which the partnership is paid.

2. Duration and planning

Both cases were affected in different ways by prior relationships among some of the parties. In the Indiana-IBM case, the government relied heavily on consultants and advisers for planning. The previous mayor of Indianapolis, Stephen Goldsmith, was a frequent adviser to the governor who also had ties to one of the main subcontractors, ACS. The Law Firm of Barnes and Thornburg also had a prominent role in planning and drafting the contract. FSSA Secretary and former vice-president of ACS, Mitch Roob, hired The Lucas Group for approximately $4 million to help write contract specifications. According to documentation from the ensuing legal activity, ACS had originally expected to be awarded the prime contract and sought at times to undermine actions taken by IBM as the prime or lead role in the MSA. In other words, rather than using this stock of "relational capital" to support a strong partnership committed to effective delivery of welfare services, it was used to opportunistically thwart actions undertaken by the prime contractor, particularly when a social norm such as "fairness" was perceived to have been breached.

In the Kirklees-KBOP case, the Council had a prior relationship with all nine of the initial subcontractors, who had been directly contracted by the Council prior to the launch of the social outcomes contract and new service arrangements. None of these longstanding delivery partners expressed an appetite to step into the role of the prime contractor or to lead an alliance of multiple delivery organizations. The intermediary, Bridges Outcomes Partnerships, established and owned the prime contractor, KBOP. Although Bridges had no prior relationship with the Council, the project spent nearly two years in joint development prior to executing the contract, allowing relational capital to be built up and establishing collaborative relationships between the partners in advance of delivery commencing.

3. Performance management: Exchange rules, control rights, and risk management

The projects had different ways of managing performance and allocating risk between the parties.

The Indiana-IBM contract relied primarily on input-based performance indicators: procedure variance rates, office staffing hours and availability, call response and hold times, document barcodes, scanning resolution, timeliness of procedures, and implementation milestones for the transition. Many of these were not under the sole authority of the prime contractor or its subcontractors to deliver on the performance expectations but rather relied on the continued cooperation and input from the state agency, FSSA. Only one of these performance input measures was related to outputs or outcomes: family work participation. All of these performance metrics suffered from an attribution issue: if performance was poor, the prime contractor assumed responsibility, without necessarily being able to ascertain which sub-contractor (or State of Indiana unit or employee) was the source of the issue.

The Kirklees outcomes contract relies on a very different performance incentive structure. A predefined "rate card" was produced, specifying outcomes to be achieved with service users, how they would be measured, and the price to be paid. Importantly, the ability to adjust these outcome metrics was allowed through mutual agreement as circumstances changed. This acknowledged that contract completeness was unrealistic: it would be impossible to tune up the contractual incentives to perfectly match the principal's desired outcomes because the exact circumstances of services delivery were not yet known and pre-existing performance data were scarce. The risk of nonachievement of outcomes is held by KBOP, as the social investment–backed prime contractor, while the risk of insufficient referrals and of insufficient connectivity to other Council services is held by the Council. Some performance risk is cascaded to the supply chain through activity-related KPIs between the prime and subcontractors. Accordingly, the risk of performance problems associated with the incomplete contract in Kirklees-KBOP is distributed across the partners, rather than falling largely on a single partner with limited control (as in the Indiana-IBM case).

The Indiana contract was rigid and included fixed "boilerplate" terms that the State was required to include according to strict guidelines. These included a "termination for convenience" clause, a "non-collusion statement," a "drug free certification," and a certification that the Vendor has "no investment in Iran" (MSA, Articles 14–21). The termination clause turned out to be particularly damaging to the contractual relationship in practice since it allowed the State to terminate without cause and assume the prime contractor's responsibilities, despite the nominal 10-year contract duration. Not only did this undermine trust, but the clause was relied upon and ultimately exercised by the State.

The Kirklees-KBOP contract also included formal contract rights, but there were no discernable attempts to exercise or enforce these. One formal right of particular importance is that the prime contractor receives compensation from the contracting authority if the latter terminates the contract early. This protects its asset-specific investment, while giving the contracting authority a strong financial incentive to maintain the contract.

4. Governance and communication

The PPPs had very different infrastructure for decision-making.

In the Indiana-IBM PPP, the State transferred responsibility for subcontractors' competence, performance, and financial resilience onto its prime contractor, IBM, while retaining the right to fire subcontractors for poor performance. This created an issue of "multiple principals," where subcontractors are beholden to the performance expectations of more than one entity (both the State and IBM in this case). One of the subcontractors, ACS, played the two principals off against one another, contributing to well-known accountability problems such as conflicting expectations, confusion, negativism, loss of control, and blame games (Schillemans and Bovens 2015). Some of the nefarious behavior of ACS employees may have also been driven by perceived unfairness:

IBM received higher compensation, yet ACS employees felt they were "picking up their work." IBM, for its part, exercised weak control over its subcontractors, constrained by the allocation of authority in the formal contract arrangements. It did not pass through liabilities and performance expectations from the prime contract to its subcontractors.

The Kirklees-KBOP contract gave the Council no right to directly intervene with subcontractors. However, forums for shared governance and decision-making were set up in practice, which included the Council, prime contractor, and subcontractors. The prime contractor retained much of the performance risk of the contract but retained the ability to manage the performance of subcontractors. To date, one subcontractor has, at mutual agreement, left the service provider role under circumstances of ongoing poor performance.

5. Social norms and principles

Social norms played different but important roles in both projects.

As we will explore in Chapter 4, actors in the Indiana-IBM case sought to bind one another to social norms, even though these were not explicitly laid out in the written contract or cultivated relationally. As a result, a perception that the norms of fairness and reciprocity were being broken triggered actions that led to the contract termination: IBM declined to shift to a plan B "hybrid" delivery model (mixed remote and physical provision) without additional compensation, and the State refused to grant the requested compensation. The actors, in turn, exhibited a whole host of negative behaviors. One of the subcontractors, ACS, engaged in willful noncooperation and appeared to connive with the state government against the prime contractor. The state government, for its part, searched for a pretext for termination (among the KPIs), publicly shifted blame onto its contractors, and sought to actively sabotage suppliers' reputations.

The Kirklees-KBOP partnership, in contrast, makes shared principles explicit in the written contract. The contract preface includes a statement of shared aims: "The Parties shall develop a close working relationship between the Authority and the Contractor at all appropriate levels, based upon openness and trust in a transparent information and data sharing environment" (Kirklees Council 2019, 15). There is evidence that social norms, both explicit and tacit, have been strongly adhered to by the parties. For example, during the COVID-19 lockdown, the Kirklees-KBOP partnership was the first service in the Kirklees area to set up a support helpline, and the Council offered more assured funding during this period. KBOP providers quickly pivoted to providing alternative models of support, including providing access to medications and food packages. Parties came together at pace and sought to cooperatively address the biggest challenges facing service users and the wider Kirklees community, even though this lay outside the direct scope of the contract.

In Chapter 4, we explore in greater depth the differing approaches in the Indiana-IBM and Kirklees-KBOP cases to the common challenges inherent in managing PPPs as their work unfolded. We then investigate in Chapter 5 how these differences shaped or contributed to the success (or failure) of each PPP in meeting its stated goals.

4

Analysis of a March Down Different Paths to Public-Private Partnership Failure Versus Success

In this chapter, we delve into the case evidence on the two PPPs introduced in Chapter 3, Indiana-IBM and Kirklees-KBOP, which pursued similarly configured partnerships to unlock public value, but yielded very different results. As shown in Chapter 3 (Figures 3.1 and 3.2), both the Indiana-IBM and Kirklees-KBOP PPPs were led by a prime contractor (contracted to the lead public entity) that managed a plethora of subcontracted partners and providers in delivering services to the public. Yet the PPPs launched on different footing in three different ways: in their relationships with subcontractors; in their efforts to develop relational mechanisms alongside formal contract structures; and in the partner orientations toward collaboration. The detailed case analysis we present will show the divergent approaches that each PPP followed in balancing the formal and relational aspects of their contracts as they sought to move away from precarious contracting circumstances and onto the path to sustained collaboration and PPP success, as illustrated in Figure 2.1 in Chapter 2. We begin below with an in-depth account of the Indiana-IBM PPP launch, progression, and demise, and we then turn to the Kirklees-KBOP implementation of a formal-relational approach

Contracting for Public Value. Carolyn J. Heinrich et al., Oxford University Press. © Oxford University Press (2026).
DOI: 10.1093/9780197763155.003.0004

to contracting. We follow with a discussion that aims to make sense of these PPPs' march down very different paths that resulted in their respective contract and PPP outcomes.

THE INDIANA CASE: THE UNFOLDING OF A FAILED PPP

In describing how the Indiana-IBM PPP unfolded and how the dynamics of the formal and informal aspects of relationships played out as the welfare modernization project progressed, we organize the narrative into four key phases. We provide a brief overview of these phases—identified based on events conveyed by informants[1] and in correspondence among key parties, press accounts, and government and court documents—and then present the case evidence and interpretation of the evidence through the conceptual lenses described in the preceding chapters.

(1) *The prelude and the promises.* This period covers early events up to the signing of the contract in December of 2006. It establishes the foundation for project decisions, including costs, roles of key participants, project scope, governance and relational rules, expectations, culture, and tone of the parties' interactions.

(2) *The brief honeymoon stage.* This short time interval follows the contract's signing, including implementation of the pilot and when problems are evident but there is still a small but detectable level of cooperation among the partners. It is also a critical period for planning and adjusting expectations. This phase ends around May of 2007.

1. We asked informants what events they thought were most important in shaping the project and in determining how the project progressed, whether positive or negative. The construction of these four project phases reflects the informants' responses: "when the contract was finally signed"; "when personnel were transferred"; "when the pilot began"; "when the rollout to 50 some counties started before we were ready"; "when the Governor was re-elected"; "when Murphy became the new head of FSSA and started shutting IBM down," etc.

(3) *The project rollout.* From mid-2007 until about November of 2008, the Indiana-IBM project implementation is underway. Investments by the partners continue, despite some mixed feedback. In this period, new challenges and contingencies emerge, and the partners attempt successive adjustments to iron out glitches in the system and respond to external disruptions.

(4) *The changing of the guard and beginning of the end.* This time period begins with the re-election of the governor and the appointment of new leadership to the FSSA. It ends with the State terminating the contract with IBM.

THE PRELUDE AND THE PROMISES

The Indiana-IBM case is a "textbook" example of the challenges in developing an effective and enduring outcomes-based contract when specialized investments are required, the outcomes are multifaceted and not simple to measure, and external forces such as economic downturns and natural disasters can upend even the most carefully laid plans for delivering public services, in this case, temporary cash assistance (Brown and Potoski 2003; Hart and Moore 1988; Williamson 1981). In such circumstances, the prelude to the design and execution of a contract is a critical period.

Among the key steps to establishing the contractual foundations of the partnership is the Request for Proposals (RFPs) that conveys the project's scope, goals, and expectations to potential private sector partners. Clear and detailed communication in the RFP is essential to fostering competition and greatly influences both the level of interest it generates and the quality of the proposals submitted. In essence, the benefits of market competition hinge in part on the strength of the RFP.

The choice of a partner is likewise a key decision. Studies suggest that the attributes of partners significantly influence alliance performance (Beamish 1987; Luo 1997), where inherent differences between public and private sector organizations, as well as cultural disparities, can negatively affect performance (Rainey et al. 2021, Chapter 3; Doz 1996). Research also highlights the challenges of forming alliances with direct competitors, noting that such partnerships often result in contentious relationships prone to deterioration (Kogut 1989). Equally important is the negotiation process, during which partners establish the terms and mechanisms for navigating the complexities of the partnership. This stage is pivotal in laying the groundwork for steering the project toward its goals and ensuring the success of the PPP (Das and Teng 2003).[2] To the extent that the partners can agree on key contractual elements—including the roles and authority of the partners, governing structures and rules and guidance, and performance indicators—they will be well positioned to address potential problems associated with unforeseen contingencies and contract incompleteness.

That said, research also suggests that focusing solely on the formal components of the contract to guard against risks and protect the parties' investments in the PPP—e.g., by building conditions (of contractual breach) into the contract, stipulations for roles and responsibilities and penalties for nonperformance of responsibilities, and procedures for dispute resolution—may be counter-productive to constructive collaboration and contribute to an antagonistic posture in future interactions (Covey and Merrill 2006; Domingos et al. 2025; Joskow, 1987). An alternative approach in the "prelude period" is to invest in developing relational mechanisms, such as trust, reputation, and reciprocity, to manage the PPP dynamics and minimize the likelihood of adversarial interactions among the partners (Bertelli and Smith 2010; Brunjes 2020; Macneil and Campbell 2001).

Indiana Governor Mitch Daniels brought an ideological vision of limited government to his plans to privatize the state's welfare system, having staked his reputation on conservative principles that viewed government as wasteful and favored private-sector solutions. FSSA Secretary Mitch Roob came to his role from the private sector—a former vice president of Affiliated Computer Services (ACS), which provided information technology and business process outsourcing to

2. Das and Teng (2003) argue that alliance performance is strongly influenced by particular characteristics of the partner firms and present an integrated approach to partner analysis.

government agencies—and consulted with privatization advocates[3] to determine how to best execute on Governor Daniels's plans. IBM, for its part, brought a long and strong record of collaboration with government agencies to the PPP, going back to the Social Security Act of 1935, in which IBM was contracted to support the accounting operation necessary to maintain employment records and deliver social security to tens of millions of people.[4] In this regard, there should have been considerable common ground for establishing a constructive working relationship between the prime (private sector) contracting partner in the Master Services Agreement (MSA), IBM, and the State.

The promise of increased public value

The deal, announced in August 2006, proceeded with little opportunity for public input (Mannix et al. 2008).[5] The new system would allow Indiana welfare recipients to apply for benefits online, by phone, or in person at designated offices, and a number of process changes promised to standardize and accelerate the pace of eligibility determinations. Some concerns were expressed about allowing a nongovernment entity to determine eligibility, which was not permitted by the Food Stamp Act, notably by Senate Agriculture Committee Chairman, Senator Tom Harkin of Iowa. Similar concerns were raised by the Indiana Coalition for Human Services; Indiana Legal Services; the American Federation of State, County, and Municipal Employees; and the Citizens Action Coalition, to name a few (Mannix et al. 2008). Attention to these concerns was crowded out, however, by the governor's pledge to increase

3. Among the advocates was Stephen Goldsmith, another former vice president of ACS and ex-mayor of Indianapolis.

4. https://www.ibm.com/ibm/history/history/decade_1930.html.

5. According to an article in the *Journal of Poverty, Law and Policy* (https://www.inthepublicinterest.org/wp-content/uploads/PublicBenefitsPrivatizationandModernization.pdf), the initiative "was put on a fast track with limited opportunity for public input. The agency held a public forum on the initiative months after the request for proposals was issued and only three weeks before the contract was awarded . . ." (Mannix et al. 2008, 8).

public value through an anticipated savings to the state of about $50 million over the life of the contract.[6] FSSA Secretary Mitch Roob, who had criticized the existing workflow process as "simply unmanageable" and pointed out that the State spent more on filing cabinets than computers (letter to Under Secretary Johner, IBM D.E. 27, March 13, 2008), likewise proclaimed that Indiana taxpayers would no longer be losing "hundreds of millions of dollars because of an antiquated and inefficient process" (*South Bend Tribune*, November 9, 2005).

Although the Indiana-IBM project was widely viewed as a groundbreaking, high-tech privatization revolution to assist the state's most vulnerable citizens, all parties to the PPP recognized its complexity and the risks at hand. FSSA Director James Robertson of the Division of Family Resources (DFR) noted that "no one has done this successfully, as far as we know" (Marion County Superior Court, Findings of Fact 2012, exhibit 3207 at 2). Apparently recognizing an important role for culture and relationships, state consultant James Maxwell said that the new system was more than a "brand-new workflow and document management system . . . [and that success would require] changing the ingrained habits of [many] employees and constituents" (Exhibit 190A at IBM-IN00255540). More than a million applicants were processed each year through extremely complex, intricate, and difficult procedures (Marais testimony, TR: 1937:19–1938:5), involving highly individualized determinations based on unique facts and circumstances (Harris testimony, TR: 1935:25–1936:1).

The State retains control over key functions in welfare services delivery

The $1.37-billion MSA signed on December 27, 2006, accorded the State final authority over eligibility determination, while IBM was to be the main point of contact for contractual matters (MSA § 14.6.2).

6. We are unable to find any specific analysis or documentation showing how the expected savings were to be derived. Court records indicate that Mitch Roob later acknowledged that no savings were expected.

The MSA detailed the overarching policy objectives as follows: (i) to provide efficient, accurate and timely eligibility determinations for individuals and families who qualify for public assistance; (ii) to improve the availability, quality, and reliability of the services being provided to clients by expanding access to such services, decreasing inconvenience and improving response times, among other improvements; (iii) to assist and support clients through programs that foster personal responsibility, independence, and social and economic self-sufficiency; (iv) to assure compliance with all relevant laws; (v) to assure the protection and integrity of personal information gathered in connection with eligibility determination; (vi) to foster the development of policies and procedures that underscore the importance of accuracy in eligibility determinations, caseload integrity across all areas of public assistance, and work and work-related experience for clients in the programs (MSA § 1.1(1).).[7] Although the MSA specified a ten-year duration with an option for renewal, it also included provisions for early termination, including closeout costs and equipment buyouts (among its 160+ pages; 24 schedules; and attachments, exhibits, and appendices).

In addition to eligibility determination, the State of Indiana also retained policymaking authority for the project and operational responsibility for county office locations:

- "The State shall make and shall retain final authority with respect to any policy changes . . . to the Services as may be necessary to comply with applicable Law or which the State in its discretion determines to be appropriate and in the best interests of the State and its citizens."
- "With respect to the Vendor Service Locations identified on Schedule 4, the State will perform those tasks and activities identified as State Retained Activities for Vendor Service

7. Importantly, while MSA § 1.1 outlined several "overarching policy objectives of the Modernization Project," MSA § 1.4(5) provided that these Policy Objectives did not impose any contractual obligations on IBM: "[I]n no event shall the Policy Objectives change or expand Vendor's obligations hereunder unless expressly agreed to by the Parties pursuant to a Change" (MSA § 1.4[5]).

Locations in a reasonably competent and timely manner consistent with its standard practice as in effect from time to time."

- "During the Term to the extent required by Law, the State will maintain at least one County Office in each County and shall staff each such office with at least one State employee for the performance of the applicable State Retained Activities."

This is also reflected in the MSA itself (Schedule 1). Various functions—from project management to business operations to applications services, quality assurance, integrated technology, program operations, and many more—had units and personnel from both the State and IBM Coalition team partners involved in making the system work (IBM-IN04133152-65; IBM-IN00828779-81, IBM-IN087864-69; FSSA1_07357871-2; FSSA1_06799643-4). More generally, the governance plan for the Indiana-IBM project established an oversight structure that kept the State informed about and involved in the key decisions on the project.

THE BRIEF HONEYMOON STAGE

At least initially, the contracting partners' efforts to specify in detail the roles, responsibilities, and infrastructure for executing the primary work of the MSA appeared to facilitate a smooth transition, as state officials and the IBM Coalition partners worked together to map out their joint vision of the Indiana welfare system privatization from January to May 2007. During this period, the parties developed a draft procedures manual, established key performance indicators (KPIs), broke down areas or phases of the project into groups of counties (reflecting unique circumstances), and agreed on dates for implementation. Some examples of cooperative governance mechanisms (Bertelli and Smith 2010) formed in the Indiana-IBM relationship include State-Coalition participation in process improvement meetings, weekly Operational Verification and Validation (OV&V) issues and risks meetings, and more generally, collaboration in the many OV&V monitoring activities and KPI reviews that were documented monthly in the OV&V monthly status reports.

Prior to these collaborative efforts, FSSA Secretary Mitch Roob asserted that no two counties followed the same approach to determining and verifying eligibility (FSSA1_08279442; letter to the Indiana General Assembly, May 29, 2008). As Roob described it, there were "92 different interpretations of the rules governing eligibility determination" that clearly made compliance and error and fraud detection a nearly impossible task. Key management personnel from the state and contractor groups worked together to develop a state-wide procedures manual to facilitate, for the first time, a consistent way of doing business, while IBM was simultaneously investing an estimated $9.5 million in hardware and software to accommodate the new workflows. Indiana's other administrative and social services–related agencies, which were involved in the planning of the proposed "privatization fix" of FSSA's inefficiencies, as well as in the selection of the vendor (Report of Interagency Review Committee 2006), also appeared to exhibit a cooperative stance in the early phase of the project. This was crucial in facilitating a "honeymoon period" for the launch of the project work, as coordination problems had also been identified with the central accounting, personnel, and contracting and purchasing systems (Eligibility Modernization, FSSA1_08279450-FSSA1_08279456).

At the same time, the literature on contracting in the public sector recognizes that beyond the initial investments of time, financial capital, and other human and organizational resources in establishing the infrastructure for project implementation, the contracting parties also need to attend to and invest in relational aspects for managing contractual and PPP dynamics over the course of the project (Bertelli and Smith 2010; Brunjes 2020; Macneil and Campbell 2001). Hefetz and Warner (2004) estimated that the pecuniary resources required to manage and monitor subcontracted relationships are, on average, 20% of the value of a given contract, although these costs are rarely explicitly enumerated or negotiated. Other research suggests that stronger government capabilities are not only associated with greater project success but also higher engagement from private sector partners (Lazzarini 2022). This is particularly critical for contracts with more than two parties, as research also shows that multiparty PPPs increase the complexity of decision-making, along with uncertainties and perceptions of risk among the contracting parties. This type of multilayered complexity also heightens the need for relational mechanisms such as "guiding principles" that allow parties to use judgment as circumstances change and sustain cooperation (Huxham and Vangen 2013; Frydlinger et al. 2019, 2021).

Shortly after the MSA was signed, Joe Loftus, a representative of ACS (one of IBM's key subcontractors), began to challenge IBM's role and performance. Loftus, who had previously served as deputy mayor under Stephen Goldsmith, expressed concerns in communications with FSSA Secretary Mitch Roob. The negative tone and critical stance toward IBM in these communications between Loftus and Roob was disclosed in court filings. In one email, Loftus wrote, "I expect to get a lecture today from IBM reminding me that they are the Prime . . . IBM really does not understand how to deliver social services" (Exhibits 244 and 245, Judge Dryer's Findings of Fact). ACS representatives also bypassed IBM by directly lobbying the governor's office to criticize IBM's performance, an act that violated contractual specifications requiring all state communications to go through IBM (Loftus, email to Roob, December 8, 2008; Exhibit 245, Judge Dryer's Findings of Fact, Conclusions of Law and Judgement for IBM, Cause 49D10-1005-PL-021451).

These actions signaled the emergence of opportunistic behavior and highlighted the relational strain among the parties, particularly a lack of trust between ACS and IBM and, to some extent, between IBM and some state officials. The willingness of the parties to engage early on in such critical banter further suggests that the formal contract (the MSA) was insufficient in curbing these behaviors. Trust, a cornerstone of successful partnerships, eroded as ACS circumvented established communication protocols, undermining IBM's authority and the integrity of the partnership. This failure to adhere to contractual norms reflected in part the lack of relational infrastructure that hindered collaboration and performance. Moreover, it is consistent with recent research showing that when contracting parties respond to complexity by layering on more rules, clauses, and schedules at the outset of the relationship, ostensibly to guard against opportunism and uncertainties, it may simultaneously depress any positive sentiments among the parties in the execution of the PPP work (Domingos et al. 2024).

The tendency to assign blame to IBM without direct communication also disrupted the norm of reciprocity, which is essential for effective collaboration. Reciprocity relies on goodwill and cooperative problem-solving, both of which were absent in this case. By criticizing IBM without open dialogue, ACS neglected its obligation to foster equitable contributions to the relationship. This behavior also violated the norm of autonomy, as IBM was denied the opportunity to respond to criticisms or address performance concerns, undermining its ability to act in its own interest.

Meeting minutes and interview data further illustrate the breakdown in trust and its impact on the partnership. ACS's actions cemented distrust, with some interviewees explicitly linking the deteriorating relationship to the early termination of the contract. When asked about the events that led to the contract's downfall, one respondent suggested that ACS "could do whatever it wanted and did not have to follow any rules." However, other perspectives on IBM's role were mixed. While some viewed ACS's behavior as opportunistic, others criticized IBM for frequently requesting change orders, which were perceived as an attempt to increase fees. These contrasting perceptions underscore how feeble relationships and misaligned expectations contributed to the partnership's failure. The breakdown in reciprocity and autonomy further undermined the effective execution of the PPP work, contributing to its premature termination.

THE PROJECT ROLLOUT

The first phase of the Indiana-IBM welfare modernization project officially rolled out in March of 2007. The parties relatively soon became aware, however, that they had likely underestimated the personnel needs of the project and been overly optimistic on timelines. Hence, early in the implementation of the project work, the parties had to rethink the transition plans and adjust targeted milestone dates. The empirical literature on social services contracting finds that in circumstances like welfare reform, where the introduction of service technology may be new or where the providers may be new entrants to the field, one should expect start-up costs to be higher and the time to develop a functioning service model longer (Milward and Provan 2000; Timmins 2016). In fact, the Food and Nutrition Service (FNS) also recognized these upfront investments in a December 2007 letter to Mitch Roob, 2 (FSSA1_08474535): "The Food and Nutrition Service (FNS) strongly supports FSSA's commitment to a careful and measured approach to implementing this innovative project, and we are in full agreement with the State's philosophy to 'do it right, not fast.'" IBM was accommodating in agreeing to defer compensation for the substantial start-up and operational costs in the initial welfare modernization rollout.

Although clients of Indiana's welfare system continued to complain about long wait times in this first phase of the rollout, it is important to bear in mind the system's baseline performance at the time the MSA was signed. Clients had to "go out of their way" to apply for benefits, often making multiple trips and waiting in lines because they were not able to access the system by phone, fax, or email during the initial eligibility application and determination process (State of Indiana's Request for Information, IBM D.E. 194). In addition, 48% of clients reported that it was difficult to reach a caseworker (Eligibility Modernization, FSSA1_08279441), and 65% rated the FSSA's services as below average, with more than half complaining that the eligibility system was too slow (Inter-Agency Review Committee Report, November 22, 2006, 10) (IBM D.E. 199). Yet as complaints continued in May 2007, with clients also objecting to what they perceived as a more impersonal system, the State hired a third-party company, First Data, to monitor contract performance (KPIs) and compliance (at a cost of $11.4 million). First Data agreed to start delivering performance reports by mid-year, although the State also sent out its own team to evaluate various aspects of the IBM Coalition's performance, including the readiness of service centers and application processing times (Court Transcript Roob, 5890:35891:1). The State's approach to addressing early client and performance concerns of the IBM Coalition—i.e., intensifying and layering on additional mechanisms of oversight and control—despite having recognized the rollout would require time to address existing challenges, is emblematic of a more adversarial (as opposed to cooperative) approach to managing the complex PPP.

Pointing fingers as problems arose

As implementation of Indiana's welfare privatization project went into full swing in the summer of 2007, the State and IBM Coalition announced plans to rapidly roll out the modernization efforts (in three stages) to fifty-nine of Indiana's ninety-two counties. A twelve-county pilot program, representing about 10% of the state's welfare caseload, was scheduled to begin in October, even as the FSSA and IBM continued to meet to try to resolve delays in processing of eligibility requests and other performance issues (as FSSA Secretary Roob testified in the Marion Superior Court). ACS continued to undermine IBM's authority as the prime contractor, pointing fingers at IBM for the performance problems reported by clients and stakeholder groups and contacting the governor's office to offer commentary on IBM's work. The State, in turn, directed ACS to hire additional personnel, apparently acknowledging that ACS shared at least part of the blame for underestimating personnel needs. ACS agreed to hire an additional 70 clerical staff (by July 1, 2007) and to pay employee relocation expenses to encourage worker retention, but it also back-channeled its objections to the governor's office about covering these costs that it attributed to IBM.[8] These interactions reflected a lack of what Macneil (1980: 39–59) characterized

8. Communication between Anne Murphy and Mitch Roob regarding ACS Lobbyist Joe Loftus's meeting with Governor Daniels to discuss "ACS having to pick up cost of recent increase in work from IBM" (Murphy, email to Roob, Exhibit 58, Judge Dryer's Findings of Fact, Conclusions of Law and Judgment for IBM, Cause 49D10-1005-PL-021451). On the one hand, Loftus's statement suggests IBM is being unfairly burdened. The perception of unfair responsibility undermines the norm of fairness, which is fundamental to any contract. On the other hand, by bypassing formal communication channels and discussing financial burdens with the governor rather than addressing the issue collaboratively, this action undermines cooperation and signals an attempt to shift responsibility. It also reflects a lack of transparency and a lack of commitment to collective problem-solving. The combined effect of violating these norms undoubtedly contributed to the contract breakdown.

as "contractual solidarity," or what Frydlinger et al. (2019) and others have described as reciprocity, in which the partners respect each other's strengths and contributions and accordingly engage with a spirit of fairness and in support of their collective interests.

At the same time, the State was alternatively reporting to the press throughout this period that all was going well with the welfare modernization project, which appeared consistent with the State's actions to expand the scope of IBM's work multiple times in 2007 and 2008. In December of 2007, the Healthy Indiana Program (HIP), a new social program to provide health insurance to uninsured low-income residents, was introduced and added to the IBM Coalition's slate of responsibilities. The implementation of HIP and its integration into the project was not anticipated in the initial MSA; thus, the parties agreed that IBM would take on the additional work for an added, fixed fee of $44.2 million. Moreover, in an apparent attempt to avert disclosure of the unanticipated budget increase so early in the project, the parties also concurred that payment of the associated costs (fee) would be deferred until fiscal year 2017, after the effective contract end date (MSA, Amendment 1, January 2008).[9] Yet none of the parties anticipated the extent to which the new HIP would burden operation of the social services benefits system and inflate its costs. In the first month alone, HIP enrollment exceeded expectations, resulting in approximately 20,000 applications, an increase of 21% from the prior year.

Despite the State's messaging to the public, a review of agency complaint records, press accounts, and court transcripts provide objective evidence that project performance was not going well. One might

9. Changes in work scope, adjusted payment amounts, and contract amendment dates appear in the change orders, amendments, and court documents, but with some discrepancies. We estimate that the State expanded the scope of IBM's work at least 11 times between September 2007 and October 2009, adding $178 million to the contract price (Marion County Superior Court Common Cause Number 49D10-1005—PL—021451; Findings of Fact, Conclusions of Law and Judgment for IBM: footnote 45, 28). Contract scope expansions are reflected in change orders 23, 33, 53, 60, 64, 67, 68, 90, 93, 119, and 133 and in amendments 1–4. According to amendment 2, $129,900,000 was added between May 2007 and March 2008 (A2 signed on March 14, 2008, with new amounts part of change orders). According to Amendment 3, $285,184 was added between March 2008 and August 2008 (A3 signed added on August 6, 2008), and Amendment 4 indicates $47,308,299 was added between August 2008 and March 2009 (A4 signed on April 15, 2009).

question whether this was a matter of interpretative uncertainty (Brown et al. 2018)—that is, where the contracting parties saw the others' behaviors differently or relied on different information. For example, the MSA included "transition key performance indicators" to assess process aspects of performance, such as the number of applications processed and timeliness of processing, that are distinct from the federal performance standards that focus on outcomes such as client work participation. As the press reported high error rates, backlogs, and calls for assistance left ringing in call centers around the state, the State announced in March 2008 that the IBM Coalition had successfully completed the pilot phase of the rollout. And on April 8, DFR Director Zach Main reported that citizens were satisfied with call-center operations, even though callers were waiting longer to speak to eligibility workers than the State originally planned.[10]

Navigating in new storms

In June of 2008, Indiana was hit by a literal wave of unanticipated events and contingencies that would test the foundations (formal and relational) of the PPP and the MSA infrastructure for withstanding external disruptions. Indiana experienced some of the worst storms and flooding in state history, just at the onset of the Great Recession that began in 2008. Of the state's 92 counties, 82 sought presidential disaster declarations, which slowed the privatization progress and vastly increased the volume of applications for economic relief. In fact, the State of Indiana acknowledged that it was seeing substantial increases in the number of clients contacting the system for services, which it attributed to the economic downturn and the natural disasters.[11]

10. https://www.govtech.com/education/102471609.html.

11. In a later July 2009 interview with the Wall Street Journal, then FSSA Secretary Anne Murphy explained: "So the roll-out started in late 2007, and then we did two more regions in 2008. At the time that we were rolling out, Indiana had two floods. So, we had two natural disasters that we were having to deal with. And so there were a lot of food stamps and particularly emergency food stamps, that were being issued in 2008. And then, of course, the recession. And so we had a lot of people coming onto the rolls at the same time, and

Still, FSSA Secretary Mitch Roob pointed out in a letter to Under Secretary for Food, Nutrition, and Consumer Services Nancy Johner that Indiana was increasing both the quality and quantity of services it was providing through its welfare modernization project during this period: "We have seen an enormous increase in the use of our call center, from 10,000 calls during the first week to 30,000 calls in week 19 of our pilot. FSSA is serving more people in a timelier manner than ever before" (letter, March 13, 2008). In an email to a long list of IBM Coalition staff and partners and State of Indiana FSSA staff, Zach Main likewise alluded to the substantial increase in application volume due to the introduction of the new HIP and complimented the modernization rollout leadership and staff on their great success in dealing with "far more applications during the initial few months" than were expected and in responding to the extra demands for services from victims of flood and wind disasters (June 13, 2008). And Governor Daniels himself stated that despite a "flood of applications, [i]f you read the front page of today's national papers, there are systems crashing in states elsewhere, and ours is performing very well" (transcript, January 9, 2009, 5). The State accordingly gave the "green light" to approve the rollout of privatization effort to another 20 Indiana counties.

THE CHANGING OF THE GUARD AND BEGINNING OF THE END

Almost immediately after the State authorized the continued expansion of the welfare modernization rollout, the FSSA decided to "slow-walk" the project. On June 13, 2008, on behalf of the state, Zach Main sent an email to the IBM Coalition, stating: "Given our immediate and extended focus on mobilizing and helping victims of Indiana natural disasters, we will delay roll out of modernization program." The original negotiation of a 10-year contract with IBM, including a detailed but *tentative* schedule for the implementation of the new system, recognized the

that is, as I'm sure you're aware, Indiana has been running above the national average on unemployment." (FSSA1741 7149).

fact that it would take time to fully implement the project as a pilot, rolling out region by region (see MSA Appendix II, Transition Plan, 20043699_1). Zach Main also emphasized this point: "Our schedule has always been written in pencil. Bottom line, until we are completely confident that we can handle the volume that rolling a new region will add, we will not roll to the next region" (email to Peggy Anthony, January 4, 2008).

The PPP parties subsequently initiated discussions to address the growing problems with the revolutionary and philosophical reboot of delivering benefits to Indiana welfare clients. In November of 2008, representatives of the IBM Coalition met with FSSA Secretary Roob to propose systemic changes to address client concerns and move forward with reasonable revisions to alleviate problems of the modernization project. The IBM Global Services Team conducted an extensive, end-to-end performance assessment (in a period of twelve weeks) to evaluate all aspects of the eligibility modernization project and develop recommendations for program enhancements. The assessment (as the project existed at the start of 2009) acknowledged the considerably higher case volumes, the disruptions from the 2008 natural disasters, and growing complaints about the loss of face-to-face contact made by opponents of modernization (e.g., unions, Indiana Legal Services). The assessment also concluded, however, that any problems arising as a result of the changed circumstances were "eminently fixable," and it produced a foundation for the State and Coalition to move forward with improvements (End-to-end assessment at 3). The findings of the end-to-end assessment were consistent with those of an analysis of the State of Florida's welfare modernization project, which faced similar challenges and client concerns about the loss of personal contact; it demonstrated how in staying the course on welfare modernization, Florida in due course achieved its goals for online application rates and application processing accuracy (Goldsmith and Kettl 2009).

The State, however, was simultaneously facing political pressures that were complicating the PPP interactions, relationships, and work in progress. Shortly after re-election in November 2008, Governor Daniels was forced to call a special session of the Indiana General Assembly to resolve a state budget shortfall of $1 billion. Moreover, more than one bill was advancing in the State Senate to halt the modernization project, although the governor and his Senior Policy Director Lawren Mills initially appeared prepared to defend the State and IBM Coalition's performance. Governor Daniels advised that the State needed to respond to the opposition with reminders of the problems with the old system: the "team needs to be armed to tee off big-time on the old system's fraud, waste, and mistreatment of deserving clients" (communication between Lawren Mills, Governor Daniels, and Deputy Chief of Staff Betsy Burdick, January 17, 2009).

The first half of 2009, as typical following an election, also set in motion a "changing of the guards" in political administration. Beginning in January 2009, FSSA Secretary Mitch Roob was appointed to a new post, CEO of the Indiana Economic Development Corporation, and Anne Murphy, the governor's former Chief of Staff, assumed the leadership role at the FSSA. When the new FSSA Secretary Murphy sent IBM a letter calling for a corrective action plan (CAP) in March 2009, she clearly invoked terms associated with a possible breach of the MSA. The State identified 36 issues for the Coalition to address, although private communications suggested that state officials did not attribute the problems to a single partner's making (Murphy, email to Daniels, March 23, 2009).

Sensing that a major political and organizational reordering was underway, the different subcontractor organizations of the IBM Coalition began to appeal to Governor Daniels and advocate for their interest in any new plans. In May of 2009, ACS went directly to the State (subverting protocol) to report what IBM was charging for its services. According to a May 2009 communication between FSSA Secretary Murphy and Governor Chief of Staff Earl Goode: "ACS believes the markup was around 50%" (transcript). In July 2009, the parties agreed to a CAP targeting 22 short-term fixes and 31 long-term initiatives to improve program performance, although it explicitly did not "relieve either party of its duty to comply with the terms of the Master Services Agreement" (Exhibit 5407, July 2, 2009). IBM appeared to approach the change of course cooperatively, participating in biweekly steering committee meetings that included monitoring and support of the execution of the CAP, while making significant progress on issues raised by the State, even those that were outside the scope of its contractual (MSA) obligations. In effect,

IBM's response appeared to exhibit one of the key principles, loyalty, that Frydlinger et al. (2019) suggest is foundational to a formal-relational contract, in which the partners are willing to look out for the relationship first, including through times of adversity. For their part, Governor Daniels and FSSA Secretary Murphy both acknowledged there had been incredible progress on the CAP and that backlogs and complaints were coming down (FSSA1741 7149).

Despite their public recognition of IBM's efforts to improve, FSSA took a number of actions that clearly signaled an adversarial and opportunistic turn in the relationship with the Coalition. Internal emails and other correspondence divulge that the FSSA leadership was more focused on trying to establish that IBM was in breach of the MSA than engaging cooperatively with the Coalition to improve performance. In an email from Secretary Anne Murphy to Roger Booth on July 2, 2009, she stated:

> "As we gear up for a potential breach of contract action against IBM/Coalition, we have asked OVV to really 'audit' performance on timeliness, accurateness, etc. I put audit in quotes because I doubt it technically falls within the definition of audit, but what I do know is that we've stretched the OVV vendor thin and they need some assistance in monitoring and documenting . . . All personnel working on the eligibility modernization are potential witnesses in court for a breach of contract case, so you'll want to keep that in mind as you are thinking about who could be deployed." (PRIV-FSSA-00009589)

There was no mincing of words in the intent of the State to halt cooperation with IBM. On August 12, 2009, Marcus Barlow, FSSA Director of Communications, corresponded with FSSA Director Anne Murphy about the State's strategy:

> "It would be the first time that we've thrown IBM under the bus like this and would definitely change the tone of our position prematurely." Barlow added in a follow-up email on the same

> day: ". . . you just need to survive until Oct., then we are going to drop bombs ala Hiroshima and Nagasaki" (FSSA1_08398771, IBM D.E. 88).

Shortly thereafter, in September of 2009, the State requested major changes in the approach to welfare modernization, known as the hybrid Plan B. Under Plan B, the State would reverse course on eligibility determination, abandoning the centralized call center and replacing it with local offices where clients could experience face-to-face interactions with case workers (Murphy, email to Barlow, September 25, 2009). IBM was willing to move forward with the State's request to implement Plan B; however, the State would not agree to pay IBM additional funds to implement these changes, apparently because of a lack of budgeted funds. IBM had already agreed to defer compensation of $44.2 million for taking on the HIP, and IBM countered that it could not implement Plan B under these terms (IBM D.E. 135, Murphy, email to FSSA colleagues, September 27, 2009).

On October 15, 2009, the State of Indiana announced it was terminating the MSA with IBM for cause, and the Indiana-IBM PPP came to an abrupt end. In its letter terminating the contract with IBM, the State suggested that progress toward welfare modernization was not adequate or happening rapidly enough. However, immediately prior to the cancellation of the contract, Governor Daniels was quoted as saying that the State was "getting more complaints in the counties that haven't modernized compared to the counties that have, at least in certain categories." During the press conference announcing his decision to terminate the contract, Daniels stated that IBM should be "commended" for its performance and described a series of benefits the State received from the project, including a paperless system, reduction in fraud, improvement in welfare to work statistics, and significant cost savings (transcript, October 15, 2009, IBM D.E. 345). Yet the governor also appeared to distance the State from the system over which it had retained decisive authority, making reference in published comments to a "so-called modernization system run by IBM" (FSSA1_08335875, email with AP story, October 15, 2009). In a final betrayal, the State subsequently signed a new contract with ACS as the prime contractor, an eight-year deal for an additional $638 million.

THE KIRKLEES-KBOP CASE: EMBARKING ON A NEW CONTRACTING APPROACH

To describe how the Kirklees-KBOP case has unfolded so far, we follow a similar structure to the Indiana-IBM case, though with key differences. Both projects shared a sense of cautious promise at the start, albeit with a few voices of concern. Rather than the honeymoon period experienced in Indiana, the Kirklees-KBOP partnership faced "teething issues" as the new outcomes contracting approach was rolled out. This likely reflects that Kirklees-KBOP started down a different path than the Indiana-IBM PPP, with a more concerted effort to develop both formal and relational aspects of the PPP contract. In the third stage of embedded project delivery, the KBOP service providers hit their stride, with encouraging advances in services delivery and community partnering.

The contract reached its initial operational end date in March 2024 (with outcomes payments being drawn down by September 2024). Following the conclusion of the Life Chances Fund, Kirklees Council has committed to continuing service provision under a new outcomes contract, based on the same contractual model that retains KBOP as the prime contractor supported by Bridges Fund Management. However, the new arrangement will operate with significantly less funding, a scaled-down service, and fewer service providers (Rosenbach et al. 2025). It is also notable that the outcomes-based partnership approach pioneered through the Kirklees-KBOP PPP has now been adopted across domestic abuse services in Kirklees (since early 2024), and there is a strong appetite to retain this form of partnership structure in the future delivery of homelessness prevention services.

(1) *Prologue to a formal-relational approach.* This period covers events up to the signing of the contract in 2019. The initial expression of interest from the Kirklees Council to the Life

Chances Fund was submitted in September 2017, and the outcomes contracting arrangement took considerable time to develop. A formal mobilization period took place between contract signing in March 2019 and service launch in September 2019, during which time the outcomes "rate-card" was revised.

(2) *Teething issues.* This follows the launch of services under the new contracting arrangement on September 2, 2019. This period was characterized by a one-year "grace period," where the performance improvement provisions in the contract had yet to be implemented.

(3) *Under new management and unexpected shocks.* From the arrival of a new KBOP director in early 2020, through the disruption of COVID-19, and to the present, the project hit its stride, and the achievement of outcomes was either at or above anticipated levels.

Our analysis is informed primarily by a series of informant interviews, observation of key meetings, correspondence, and documentary analysis carried out by the Government Outcomes (GO) Lab research team. The research team also facilitated an interactive workshop with the KBOP service provider network to validate and contextualize the interpretation of findings.

PROLOGUE TO A FORMAL-RELATIONAL APPROACH

As well described in theory and unpacked in Chapter 2, the preface to a complex PPP contracting arrangement may be characterized as a balancing act between two approaches, formal and relational. The parties strive to have the right formal protections against key risks and to protect their investments, while also drawing in relational mechanisms—trust, reputation, and reciprocity—to avoid serious contracting difficulties. As we will explain, the parties to the Kirklees-KBOP contract attempted to bring these two imperatives together explicitly in the way the contract was designed and negotiated. The contract was set up with certain features that were intended to bring about improvements in how the service was to be managed; how performance would be assured; and how discretion and personalization would be unlocked in delivery.

Taking time to lay the foundations for a new contracting approach

Considerable time was taken to prepare for the introduction of a new outcomes contracting model in Kirklees. This involved both relational and technical work. In terms of culture and relationships, the Council encouraged service providers to come together as an "alliance" to better map the complementarity between services. Professional facilitation of dialogue within the prospective alliance of existing providers brought greater cohesion but also revealed that none of the provider organizations had an appetite to take on the role of lead delivery organization or "prime" provider. Instead, the Kirklees Council ran a procurement exercise and identified Bridges Fund Management as a suitable partner to co-design and develop the social impact bond (SIB). The purpose of this co-design stage was to "develop the intervention and support service to improve outcomes and life chances for vulnerable people, which will then reduce the likelihood of their future need to access costly crisis interventions." Bridges Fund Management invested in this process "at risk," meaning they had no guarantee that they would go on to win the contract.

On the technical side, considerable attention was paid to the preparation of a "rate card" of outcome measures to guide the partnership (discussed further below). Several of the key actors involved were able to draw on experience from another outcomes contracting pilot—the Fair Chance Fund. Bridges Outcomes Partnerships had experience with this fund, and so did one of the longstanding service providers in Kirklees—Fusion Housing—which had successfully delivered an outcomes-focused project for homeless young people (with support from Bridges) in 2015–2017. The lead commissioner at Kirklees Council had sat on the steering group for this youth homelessness pilot and was inspired by the potential of the flexible, personalized support. Research on outcomes-based contracting has shown that having experienced partners with existing knowledge and capacities for managing complex contracting relationships in PPPs is important for navigating risks and managing challenges in the launch of a SIB (Heinrich and Kabourek 2019; Lazzarini 2022).

How the contract was to be managed

The single prime contractor was intended to greatly simplify contract management for the under-resourced Kirklees Metropolitan Council. The prime contractor was also expected to introduce additional capacity alongside new management competencies—chiefly, performance and information management. All the parties expressed considerable excitement about the potential of a proposed central information system. Clients had complained that they needed to retell their often highly traumatic life story again and again as they were bumped around an uncoordinated service system. The new system would collect the required information once to be reviewed by a central "referral panel," which would oversee the transition of people into and out of support and manage overall service demand.

The necessity of granular outcomes achievement data for the smooth functioning of the "payment-for-outcomes" model justified the Council's procurement of a dedicated case management software: CDPSoft. This crucial piece of technical infrastructure was purchased by the Council independently of the Kirklees-KBOP contract. This system is used by the Council for monitoring and validating outcome payments; by KBOP for managing referrals of potential program participants and underlying performance management data on relative provider performance; and by providers themselves for collecting and maintaining key case management information. The Council retained overall responsibility for procuring the system but engaged heavily with KBOP and the delivery teams to develop CDPSoft's functionality and make any changes.

The introduction of the prime contracting structure, similar to the Indiana-IBM PPP, marked a shift of responsibilities. The "rules of the game" were reoriented by the Council commissioner to place greater emphasis on being person-centered and focusing on long-term outcomes. The availability of the Life Chances Fund top-up funding and the involvement of Bridges Outcomes Partnerships enabled a more substantial and dedicated team to manage the provider network and to provide training and development around asset-based working. Furthermore, as we discuss in the next section—and *unlike* in the Indiana-IBM case—the prime contractor was given considerable discretion to manage the constellation of provider organizations and their entry, exit and relative "market share."

How performance would be assured

Alongside improved provider coordination, Bridges Outcomes Partnerships and the Kirklees Council designed both formal and relational mechanisms to ensure that providers were performing well in meeting service user needs and moving toward improved long-term outcomes. The lead Council commissioner was dissatisfied by the superficial support offered in legacy floating support arrangements, noting that at times the service was "trapping people in a bit of a cycle" instead of enabling them to progress and "trying to work with people to see where they want it to go next" (K28). There was a shared view that the KPIs under the old contracts were not meaningful.

Establishing an objective and meaningful set of outcome measures to assess performance was therefore an integral stage of both technical contract development and for honing a shared sense of purpose for the partnership. The Council team drew on previous examples of outcomes-based projects to tackle homelessness and worked with a specialist consultant to refine the proposed outcome measures. Negotiations took place around the perceived level of challenge, both in the specific measures chosen and intended performance levels. One advisor noted that Bridges Outcomes Partnerships preferred more tried-and-tested and near-term measures, such as accessing a general practitioner or undertaking a well-being assessment, "that they had the experience to solve."

The Council and Bridges Outcomes Partnerships teams acknowledged that with limited data to inform the initial outcome measures and performance expectations, these features of the contract might need to be revisited. In fact, the literature on performance management suggests that contracting parties will rarely ever get the performance measures and standards "right" on the first attempt and that they will necessarily evolve with learning over time (Bevan and Hood 2006; Heinrich and Marschke 2010). In terms of reducing the experience of domestic violence and overcoming mental health challenges, the project was "going into uncharted territory in terms of anybody ever having measured how successful you could expect an intervention to be" [independent advisor to Kirklees Council]. Although performance measures are formalized and articulated through the outcomes payment mechanism, the joint development of these measures and the willingness to revise them is an important foundation for the open learning culture surrounding the partnership, as discussed in more detail in Chapter 5.

The high-powered payment for outcomes contract undergirding the PPP sits between the Council and KBOP, but the outcome measures were also clearly articulated for the service provider network, albeit without the heavy financial incentives. Some of the work to uphold performance standards across providers was positively framed: for example, providers were to be encouraged to share good practices with one another, in addition to the formal monthly performance review meetings stipulated in the contract. But the contracts between the prime contractor and subcontractors also stipulated escalating punitive action in case of poor performance: a formal improvement notice, a reduction in allocated cases, the withholding of payments for "central overheads" (though payment for delivery cost was always assured), and ultimately, exit from the delivery partnership. The prime contractor could exercise these rights with the Kirklees Council's written approval (which was not to be unreasonably withheld).

The considerable powers granted to the prime contractor over subcontractors may at first seem heavy-handed and inconsistent with the principles of relational contracting. Yet the providers accepted these terms, despite some claiming to be unfamiliar with the potential application of high-powered performance contracting. Two factors can explain why these powers might in fact align with the relational principles of reciprocity and fairness:

(1) The prime contractor's ability under the promised central intelligence system to benchmark provider performance gave an objective and verifiable basis for decisions related to provider performance. This sense of equal treatment was explained by one provider in this way: "It was introduced as one contract, e.g., 'if one provider fails, the rest of us do'. Because it's a partnership, we're all working towards that same common goal." (Rosenbach et al. 2023, 74).
(2) The fact that the prime contractor itself would be working under a high-stakes performance regime through the payment mechanism agreed with the Council, which paid most of the contract value only when clients (service users) met key progress milestones related to accommodation, training/education, and employment.

Discretion in delivery

One of the principles of relational contracting is autonomy—partners should not try to constrain or control each other's activities (Frydlinger et al. 2019). Subcontracted providers were excited by the flexibilities that the outcomes-focused contract might unlock for them. Rather than support being driven by activity-based KPIs—defining prespecified numbers of people with prespecified amounts of support—providers felt that the focus on long-term outcomes would enable them to be "focused around [peoples'] needs and doing what we need to do to support them rather than being concerned about the contract that is more about numbers" (Rosenbach and Carter 2020, 39). The prime contractor, too, welcomed the discretion unlocked by the contract that would enable them to adjust the type and intensity of support according to service user needs and aspirations through its central referral system.

Those affected by the new contract—whether they were involved in setting it up or not—were generally positive about the implications of the new approach. This might be expected from the prime provider, who led on the contract design, and to a lesser extent perhaps also the officials in the Kirklees Council directly involved in negotiating the contract. But cautious optimism was also expressed by the subcontractors, even though they were not directly involved in contract design and were to work under a new and unfamiliar contracting principal. One noted, "The experience in developing the SIB model has been extraordinarily positive, in the respect that the management team involved in [KBOP] have been very collaborative in their approach" (Rosenbach et al. 2023, 28). Third parties who were not party to the contracting arrangements but would be making referrals of clients to the service and receiving referrals from it were also hopeful.

Perceived benefits were framed in direct response to the challenges experienced by each stakeholder in the "legacy" activity-related housing support contracts, described in more detail in Chapter 3. The challenges of insufficient Council resources, constrained management capacity, poorly articulated KPIs, questionable service effectiveness, and disconnected provider networks were all expected to be overcome by the new outcomes contract. This perception indicates a risk—if each stakeholder saw the new contract as being able to solve their fundamental issues, would they be disappointed during delivery? Could a change in the contract be expected to fulfill so many reform promises? Surely, there would need to be trade-offs between the preferences of different stakeholders with quite different motivations and concerns.

TEETHING ISSUES

For year one of delivery, the contract between the Council and KBOP intentionally dialed down the punitive implications of poor performance. In the early stages, if performance did not meet the satisfactory level of outcomes, there would *not* be an immediate resort to a Performance Improvement Plan or contract default procedure. This simultaneously acknowledged that performance levels for some of the outcome measures had been difficult to gauge, given the paucity of granular pre-existing data, and sent a strong signal that the project would be a solutions-focused partnership, where parties came together to understand poor performance and identify a better way forward. In effect, this need to periodically revisit the key performance measures was *formally* built into the contract through an unanimously agreed change procedure, a *relational* mechanism.

The contract and Council strategic lead placed a high priority on the support being person-centered. The senior Council officer responsible for the project was keen to use the contracting reform as an opportunity to reshape services so that delivery teams listened more intently to participants' aspirations and went beyond a superficial but temporary fix, instead working toward long-term independence. Even though that was the original intention, a Council officer explained that early in the implementation, it was "very kind of needs and risk assessment, and ticking boxes. It was really uncomfortable . . . It's the opposite of what we wanted" (Interview transcript, senior Kirklees Council official). Indeed, it was perfectly possible to interpret the Kirklees-KBOP outcomes contract as an exercise in "tick boxing" for the production of outcomes achievement data, and this frustration was also expressed by frontline delivery teams. Frontline staff bemoaned the onerous evidence requirements. Now they needed to collect and compile evidence underpinning each of the intermediate outcome measures in the payment schedule. This was seen as intrusive for program participants who were asked to share details of tenancy agreements and new jobs in order to validate payments. There was also concern that chasing evidence was corrosive to the trusted dynamic between frontline staff and those who were participating in the service.

These changes led to some heated conversations between the strategic leads of the Council and KBOP teams. The Council team became frustrated by the perceived risk aversion and the cautious approach to service reform, as they realized that the outcomes contract alone was insufficient to bring about the changes they sought. Instead of immediately bringing in a more asset-led approach, the Council saw the KBOP team as bringing a *protective* and risk averse mindset to the challenges at hand. The KBOP team pursued what they were comfortable with, limiting the service to "where there was an evidence base, which was the old way of working," perhaps seeking to protect the considerable financial investment they had made (Interview transcript, senior Kirklees Council official). From the perspective of Bridges Outcomes Partnerships, this was the biggest SIB project that had ever been launched in the UK (both by investment value and number of intended participants); an investment of this size needed to be closely managed and protected. But from the perspective of the Council, the contract was relatively small—the team was used to managing much larger and more precarious social care contracts. Although the partners' perspectives on service reforms diverged here, perhaps because of the relational foundations established at the outset of the PPP, this misalignment of interests did not descend into outright opportunistic or shading behaviors, as seen in the unfolding of the Indiana-IBM PPP.

UNDER NEW MANAGEMENT AND UNEXPECTED SHOCKS

During the initial implementation period, KBOP was being run by a temporary director, while Bridges Outcomes Partnerships searched for a suitable candidate to appoint to the role permanently. Taking time to find the right person came to be crucial in moving the project into a more progressive, genuinely person-centered service. Yet "they really struggled to recruit" an appropriate person for this role (interview with Council staff member). A new, permanent director arrived in January 2020, a seasoned nonprofit sector leader who had an impressive portfolio working across housing, homelessness, and justice services in charities delivering public contracts. The new director was familiar with outcomes-based contracts and was an advocate for the flexibility of the approach. As described by the commissioner, "the advantage with [the new director] was she was in similar programs elsewhere, and can see that it is transferable, and what's transferable and what's not" (K28).

Less than three months after the new director's arrival, a large, unanticipated shock hit Kirklees, as a series of stay-at-home orders forced the UK into a lockdown in response to the coronavirus pandemic. The COVID-19 pandemic necessitated unprecedented changes in the way that all health, social, and housing services were delivered. The KBOP service providers reacted quickly to the changed operating environment and dramatic escalation in demand for support. At the outset of the pandemic, referral agencies in Kirklees were not operating as usual, and there was some anxiety that the KBOP-backed services would be affected by reduced referrals, in addition to the challenge of operating in line with guidelines for limited face-to-face contact. Exhibiting the flexibility of the PPP infrastructure, the Council team quickly offered assurances regarding funding and the potential to decouple payments from the outcome measures to offer more guaranteed resources if required.

The Kirklees-KBOP partnership was the first service in Kirklees to set up a support helpline in the early stage of the pandemic. The helpline resulted in the KBOP delivery partnership being the first point of contact for requests from individual service users, as well as for referral agencies and social sector organizations beyond its target group. To manage the high demand for the helpline, KBOP liaised with other local partners and services and started to support, coordinate, and advise other services across Kirklees, such as community hubs, the social prescribing team, the probation service, and more. This effort helped build KBOP's knowledge about the landscape of potential local partners and services in Kirklees. At the same time, this approach positioned KBOP to become known and embedded as a relevant local service delivery partner. The KBOP director explained how, soon after the establishment of the helpline, KBOP began receiving requests for support from other statutory services and nonstatutory services in the area.

Ultimately, the shifts made to the service during COVID-19 reflected the highly adaptive, responsive, and solutions-focused approach of both the Council and KBOP teams. Notably, there was a move away from the outcomes-payment approach in order to stabilize funding, in recognition of the highly uncertain operating environment. Frontline staff teams developed an ability to support far higher numbers of potential program participants than initially expected. Although there is a longstanding preference for in-person support, the uptake of new technologies brought additional tools to help staff and service users stay connected while cutting travel times, increasing efficiency. Crucially, the early move to set up a helpline not only brought KBOP deeper knowledge of the local service landscape, but it also raised awareness of the KBOP service, thus broadening the network of referral agencies that would later make referrals to the service. During COVID-19, the Kirklees-KBOP partnership was understood to have become increasingly well known and embedded as a relevant local service delivery partner. Once again, this approach stands in contrast to how the Indiana-IBM PPP weathered its unanticipated, "stormy" events, which similarly increased service demands but resulted instead in strained and fractured partner relationships.

A new approach emerges

The new program director's approach to managing the partnership signaled a shift from that of her temporary predecessor. While the centrality of performance measures and outcomes-based payments to the contract remained, the way in which these were used to guide practice shifted significantly. The new director oversaw changes in the leadership and governance of the program and increased the level of flexibility in the approach to supporting service users at the frontline. She also attempted to reach out to the wider local public services ecosystem to address more systemic issues.

In terms of the direct performance management of their subcontracted providers, the KBOP team sought to move away from a rigid, target-driven approach. According to the program director, "Although there is a very clear contract management process in place . . . where there's very clear accountability and reporting and governance, it is all done in a very open, honest and collaborative way" (Rosenbach et al. 2023). While quantitative measures of performance relative to targets continued to shape discussions, they did so as part of a much more holistic understanding of how the contract was working. At contract management meetings, referral and outcome achievement statistics were presented alongside case studies of service user experiences to facilitate a wider discussion around how the service was working. As part of this open and collaborative approach, the new director led a major review and reworking of the rate card so that the outcome measures themselves were revised in a way that incorporated feedback from providers. Thus, the rate card adjustments allowed the informal mechanisms the director instituted to be supported by stronger formal levers.

The changing approach to formal performance targets was mirrored at the frontline through the adoption of a personalized, "strengths-based" approach to support service users. The focus of support for service users shifted from addressing someone's needs to supporting them to achieve their aspirations. Frontline staff undertook training by the Mayday Trust, a charity specializing in person-led, transitional support approaches. Training in active listening and coaching underpins a tailored, integrated service model that gives people choice and autonomy (Baraki and Phagoora 2022). Participants are able to set the goals they want to achieve in collaboration with support workers, and frontline staff are also given significant discretion in determining the type and frequency of support, including the duration and location of their sessions (Rosenbach et al. 2023, 76–85).

Again, this new service model required a de-emphasis of the formal contractual incentives. Indeed, there is evidence of provider managers "shielding" frontline staff from the contract's targets (Rosenbach et al. 2023, 67), although doing so created a tension with the hard outcomes-based performance management and payment incentives. KBOP's managers relied on an implicit assumption that person-centered support would ultimately lead to the achievement of payable outcomes, even when those payable outcomes were not the focus of frontline staff.

In addition, there has been a greater recognition of the inherent limitations of the core KBOP services in achieving the program's broader objectives. The investment fund director, which supports KBOP, emphasized, "If KBOP is going to work, we can't just deliver our own service. We have to go out and change the way all these other services interact with the people we're trying to help." Often, the front-line KBOP services operate against a backdrop of much deeper, systemic challenges, such as constrained access and long waiting lists for therapeutic mental health support. Individual provider organizations have little incentive or ability to address these alone, and yet in the context of the overarching goal of the partnership, they serve as significant barriers to achieving service goals. Under its new management, the role of KBOP shifted from pure performance management taskmaster to something more akin to what Alnoor Ebrahim has described as an "ecosystem orchestrator" (Ebrahim 2019, 161). Beyond its direct role in managing subcontracted provider organizations to deliver the floating support housing services, KBOP started helping to coordinate the wider support ecosystem in Kirklees. Managers are involved in a variety of local and regional boards covering housing and homelessness, health and well-being, and criminal justice. These strong networks allow them to communicate challenges faced by providers to those better placed to address them, as well as to build and pursue more formal collaborations (with associated funding) to tackle systemic issues (Rosenbach et al. 2023, 87–91).

This quite significant reframing of the approach to the Kirklees-KBOP partnership was in part driven by the director's expertise and social capital. She had significant practical experience working at the sharp end of outsourced service provision in the nonprofit sector and had previously managed another SIB. As a result, she recognized the tensions between the traditional ways of working within provider organizations and the structures and processes embedded in the formal contract. However, while the new director undoubtedly played a key role in the change of approach within the KBOP program, it would be a mistake to suggest that other parties, and the contractual framework within which they interacted, were also not important. Within the Kirklees

Council, the program's commissioners embraced a more flexible and collaborative approach from the outset of the contract and pressed for the shift toward more person-centered support. In a sense, the shift driven by the new KBOP program director is merely a realization of this original vision from local government leaders. Independent provider organizations have also had to buy into this approach, often quite significantly adapting their standard service delivery models and broader organizational structures, requiring significant investment in human and technical resources.

The contract itself also facilitated this shift in approach. A detailed analysis of the features of the Kirklees-KBOP contract (van Lier et al., forthcoming) highlights the key role of specific contractual clauses, alongside the formal and informal governance arrangements that arose from them, in supporting more relational working in Kirklees. It suggests that the overarching contractual commitment to "develop a close working relationship between the Authority and the Contractor at all appropriate levels, based upon openness and trust in a transparent information and data sharing environment" (Kirklees Council 2019, 15) helps to provide a foundation for collaboration and flexibility. This is embodied in the formal change procedure, which has been used to co-develop adaptations to the outcomes framework, and in the informal governance structures that have helped to include a wide range of stakeholders in contractual oversight.

In 2022, the Kirklees Better Outcomes Partnership received an award for Best Procurement Delivery at the UK National Excellence in Public Procurement Awards (the "Oscars for public procurement"), during which the team was commended for a pioneering "social outcomes contract" that focuses on creating closer collaboration and partnership to deliver better outcomes for clients. The KBOP also made the finals at the 2022 Local Government Chronicle Awards.

The initial Kirklees-KBOP contract was due to conclude in March 2024, but the Kirklees Council announced a 6-month extension to the initial contract (to September 2024). This extension would allow them to retain provider staff while a longer-term settlement could be developed to support a new "KBOP2" program. The extension and pursuit of a new contract suggested a vote of confidence from key stakeholders in the Kirklees Better Outcomes Partnership. However, challenges remain. The budget for the extension was significantly reduced compared with the original budget, owing to the end of central government co-funding at the conclusion of the initial contract. Meanwhile, like many local authorities in England, the Kirklees Council faced significant budgetary pressures at the time and had to implement significant spending controls to avert potential bankruptcy (Marlow 2023). These headwinds show that even a PPP that is deemed a success by its partners and its public sector peers can face continued uncertainty on the path to sustainability.

PROCESS TRACING EVIDENCE AND TESTS OF KEY CASE DIFFERENCES

Allocation of formal and real authority

The Indiana-IBM and Kirklees-KBOP cases present starkly contrasting approaches to the allocation and exercise of formal and real authority within PPPs. Formal authority (i.e., the contractual right to make decisions) often differs from real authority (actual control over decisions) (Aghion and Tirole 1997). The cases provide rich empirical evidence demonstrating how written agreements can be fundamentally disconnected from actual decision-making dynamics, with far-reaching implications for potential loss of control, as well as the effort and incentives of agents. In the Indiana-IBM case, formal authority was meticulously defined in the MSA, with the State retaining explicit decision-making rights through a detailed governance plan. However, the real authority dynamics were fundamentally fragmented and consistently contested, characterized by a complex network of subcontractors and shifting leadership that created persistent accountability challenges. Additionally, the communication dynamics in the Indiana-IBM partnership were strategically opportunistic, with subcontractors like ACS systematically bypassing formal authority structures by directly engaging state officials. These actions undermined the prime contractor's position and created an environment of strategic information sharing that deteriorated as conflicts escalated. The large span of control, involving as many as twelve subcontractors, further complicated authority allocation and created significant coordination challenges.

In contrast, the Kirklees-KBOP case evidence elucidates a more collaborative and adaptive approach to authority. While maintaining a clearly defined contractual framework, the partnership emphasized flexibility, transparent communication, and user empowerment. The real authority was distributed more equitably, with structured communication channels and a focus on building trust and alignment among partners. This approach allowed for more dynamic decision-making and responsive service delivery.

In effect, the fundamental distinction between these cases lies not just in their structural differences, but in their philosophical approach to governance. The Indiana-IBM model represented a top-down, control-oriented paradigm, while the Kirklees-KBOP approach embodied a more relational, collaborative model of public service delivery. Collectively, the evidence suggests that successful authority delegation requires low interdependencies, high trust, clear communication, and the ability to adapt to emergent needs—qualities most prominently displayed in the Kirklees-KBOP partnership. This analysis also reveals that formal authority, when rigidly implemented without consideration of real-world complexities, can become a hindrance rather than a facilitator of effective public services delivery. The Kirklees model demonstrates that true effectiveness emerges from creating flexible governance structures that prioritize communication, trust, and user-centered outcomes over strict hierarchical control.

The allocation of formal and real authority in the Indiana-IBM and Kirklees-KBOP PPPs reveals profound differences in how organizational incentives and control mechanisms function. In the Indiana-IBM case, the misalignment of authority created a complex landscape of perverse incentives that systematically undermined the partnership's effectiveness. Subcontractors like ACS were strategically positioned to exploit gaps in the governance structure. The incentive distortions were particularly evident in the punitive performance monitoring approach, which encouraged opportunistic behavior rather than collaborative problem-solving. The State of Indiana maintained a control framework that paradoxically reduced its real control, with multiple principals creating conflicting directives and leadership changes constantly disrupting project continuity. The large span of control further exacerbated these challenges, reducing organizational visibility and coordination capabilities.

Combining theoretical insights discussed in Chapter 2 with the case evidence presented above leads to the following proposition for our first process tracing test:

> **Proposition 1**: Real authority dynamics may reinforce or undermine the formal contractual framework.

The test evidence and test results for Proposition 1 appear in Table 4.1 and are briefly summarized here. The process tracing tests provide strong support for Proposition 1. The initial *straw in the wind test* provides suggestive evidence of authority divergence, highlighting preliminary indicators of how real authority was beginning to deviate from the formal contractual structure in the Indiana-IBM case. The *hoop test* demonstrated more robust support, establishing clear criteria required to meet the hypothesis. In documenting communication bypasses, strategic information manipulation, and measurable deviations from contractual provisions in the Indiana-IBM PPP, the test confirmed that the hypothesis passed critical threshold requirements. Alternatively, the evidence from the Kirklees-KBOP PPP demonstrates a fundamentally different approach to authority allocation. By establishing clear, transparent expectations, the partnership aligned organizational incentives toward mutual benefit. The governance structures prioritized flexibility, trust building, and adaptive service delivery, which naturally encouraged more cooperative behaviors aligned with the formal contract framework.

The *smoking gun test* produced particularly compelling evidence for Proposition 1, uncovering decisive markers of authority subversion in the Indiana-IBM case. The placement of Richard Rhoad, an ACS

Table 4.1 Test Evidence for Proposition 1: Real Authority Dynamics May Reinforce or Undermine the Formal Contractual Framework

Test	Evidence	Results
Straw in the Wind Test	Preliminary indications of authority's impact. Easily passed with anecdotal evidence.	PASS
Hoop Test	Looking for documented variations in authority allocation and their measurable impacts on partnership outcomes. Kirklees-KBOP: Contract outlined (reinforced) clear collaborative authority structures; structured yet flexible communication protocols; transparent communication channels (even when not fully outlined in the contract, they were clearly communicated across the delivery network); partnership sustained and performing above expectations; contrasting performance on key social service metrics; measurable differences in service delivery effectiveness. Indiana-IBM: MSA specified formal authority; fragmented authority in practice (communication channels systematically undermined is evidence of real authority); multiple principals with conflicting directives; span of control up to twelve subcontractors; leadership changes disrupted (undermined) governance; quantifiable performance measurement differences; partnership terminated after less than three years. Specific documentable indicators for both cases: Formal contract provisions; communication pathway documentation; leadership transition records; performance measurement frameworks; subcontractor relationship management approaches.	PASS Demonstrates necessity

Test	Evidence	Results
Smoking Gun Test	Looking for evidence that the proposition would be highly unlikely to exist unless the proposition is true; evidence of a causal path. Kirklees-KBOP: Clear, collaborative authority distribution with user-centered approach (changing the system, not the person, returning power to individuals); role clarity (contract terms and board meeting notes); central hub for communication; aligned organizational objectives; flexible governance structure; sustained and successful partnership (multiple interviews and validated performance data submitted to Life Chances Fund team in central government). Indiana-IBM: Unclear principal-agent relationships (Interview: ACS never had to answer to anybody); direct evidence of authority manipulation and communication manipulation (ACS Lobbyist Joe Loftus directly contacted the governor's office); systematic undermining of IBM's prime contractor status; Richard Rhoad (ACS) maintained an office with the state executive team; interviews reveal constant management changes (when Anne Murphy took over, IBM was no longer needed); opportunistic communication to undermine partnership; selective and conflicting information sharing; strategic timing of leadership transitions; exploiting governance ambiguities; partnership ultimately terminated.	PASS Strong causal evidence. Multiple complex causal paths.
Doubly Decisive Test	Need to rule out alternative explanations. Kirklees-KBOP: Definitive success indicators: partnership and organizational effectiveness; performance exceeding expectations, contract extension.	PASS

Continued

Table 4.1 CONTINUED

Test	Evidence	Results
	Independent validation for distribution of authority (GOLab research, longitudinal evaluation reports, stakeholder testimonials, performance audit confirmations).	
	Indiana-IBM: Definitive failure indicators: Quantifiable indicators of leadership/authority changes with links to project delays and partner conflicts; principals and agents jockeying for position; State unilaterally terminated partnership, multiple legal proceedings, explicit court findings of failure with testimony connecting failures to authority structure and related behaviors.	
	Independent sources confirmed a consistent pattern of authority manipulation, demonstrating how communication dynamics and strategic behaviors could fundamentally reshape organizational control structures. Specifications of real authority in the formal contract were not merely inadequate, but actively circumvented.	

(subcontractor) representative, in the state executive team's office exemplified a striking manifestation of how real authority could operate independently of formal contractual boundaries. Direct communications between subcontractors and state officials, systematic undermining of communication protocols, and strategically timed leadership changes emerged as powerful mechanisms of organizational control that transcended written agreements. Evidence for Proposition 1 was also clear in the Kirklees-KBOP case, in which real authority (in contrast to the Indiana-IBM case) was aligned with the flexible governance structures and user-centered approach and facilitated collaboration that supported the success of the partnership.

The *doubly decisive test* provided definitive proof of the proposition, presenting conclusive documentation of governance subversion in the Indiana-IBM case. Multiple independent sources confirmed a consistent pattern of authority manipulation, demonstrating how communication dynamics and strategic behaviors could fundamentally reshape organizational control structures. The test suggested that the written contract was not merely inadequate but was actively circumvented through sophisticated organizational maneuvering. The mechanism of breakdown centered on strategic information sharing, power redistribution, and opportunistic organizational behaviors. By exploiting governance ambiguities, organizational actors systematically dismantled the formal contractual framework, revealing it as a relatively weak constraint compared with the dynamic, strategic reallocation of real authority. Conversely, control maintenance in the Kirklees model was achieved through carefully designed communication protocols, a centralized coordination hub, and regular performance review mechanisms. These structural elements created an environment where information sharing was encouraged, strategic decision-making was collaborative, and organizational trust could flourish within the formal contract structures.

In sum, the process tracing tests of Proposition 1 provide strong, suggestive evidence that the success of PPPs critically depends on the allocation and implementation of both formal authority (contractual decision rights) and real authority (actual decision implementation), with independent verification across multiple dimensions. At the same time, we acknowledge that there may be additional mediating factors (e.g., external constraints, leadership decisions, incentives) and moderating factors (e.g., service complexity, organizational size, political context) that could further illuminate plausible causal relationships that we are not able to explore with the data available.

The role of relational mechanisms versus formal contractual provisions

When considering the spectrum of formal to relational in developing the infrastructure to scaffold a PPP, our case evidence suggests that particularly in the context of complex, multiactor PPPs, leaning toward the formal end is less likely to set a PPP on the path toward sustainability and success. The reality is that a detailed and explicit contract that aims to fully delineate expectations and rights will offer only limited protection from risks and may unintentionally elevate them. More formalized contracts with their meticulous stipulations often fall short in deterring rent-seeking tendencies and ensuring effective enforcement (Rogerson 1992; Klein et al. 1978). Given the many challenges experienced in human services delivery due to their intricate nature and the external forces that confront them (Brown et al. 2016; Macneil 1978), our case evidence suggests it is imperative to center and integrate relational governance mechanisms into PPPs. Mechanisms such as those we have described—grounded in social processes like trust building and reciprocal exchanges—foster norms of flexibility, solidarity, and information sharing, protect against transactional hazards, and ultimately bolster the enforcement of obligations that formalization is intended to promote (Baker 2002; Granovetter 1973, 1985; Gulati 1995; Ring and Van de Ven 1994).

The role of relationship building in meaningful and constructive performance management in a PPP, an essential function of any outcomes-focused contract, was also illustrated in our case evidence, particularly in the Kirklees-KBOP PPP. The Council commissioning team acknowledged that their ability to define every contingency and control right ex ante was necessarily constrained and that these would need to be navigated through dialogue. The KBOP Board actively sought to maximize outcomes by amplifying mechanisms that would facilitate a collaborative approach to performance management and to improving service delivery. This included the creation of the co-production forum, which brought together service providers and service users for productive discussions of performance data and encouraged the sharing of ideas for enhancing the service experience. The ideas for service innovations that emerged from these forums were genuinely advanced through the Kirklees-KBOP governance structures, which embedded learning and adaptation into the delivery of services and the contractual relationship itself at all levels.

Alternatively, with a lack of trust and collaborative structures undergirding the Indiana-IBM PPP, the contracted performance measures that were intended to promote transparency and accountability became a tool of animosity and retribution exercised through inspections and audits (further illuminated in Chapter 5). The frequent audits not only consumed time, resources, and attention that could have been directed toward more productive endeavors (e.g., addressing the external crises impinging on services delivery), but because they could occur at any time and at the discretion of only one party, they also undermined trust and amplified an imbalance of power. As a result, rather than supporting productive discussions among the parties of how to improve the PPP's performance, the parties became resistant to sharing information freely, fearing that such information could be used against them, even if they were acting in good faith. The Indiana-IBM partnership relied heavily on rigid formal provisions, such as process-based KPIs, which precluded flexibility when problems emerged. Disputes over metrics and a lack of reciprocity further exacerbated tensions, ultimately leading to litigation and termination.

Combining theoretical insights discussed in Chapter 2 with our case evidence leads to the following proposition in our second process tracing test:

> **Proposition 2**: The success of PPPs depends equally if not more on the strength of relational mechanisms, such as trust, autonomy, and reciprocity, as on the formal contractual provisions.

The test evidence and test results for Proposition 2 appear in Table 4.2. The evidence easily passes the *straw in the wind test*, requiring only that both relational and formal mechanisms are present in both cases. There is also clear evidence that formal and relational factors affected the outcome of passing the *hoop test*. The evidence is more mixed for the smoking gun test and the doubly decisive test. The *smoking gun test* requires evidence that would be highly unlikely to exist unless the proposition is true and there is a direct causal path. In the Kirklees-KBOP case, the partnership demonstrated flexibility, adaptability, and sustained success by prioritizing shared governance, relational trust, and mutual respect. These factors allowed the partners to collaboratively address challenges and remain focused on long-term, client-centered goals. In contrast, the Indiana-IBM partnership, despite its detailed formal contractual provisions, experienced significant conflict and eventual failure. The over-reliance on rigid metrics and performance measures created an adversarial environment, highlighting the

Table 4.2 Test Evidence for Proposition 2: The Success of PPPs Depends Equally If Not More on the Strength of Relational Mechanisms, such as Trust, Autonomy, and Reciprocity, as on the Formal Contractual Provisions

Test	Evidence	Results
Straw in the Wind Test	Looking for evidence that both relational and formal mechanisms are present in both cases and that they may have affected outcomes. General pattern present in both cases. (Low Bar)	PASS
Hoop Test	Looking for clear evidence that relational mechanisms or lack of relational mechanisms led to success/failure. Kirklees-KBOP: Documented investment in relationship building prior to contract signing; success in adapting during COVID-19 through a collaborative approach; autonomy given to frontline staff; reciprocity shown in mutual adaptation of performance measures; improvements linked to trust-based interactions; trust built through open governance and collaborative problem-solving; successful contract extension following relational approach. Indiana-IBM: Breakdown in relationships preceded contract failure; trust erosion led to defensive behaviors despite formal provisions; trust undermined by subcontractor and State bypassing formal structures; autonomy limited by the State's tight control and unilateral termination rights; reciprocity failed as the State used performance metrics antagonistically rather than collaboratively; contract termination despite comprehensive formal provisions.	PASS Demonstrates necessity

Test	Evidence	Results
Smoking Gun Test	Looking for evidence that the proposition would be highly unlikely to exist unless the proposition is true; evidence of a causal path. Kirklees-KBOP: Well-designed governance forums provided foundation; forums preceded productive adaptation of measures; open performance discussions enabled service improvements; shared problem-solving during COVID-19 points to strength of relational norms. Partners operated with mutual respect and shared decision rights, ensuring the partnership focused on long-term, client-centered goals. Indiana-IBM: Used performance audits as a solution in search of breach; no evidence of trust building. The State "geared up" for potential breaches rather than working collaboratively; communications show intent to "throw IBM under the bus"; termination followed breakdown in relational norms.	PASS At least one direct path, but multiple causal paths possible.
Doubly Decisive Test	Need to rule out alternative explanations. Key test: Did PPPs with strong formal mechanisms but weak relational elements succeed? Kirklees-KBOP: While strong relational mechanisms were present and the PPP succeeded, partners' careful attention to formal contract design contributed to success (e.g., the contract explicitly recognized the autonomy of each partner and valued their unique capabilities, outcome measures provided formal metrics for understanding performance). Success achieved through contributions from both formal and relational elements and the balance between these approaches.	NEED MORE RESEARCH Cannot fully eliminate other explanations.[a]

Continued

Table 4.2 Continued

Test	Evidence	Results
	Indiana-IBM: Both formal and relational factors cited in court documents as reasons for failure. Breakdown in relational mechanisms (trust, reciprocity, etc.) coincided with other issues (e.g., complex performance metrics; external pressures from recession and natural disasters; political changes and leadership transitions). We cannot definitively say the relational breakdown primarily caused the failure.	

[a]The differences in political or economic contexts may have influenced the outcomes. While context matters, the evidence from both cases highlights the centrality of relational mechanisms in shaping partnership dynamics and success.

limitations of formal contracts in fostering cooperation and adaptability. This evidence aligns with the proposition that strong relational mechanisms are equally if not more critical to success. In Kirklees-KBOP, trust, reciprocity, and shared decision-making played a central role in navigating challenges, whereas the Indiana-IBM case underscores how the absence of these mechanisms led to adversarial dynamics and contract termination.

Temporal evidence adds further support. In the Kirklees-KBOP PPP, relational mechanisms were consistently leveraged over time, enabling the partnership to adapt to challenges such as economic shocks. The Kirklees-KBOP partnership was built on a foundation of trust, autonomy, and shared governance, which were emphasized in the contract from the outset. These relational elements were consistently applied as the partnership addressed challenges, including initial service delivery issues and economic disruptions. By relying on these mechanisms, the partnership maintained its stability and effectiveness over time. Conversely, the Indiana-IBM partnership quickly disintegrated when faced with implementation challenges, as conflicts escalated without the support of strong relational foundations. In the absence of relational mechanisms, the partners depended entirely on formal provisions, which proved inadequate for resolving emerging issues and evolving needs of the partnership and led to the eventual termination of the partnership and litigation.

While plausible causal paths can be identified, there are also multiple alternative paths. The most stringent test in process tracing is the *doubly decisive test*. There is some supportive evidence from both cases for this test, but it may be insufficient to pass the highest standard of this causal test. For example, contextual factors, including politics and changes in leadership, also played a role in the evolution and outcomes of the PPPs. Overall, the evidence suggests the need for further research that can illuminate alternative causal paths and the influence of contextual factors in the success of complex, multiactor PPPs such as these.

CONCLUSION: MAKING SENSE OF THE PPPs' MARCH DOWN TWO DIFFERENT PATHS TOWARD FAILURE VERSUS SUCCESS

In the emerging research on formal-relational contracting, one of the key recommendations for success is the development of a set of "guiding principles" that support or reinforce desired social norms. These can be used to shape the contracting parties' interactions when they encounter frictions, major shocks, or other noncontracted contingencies. As described by Frydlinger and Hart (2023), and as was observed in the Kirklees-KBOP case, when activated, the guiding principles serve as the scaffolding (Hadfield and Bozovic 2016) that helps to sustain the partnership when it confronts difficulties, whether they manifest internally or externally. But these principles are not something that the partners pull out of a consultant's or intermediary's playbook. They have to be mutually discovered and agreed upon in the context of relationships that are formed among the contracting parties and strengthened as they start down the path to developing a formal-relational contract (Frydlinger et al. 2021). In addition, they need to be accompanied by other PPP structures (formal and relational)—such as well-defined, mutually aligned goals and effective communication channels and practices—that increase the likelihood the principles will be given weight in the face of disputes and difficulties and reduce tendencies toward shading and other negative responses.

Although not a typical step in public procurement, in both the Indiana-IBM and Kirklees-KBOP cases, there were opportunities to cultivate shared social norms and work toward the development of guiding principles among the partners. As described in the Indiana-IBM case, the major contracting partners, IBM and the State, were on solid common ground in their motivations and vision for how the PPP could transform welfare services delivery in Indiana and their beliefs about what a private sector partner would bring to the benefit of the public. Perhaps in part for political reasons and also impelled by the State's bottom-ranked standings in performance on welfare state effectiveness, Indiana and IBM moved relatively swiftly to formalize the partnership and establish the MSA with great fanfare.

In contrast, the Kirklees-KBOP partners took their time over the reorganization of services delivery and drew on the expertise and experiences of various independent actors to collaboratively construct relational mechanisms alongside the development of formal PPP structures. Moreover, the preparatory work undertaken ahead of the formal contract advanced with the humble acknowledgement that things would inevitably need to change with time, and with the recognition that relational mechanisms would be critical to navigating the uncertainties that lay ahead. In the rigidly structured MSA that launched the Indiana-IBM PPP, there appeared to be less space for accommodating the "known unknowns" and any mechanisms that might evolve to cooperatively address them.

This rigidity also undoubtedly relates to the fact that the prime contractors in the Indiana-IBM and Kirklees-KBOP PPPs were conferred differing levels of discretion in their formal contractual arrangements. The State of Indiana kept tight reins on a number of functions core to the PPP's work, including determination of client eligibility for welfare services and other areas of policymaking authority and operational responsibility, down to the local (county) level. There were also contractual clauses that gave the State further leeway to assert its authority over the prime contractor and subcontractors, including the ominous early termination clause that the State ultimately used to bring down the PPP. In contrast, from the start, the Kirklees-KBOP contract explicitly recognized the importance of the partners' autonomy and valued the varying capabilities the partners would bring and the collaboration that could be unlock. The focus on mutually agreed, long-term and client-centered goals naturally required the Kirklees-KBOP partners to approach the work flexibly and to accommodate changes over time to preserve their focus on the people being served. Thus, whereas the Indiana-IBM PPP became mired in process- and activity-based KPIs that were used in adversarial ways to point fingers and apportion blame for the problems that arose, the Kirklees-KBOP partners leveraged the relational mechanisms and flexibility they afforded to cooperatively guide and fine-tune the PPP work.

Perhaps the overarching distinction between the progression of the two PPPs is how the formal and relational elements in each were nurtured and balanced. In the Kirklees-KBOP outcomes contract, the formal contractual clauses appeared to intentionally facilitate the effective working of the informal governance arrangements that the partners cultivated, whereas in the Indiana-IBM MSA, the formal contractual provisions eclipsed and inhibited the partners' use of relational mechanisms to manage PPP challenges. In effect, in the face of divergent perspectives or unanticipated shocks, the Kirklees-KBOP partners relied on the relational elements of their PPP to protect against opportunistic or shading behaviors and further cultivate trust and cooperation. Alternatively, in the Indiana-IBM case, the State invoked the formal MSA performance requirements and stipulations (e.g., audits, penalties) to assign blame for shortcomings and chastise the prime contractor, which only hastened the partners descent into conflict and the termination of the PPP.

In Chapter 5 that follows, we describe in greater detail the performance expectations and accountability provisions that were (or are) core elements of the Indiana-IBM PPP and Kirklees-KBOP contracts and by which the success of the PPPs in generating public value were (or are being) judged. We show how the differing governance structures and partner approaches to collaboration described in this chapter influenced the design and implementation of the performance management tools and their use dynamically to guide the work of the Indiana-IBM and Kirklees-KBOP PPPs.

5

Performance and Accountability

A tyranny of metrics versus a tool for learning

Public aspirations for what governments can achieve and for holding them accountable for results continue to rise (Hevenstone et al. 2023). Accountability to the public compels the appraisal of government performance in generating public value, and in many social outcomes contracts, the government only pays when the intended outcomes are realized. In complex PPP arrangements such as those we examine in this book, governments may effectively pass responsibility (or accountability) for generating public value onto their contractors. This requires them to translate expectations for delivering value to the public into formal contract specifications. Most often, this translation has involved outlining specific outputs and outcomes and attaching monetary value to them, to align financial incentives with public imperatives. But as we have discussed throughout this book, this may not be sufficient to keep a PPP on the path to sustainability and success in achieving public goals. It is frequently challenging to convert expectations into complete contract terms, or to determine the appropriate balance between goals that may be competing, such as a public duty to promote equity and accessibility versus boosting efficiency through resource targeting. That is why expectations also need to be embedded in informal structures and facets of the relationship that the partners cultivate in the PPP, such as assurances of ongoing cooperation toward achieving PPP goals and relational

Contracting for Public Value. Carolyn J. Heinrich et al., Oxford University Press. © Oxford University Press (2026).
DOI: 10.1093/9780197763155.003.0005

mechanisms for joint problem-solving. As Pearl Zhu (2017) has argued, "Most organizations fail to manage performance effectively because they fail to look into the system holistically."

In this chapter, we compare how the parties in our two cases developed and managed contractual performance standards in the PPPs and examine the role that these standards played in determining the fate of the contracts. To enforce these contractual terms, the contracting parties typically design mechanisms—formal and/or relational—for monitoring performance and holding the service providers accountable for the outcomes. In the Indiana-IBM PPP and Kirklees-KBOP contract, the performance expectations and accountability provisions were core elements by which the success of the PPPs in generating public value were judged. The two PPPs differed considerably, however, in their purposeful use of performance information.

More specifically, we identified three key areas in which the Indiana-IBM and Kirklees-KBOP PPPs differed in their approach to using the contractual performance standards. Firstly, the PPPs differed in whether they treated performance standards as fixed or negotiable. Both had complex, onerous sets of KPIs and evidence requirements, but in the Kirklees-KBOP PPP, the parties realized the risks associated with rigid and taxing KPIs—with the potential for undermining the contract goals—and revisited them midway. Secondly, the cases differed in what the performance information was used for: the State of Indiana treated it as a means of reproving its contractor, IBM, while in the Kirklees-KBOP PPP, the parties used the information collaboratively to guide ongoing learning and adaptation of the services delivery model. Lastly, the cases differed in the reasons for their contrasting fates. The State of Indiana ignored and even obscured performance data that reflected value to the public, instead using KPIs focused on minutiae or process as a pretext for terminating the contract. Kirklees-KBOP, by contrast, built intensive forums for collaboration and channeled performance information to foster meaningful discussion. KBOP also espoused a different style of leadership that sought to widen access to performance information to unlock greater inclusivity and appropriately delegate decision-making.

CONTRACTED PERFORMANCE INDICATORS AND STIPULATIONS

The literature on performance management (Hatry 1999) distinguishes among six basic types of performance information that can be used for performance monitoring, evaluation, and improvement in PPPs. These types include

- inputs e.g., technology, financial resources, staffing;
- process e.g., wait times, error rates;
- efficiency e.g., costs per application processed;
- outputs e.g., claims processed, services delivered;
- outcomes e.g., welfare recipients entering unsubsidized employment; and
- impacts e.g., increases in client self-sufficiency attributable to program participation.

PPP contracts may articulate performance expectations that draw from one or more of these performance information types.

Indiana-IBM

In its decision on the Indiana-IBM case (No. 49S02-1408-PL-00513), the Indiana Supreme Court wrote that the MSA (contract) "provides performance standards and indicators to measure IBM's performance," and "the policy objectives of the MSA are incorporated into those performance standards," which set forth the standard for assessing the PPP outcomes. The MSA performance regime was lengthy, highly formalized, and rigid. It focused on many detailed process measures that reflected an orientation toward micromanaging the work of the PPP—that is, a top-down, hierarchical approach to the relationship rather than relying on professional accountability or cultivating norms such as trust and reciprocity to guide execution of the work (Romzek 1998; Williamson 1985). The insertion of sizeable penalties for each performance indicator—many addressing minutiae of the daily PPP work—likely reinforced an inimical orientation to addressing challenges encountered in the intricate project.

The performance metrics primarily included process measures of program administration, a few input measures, and only one measure that could be characterized as an outcome measure (the work participation rate). The PPP contract formalized these performance expectations and mechanisms for accountability in a detailed schedule (MSA Schedule 10, Performance Standards) of indicators and standards that are summarized in Box 5.1. Schedule 10 also defined penalties for failure to meet each performance standard: (1) those that placed a specific percentage of the contract payment "at risk," and (2) liquidated damages of a defined amount per weekday or month that the vendor (IBM) had to pay when a performance standard was not met.

Box 5.1

Indiana-IBM PPP Contract Performance Measures

Schedule 10 of the MSA specifies the following performance measures:

Service Levels (including process measures and one outcome measure)

- Process measures (Procedure Variance Rates): Medicaid Long Term Care Procedure Variance Rate, TANF Procedure Variance Rate, Food Stamp Procedure Variance Rate, where the variance rate (a percentage) is calculated as the number of cases which are incorrect in the case sample over the total number of cases.
- Outcome measure: All Family Work Participation Rate

Statewide Key Performance Indicators (KPIs)

- Performance reporting

Transition Key Performance Indicators (TKPIs)

- TANF, Food Stamps, and Medicaid Timeliness: % of applications (of each type) completed within Federal timeframes (3 separate measures)

- TANF, Food Stamps, and Medicaid Application Volume: % of variance of applications processed per office (and in aggregate) compared to the same period the prior year (3 separate measures)

Service Center KPIs (process measures)

- Office hours
- Call center call response time, hold time, abandonment rate, blockage rate
- Workflow Management System Availability, Eligibility Web Site Availability, System of Record SOA Interface Availability, Telephony System Interactive Voice Response System Availability
- Disaster Recovery Testing completed
- Non-Index Document Processing Rate
- Constituent Care Response Time

Document Center KPIs: Document Scanning Rate, Scanning Quality

Program Specific KPIs

- Food Stamp Case Actions
- Medicaid Case Actions
- Medicaid Disability Applications
- TANF Case Actions

State Managed Office KPI: Call Operations Availability

Operational Verification and Validation (OV&V): Monthly status reports tracking new and ongoing issues that the parties to the contract are working to resolve.

Moreover, Schedule 10 of the MSA stipulated that the State "shall select no less than eight Transition Milestones set forth in the Transition Plan that are critical to the State with respect to the success of the Transition." Like the transition key performance indicators (TKPIs) shown in Box 5.1, the critical "Transition Milestones" were primarily task- and process-oriented, including, for example, 100% of transferred employees rebadged and receiving payroll checks and benefits enrollment opportunities; delivery of a "steady state" procedures manual; software releases, and completion of Region 2A, 2, and 3 program rollouts. And consistent with the largely transactional nature of the agreement, liquidated damages were also assigned for each Critical Transition Milestone, with a total penalty not to exceed $2 million.

Despite hefty lawyering on both sides in the negotiation of the MSA, the resulting contract was little more than an expanded version of the two-party contract template in Indiana's Manual for Professional Service Contracts, with exhaustively detailed written specifications that clearly allocated authority and stipulated recourse (e.g., penalties). It disregarded the PPP's complex, multiactor context and discounted the potential benefits of fostering trust, which can encourage risk-taking, information sharing, and collaborative problem-solving, while counteracting the pursuit of short-term, individual party gains (Ostrom and Walker 2003).

In a contractual relationship, trust involves a reciprocal dynamic, wherein parties foresee future gains even if experiencing short-term losses (Helper and Levine 1992, 563). Moreover, trust is not necessarily static over the course of a PPP's work; even if present at the outset, it can deteriorate over time. In the Indiana-IBM case, the subcontractor ACS began undermining IBM as the prime contractor almost immediately after the MSA was signed. ACS personnel and its lobbyist subverted the contract structure to secure consistent and direct contact with the governor's office and top FSSA officials. ACS and State personnel testified in court that they were aware that such contacts were contractually prohibited, but they nevertheless continued the practice throughout the project. It is when trust is lacking at the start (as in this case) that the parties often resort to additional risk-mitigating clauses, such as stringent performance requirements and payment terms, penalty clauses to safeguard interests, audit rights, renegotiation triggers, or shorter contract durations. In fact, the Indiana-IBM MSA also included a termination-for-convenience clause—giving the State discretion to end the contract unilaterally, without cause—which is perhaps the ultimate manifestation of this type of risk mitigation in the absence of a foundation of trust.

Kirklees-KBOP

The Kirklees Council-KBOP partnership is underpinned by an outcomes-based contract, as part of a social impact bond (SIB), and so payment is (primarily) tied to the achievement of prespecified outcome measures. The positive outcomes that the Kirklees-KBOP PPP aims to achieve through its support of service users include improved well-being; stable accommodation; occupied in education, training and employment; improved emotional and mental health; reduced or eliminated drug and alcohol misuse; and reduced experience of domestic violence.

Key performance measures against each of these desired outcomes were set out in a "rate card": a menu of participant-level indicators that determine payment from the Council to KBOP, articulated in an annex to the head contract. However, initially, rather than seeking to measure these long-term positive changes, the rate card heavily weighted near-term output-type measures (see Figure 5.1 for a high-level overview and Table 5.1 for details). It included an "initial well-being assessment," which confirms that a client meets the criteria for the service and has completed an initial support plan and self-assessment.

At the outset, the rate card was extremely complex, offering different targets and payment levels across two dimensions:

(1) *Higher payment and lower targets for longer-term sustained improvement.* Payments were split between the initial step toward an outcome (such as entering education or training) and sustaining the outcome over a specific period of time (e.g., sustaining stable accommodation over twelve months). The short-term output type measures were intended to function as milestone payments. To incentivize KBOP to work with service participants toward long-term change, the outcome payment level increased if the outcome was

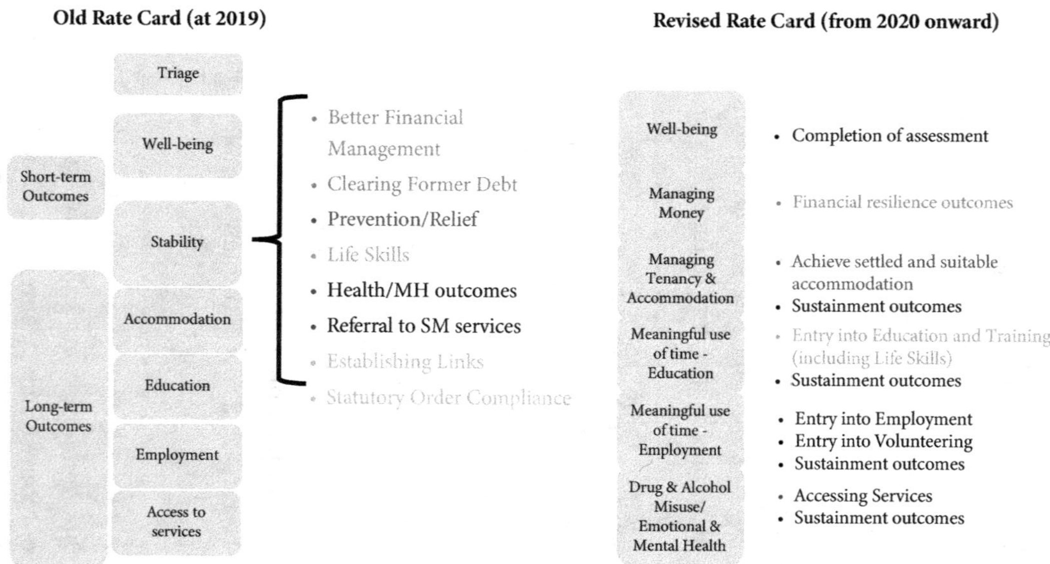

Figure 5.1 Kirklees Council-KBOP Rate Card Before and After Renegotiation

Table 5.1 Initial KBOP Rate Card Performance Measures, 2019

Payment-linked outcome performance measure	Definition
Assessment, stability, and well-being payments	
Successful triage	Only clients that are not referred onto the full service are eligible for this payment. This will be paid for the successful completion of an immediate action that prevents a referral from being placed onto the full service. This must have included at least two face-to-face appointments following the initial referral.
Initial well-being assessment	Assessment should be face-to-face and should cover the following: i) confirmation that the client meets the criteria for the service; ii) completion of an initial support plan and initial well-being assessment (Homelessness Star) that is agreed with the client.
2nd well-being assessment (at 3 months+)	Well-being assessment can take place at any time from 3 months after the initial well-being assessment. This should include an assessment as to whether the client is ready to be moved on from the service.
3rd well-being assessment (at 6 months+)	Well-being assessment can take place at any time from 6 months after the initial well-being assessment. This should include an assessment as to whether the client is ready to be moved on from the service.
Health outcome	This can be claimed once an individual with a long-term health condition that requires treatment, who was not engaging with health services before referral, and is attending GP/hospital appointments for their condition.

Continued

Table 5.1 Continued

Payment-linked outcome performance measure	Definition
Successful prevention or relief	Payment made for successful relief or prevention of homelessness. This can only be claimed where an individual has been identified as having an immediate housing need. This could be from 1) threat of eviction (within 56 days); 2) they are already homeless; or 3) their current property is unsuitable for their support needs (e.g., property has stairs).
Successful referral to mental health or substance misuse service	This can be claimed for individuals who are not currently receiving an appropriate service in relation to substance misuse or mental health. It can be claimed on the acceptance of the referral by the third-party service and attendance at an initial appointment.
Establishing links	This outcome can be claimed once one or more of the following outcomes has been achieved by the client, where isolation and social engagement have been identified as a need at the full assessment: (i) participation in a peer-support networking group or self-help group (3 or more events); (ii) participation in a be-friending service (3 or more occasions); and (iii) participation in a community activity (e.g., faith/leisure) (3 or more events).

Life skills training (including employability)	This outcome can be claimed for completion of a training course relating to improving life skills. This can include courses related to (i) healthier living; (ii) maintaining tenancies; or (iii) IT skills and employability. These courses must be classroom-based (i.e., delivered outside normal meetings with support workers) and can include courses internally run by the relevant subcontractor.
Better financial management	This outcome can be claimed for clients where financial management is identified as a support need. This can be claimed through (i) supporting the client to maximize their income (including benefit entitlement) (if not already doing so); **OR** (ii) the client completing a financial management training course (e.g., in household budgeting, managing the benefit system), either through the relevant subcontractor or a separate course.
Clearing former debt	This outcome can be claimed where the client has rent arrears from their current or previous property, or other outstanding debt. This can be claimed by (i) evidencing that a sustainable repayment plan is in place and is active (two months' worth of payments made); and/or (ii) evidencing that former tenant arrears have been reduced to a level required for consideration for housing (this is set at £341.75 equal to 5 weeks average rent in line with the authority's policy). This outcome can only be claimed where outstanding debt has been identified as a blocker to accessing housing **OR** the client is at risk of losing their current accommodation.

Continued

Table 5.1 CONTINUED

Payment-linked outcome performance measure	Definition
Compliance with statutory order	This outcome can only be claimed for a client who is recorded as being under a statutory order. It is payable if the client has complied with the order while being a participant in the program and has then successfully transitioned away from needing support from the program or has successfully complied with the order up to the expiry date of this contract.
Significant reduction in domestic violence risk levels	This outcome can only be claimed for a client in the domestic violence cohort. This will be self-assessed by the subcontractors providing domestic violence services using the DASH risk assessment framework. A client's score in DASH risk assessment must have reduced by a minimum of three points from the initial score captured at referral stage.
Well-being improvement	The measurement for this is yet to be defined. During the mobilization phase, we will review available tools and based on feedback from KBOP members and with agreement from the Council, we will select an appropriate tool. During the first year of delivery, we will baseline performance using the selected tool and set the rate card at the end of year one.

Longer-term outcome measures	
3 months' accommodation outcomes 6 months' accommodation outcomes 12 months' accommodation outcomes	Payment made for successful sustainment of accommodation over time paid at specific intervals following referral or entry into suitable accommodation (3, 6, and 12 months). This can be claimed for all clients, regardless of whether they had an immediate housing need on referral. The client can move between tenancies over the course of the period if each is a planned move and not an eviction or abandonment.
18 months' accommodation outcomes	Payment made for successful sustainment of accommodation over 18 months. This can be claimed for all clients, regardless of whether they had an immediate housing need on referral. The 18- Month Sustainment Checklist must be completed to claim this outcome. The checklist can be completed at any time during tracking, but this outcome can only be claimed after 18 months in stable accommodation.
Entry into education	A client enters education or training that will lead to a fully or partly approved qualification at any level (including entry level). An individual must complete at least the first two sessions of the course. This payment can only be made once per client.

Continued

Table 5.1 Continued

Payment-linked outcome performance measure	Definition
Part completion of Ofqual approved qualification	A client completes a course or units of a course, which count toward a full Ofqual qualification, Level 1 or above. The course or units must be worth at least three credits in total. This outcome can be claimed up to a maximum of two times as long as the second qualification is of a higher level or in a different subject.
Completion of full Ofqual approved qualification	A client achieves an Ofqual approved qualification, Level 1 or above. The course must be fully complete and worth at least nine credits in total. This outcome can be claimed up to a maximum of two times as long as the second qualification is of a higher level or in a different subject. The full and part qualification outcome can be claimed for the same course (i.e., the Part claimed when three credits are achieved, and the Full when the course is completed).
Entry into employment	To claim this outcome, the client must have been made, and have accepted, an offer of employment. They must also have attended at least the first day of employment. Self-Employment: starts trading. Apprenticeship: Where a client is enrolled on an apprenticeship and the contractor can claim both the employment and the education outcomes if they each meet the relevant outcome requirements. The payment for entry into employment can only be made once.

6.5 weeks' equivalent employment F/T 13 weeks' equivalent employment F/T 26 weeks' equivalent employment F/T	Employment: There must be a contract in place. Employment does not have to be in the same place of work, but each client **must achieve** the relevant **accumulated gross earnings detailed in the Earnings Table.** Self-Employment: Triggered when a client has invoiced revenue as detailed in the relevant section of the Earnings Table or achieves a cumulative period of not less than eight hours of self-employment per week in a period of thirteen weeks. Apprenticeship: Where a client is enrolled on an apprenticeship and the Contractor can claim both the employment and the education outcomes if they each meet the relevant outcome requirements. The payment for each duration of ongoing employment can only be claimed once. Unless otherwise agreed between the contractor and the authority, this outcome cannot be claimed for clients who were in stable employment (consistently in work or with no more than a two weeks' gap in between roles) for six months or more at the point of referral to the service.
6 weeks of volunteering 20 weeks of volunteering	A client enters and carries out volunteering or work experience placement(s) averaging at least six hours per week. Payments are made at six and twenty weeks. This payment can be made up to two times (once for volunteering and once for work experience).

Continued

Table 5.1 CONTINUED

Payment-linked outcome performance measure	Definition
Mental health sustained engagement with services	Payment made for engagement with a mental health support program. This may include any clinical commissioning group– or authority-funded service. Engagement must include attendance at appointments for a period of three months or until discharged from the service (whichever is the sooner). This includes cases where the individual was already engaging with a treatment program at the point they were referred to the service, where further support is needed to sustain engagement.
Drugs/alcohol sustained engagement with services	Payment made for engagement with a drug and alcohol support program. This may include any clinical commissioning group– or authority-funded service. Engagement must include attendance at appointments for a period of three months or until discharged from the service (whichever is the sooner). This includes cases where the individual was already engaging with a treatment program at the point they were referred to the service, where further support is needed to sustain engagement.

Well-being improvement	The measurement for this outcome is yet to be defined. During the mobilization period, the contractor will review available tools and based on feedback from the subcontractors (and with agreement from the authority) will select an appropriate tool. During the first year of delivery, the contractor will baseline performance using the selected tool and set the rate card at the end of the first year.
Chaos Index Improvement	The measurement for this outcome is yet to be defined. During the mobilization period, the contractor will review available tools and based on feedback from the subcontractors (and with agreement from the authority) will select an appropriate tool. During the first year of delivery, the contractor will baseline performance using the selected tool and set the rate card at the end of the first year.

sustained for longer (for example, around £450 was paid for "entry into employment" and around £2,000 for twenty-six weeks sustained employment).

(2) *Higher payment and lower targets for participants deemed to be at a higher need at the point of referral.* The performance measures and consequent payment levels were further demarcated according to four distinct cohorts of participants according to the perceived level of need. The "Complex Needs Cohort" described people in crisis with a history of poor engagement with services, assessed using something called the Chaos Index (this classification was expected to describe 10% of total referrals). The General Needs Cohort were people with a track record of relatively good engagement with support services (expected to be 53% of total referrals). The Low Needs Cohort were people who either have not required support previously or have a history of good engagement with service (expected to be 15% of referrals). And the Domestic Violence Cohort were people whose primary support need was related to domestic violence (KPOB Head Contract, 51).

Allocating participants to needs-based cohorts is a technical response to known challenges of gaming in outcomes-based contracts. In the broader literature on payment-by-results contracting, this approach is referred to as "differential pricing" or payment variation by client group. The intention is to incentivize providers to work meaningfully with all clients, irrespective of their support needs/costs because the outcome payments increase in line with perceived support needs/costs (Carter and Whitworth 2015; Koning and Heinrich 2013). This formal incentivization approach aligns with principal-agent theory by assuming goal divergence on the part of the contracted agent and uses additional payment levels for participants who are understood as "harder to help" to ensure appropriate support for all participants.

The KBOP Board, who chiefly represented the views of investors, via fund managers, tended to assume that the outcomes-based performance measures provided a very close proxy of meaningful real-life impact for service users. By linking payment to these outcome measures, there was an assumption that the contract succeeded in aligning investors' interests with the social purpose of the contract. The Chair commented that the board's task was "holding the service to account effectively on behalf of service users to ensure that it maximizes the outcomes" (interview transcript, Chair of KBOP board). This view—that the measured performance equated to the real-world outcomes—was not always shared by frontline staff. They felt the narrowly defined metrics, designed around what was reliably measurable enough for payment, might crimp their ability to respond meaningfully to the diverse issues and complicated circumstances that service users often presented with. The large number of short-term outcome measures, high caseloads, and perceived onerous evidence requirements for outcome validation conveyed a sense of delivery being excessively target-driven across provider staff (Rosenbach et al. 2023). A board member from the social investment fund explained, "In the eyes of frontline staff, too much emphasis was placed on these kinds of numbers . . . and not actually enough on those long-term outcomes" (interview transcript, investment fund manager and member of KBOP board).

In response to these concerns, the rate card was altered. This was done through an inclusive redesign process led by the KBOP management team. The KBOP director hosted "change panels" with provider managers and frontline staff to listen to concerns, which were fed into discussions at board level. Space was actively created for reflection and discussion in response to concerns directly raised by those working with participants every day.

Figure 5.1 shows the key shifts in the rate card, which fall under three broad categories.

1. *Removal of short term/long-term distinction.* The rate card was redesigned to eliminate the separation between short-term measures and indicators of more sustainable change. This was felt to better reflect the reality of the ups and downs of participants' lives.
2. *Removal of needs classifications.* In the reformulated rate card, needs classifications are no longer used, enabling participants

to aim for any outcome measure, irrespective of their overarching level of need. This change has removed a formal approach to stratifying outcome payments and instead relies on the relationship between frontline staff and program participants to understand which outcome measures will function as meaningful markers of change. The sorting of participants into needs-based cohorts was viewed as inconsistent with the overarching purpose of the partnership to shift the focus from participants' deficiencies to their strengths.

3. *Streamlining of evidence requirements.* This shift in practice was intended both to reduce the administrative burden experienced by frontline staff and to overcome concerns that evidence requests were intrusive for participants. For example, rather than asking participants to produce pay slips, longer-term employment outcomes were to be validated by using administrative data from the UK tax authority. For other outcome measures, participants were allowed to self-certify the achievement through emails or text messages.

The formal contract allows for such adaptations without the need for formal renegotiation. It lays out a change procedure, inviting the parties to consider "in good faith" anything that might "improve the prospect of achieving the Objective without having a material adverse effect on the Parties, the Investor or the Service Users" (KBOP Head Contract 12.1.4). This procedure provides a mechanism through which the parties can formalize contractual changes they might negotiate and agree upon throughout the duration of contract delivery, including, if necessary, adjusting the performance measures.

These adaptions align with the concept of "incentives flexibility," which is implicit in much recent theorizing on governance mechanisms (Feiock et al. 2003; Brown and Potoski 2004; Turner 2004). This flexibility has two components: i) the capacity to vary the intensity of explicit and implicit incentives offered to agents (Turner 2004) to surmount behavioral and opportunistic factors; and ii) the ability to move resources between the explicit and implicit incentive categories to maximize the value-adding yield from those incentives.

THE DIVERGENT USE OF PERFORMANCE INFORMATION AND PERFORMANCE MANAGEMENT

Indiana-IBM: The use of performance information in initiating contract termination

In theory, the regular sharing of accurate information on PPP performance among the parties should facilitate their work efforts and enable them to address problems as they arise (Moynihan 2008). As described in Chapter 4, however, a large number of MSA performance indicators and standards (in various categories) contributed to mixed messaging by the State on IBM's performance, although this communication was also tempered by politics.

Overall, throughout most of the project, the State of Indiana was improving in its performance toward a core program goal—client work participation (or self-sufficiency). This improvement in work participation rates occurred in tandem with increased access to programs, growing economic need, and expanded programming (the Healthy Indiana Program [HIP]), which were contributing to rising caseloads. In our analysis, we classified 2005 and 2006 as pre-welfare modernization years, and 2007 and 2008 as the early modernization years, with IBM leading the Coalition's work. We characterized 2009 as a transition year, because in the first half of that year, the State began to redirect IBM away from its modernization efforts that were in progress, and it terminated the contract with IBM early in the fourth quarter of 2009. Table 5.2 presents a summary of Indiana's performance on the all-family work participation rate, the single outcome measure included in the MSA and Schedule 10, over these three different periods of the State of Indiana-IBM relationship.

The results for the core federal performance measure (all-family work participation rate)—which the Request for Information (RFI) for this contract suggested was aligned with Indiana's overarching goal to help clients find employment and become self-sufficient—showed substantial improvements in the State of Indiana. It moved up sixteen positions in rank in 2007 (from being the worst performing state in 2005 and 2006), and then reached the national average in 2008, meeting

Table 5.2 INDIANA'S PERFORMANCE ON A KEY FEDERAL PERFORMANCE MEASURE, 2005–2009

Pre-modernization years
2005 and 2006: Indiana ranked 50th among the states—only Indiana and Guam did not meet the (adjusted) all-family work participation performance target.
Early modernization years (MSA in effect)
2007: Indiana did not meet the (adjusted) work participation performance target, but it was no longer ranked at the bottom in its work participation performance; it advanced ahead of sixteen other states/territories in the all-family work participation rate.
2008: Indiana met the all-family work participation performance target and was exactly at the average for all US states and territories in its performance (29.4%).
Transition to the MSA end
2009: Indiana met the all-family work participation performance target but dropped in its work participation performance ranking among the states (ranked above seven other states).

the federal adjusted performance target. An additional federal performance measure that tracks "Changes in Combined Work Participation Rates" confirmed that the State of Indiana had significantly improved its performance toward this core program goal between FY 2007–FY 2008. Work participation rates increased in Indiana, even as twenty-four other states reported declines in work participation, and Indiana was ranked 20th among the states and territories on this measure of program performance.

These performance improvements were particularly remarkable given that between 2007 and 2008, Indiana's economic fortunes changed with the advent of the Great Recession, worsening much faster than other states. Indiana dropped thirty-one places to rank 37th in its change in unemployment rate, and its unemployment rate further increased from 2008 to 2009 (dropping to a ranking of 45th). The fact that the State was still meeting its work participation performance targets in 2008 and 2009 and that it managed to improve its work participation rate relative to other states during the launch of the modernization project was a significant achievement, publicly recognized by Governor Daniels: "Our folks are doing a vastly better job than most states . . . if you read the front page of today's national papers, there are systems crashing in states elsewhere, and ours is performing very well" (transcript, January 9, 2009, 5).

Indeed, in multiple interviews with the press and in many press releases, the governor's office recognized the improvements led by IBM and the Hoosier Coalition and signaled that the project was going well. As noted in Chapter 4, FSSA Secretary Mitch Roob explicitly conveyed to Under Secretary Nancy Johner that Indiana was providing better service to a greater number of clients through its welfare modernization project. The TKPIs tracking the number of applications that were processed and the timeliness of processing—comparing the March 2006–February 2007 (baseline) period with the measures following the first year of the modernization rollout, March 2007–February 2008—showed substantial increases in the volume of cases at the same time that timeliness in processing (measured over all programs) was improving (PRIV-FSSA-00007093, IBM D.E. 229). Two recession-related dips in the proportion of timely processing in late 2008 and early 2009 corresponded with substantial surges in application volumes in October 2008 and March 2009, and yet despite this, absolute numbers of applications with timely processing still exceeded pre-modernization averages.[1]

The State of Indiana recognized that the project contributed to eliminating fraud, generated cost savings, and developed infrastructure—human, capital, and technological—for modernizing the State's public assistance eligibility determination system, which extended to other services such as the HIP. As Governor Daniels conceded (in announcing the termination of the contract), the modernization project successfully

1. In multiple documents, including a December 2009 presentation by Secretary Anne Murphy to the Indiana General Assembly, the State of Indiana acknowledged the substantial impact of the economic recession on FSSA program enrollments/caseloads: FSSA enrollments increased by 31% since 2005.

reduced fraud that had plagued the old eligibility system: "The fraud that was rampant in Indiana's welfare system has apparently stopped. There hasn't been a single allegation, let alone conviction, whereas there were dozens. And the official reports say over $100 million was stolen in the last year before we began to try to make this change" (IBM D.E. 345, 2). In addition, in contracting with IBM, the State had anticipated a savings of $340 million in administrative costs over the 10-year project, and Governor Daniels attested that the State was on track to realize those savings: "Again, we are saving—we projected initially maybe 50 million a year over the first 10 years. Now it looks more like 40. But this is much less expensive . . . more savings than that compared to if we tried to fix the old system in place" (transcript of audio recording, File No. 38,399, IBM D.E. 345, 6). In the same press conference, the governor also acknowledged that IBM "poured people and resources into this," and FSSA Secretary Anne Murphy reported that FSSA would expend more than $65.8 million to bring the delivery of those services back in house (IBM D.E. 54).

In light of the State's public praise of the IBM Coalition's contributions to creating value for the public, it is reasonable to question how IBM's performance (on operational metrics) became the justification for terminating the contract. One of the few publicly expressed concerns was that progress on timeliness in processing of applications wasn't happening fast enough, but the State repeatedly characterized the delays and setbacks as adjustments to rapidly changing conditions, some of which were outside the vendor's control (FSSA1_07511406).[2] Moreover, where timeliness was discussed in the MSA, it was only one of many metrics listed as applicable during "steady state,"[3] and the express remedy under the contract was for a fairly limited amount of liquidated damages.

2. Further complicating the performance review were discrepancies in calculations of timeliness, as indicated by exchanges between the USDA Food and Nutrition Service (FNS) USDA and FSSA in Indiana in July and August 2008 (PRIV-FSSA-00008988-91). The revised FNS calculation reported by the State in September 2008 indicated that the State was meetings its 90% threshold, satisfying federal performance requirements (email message from Jim Maxwell, September 5, 2008, IBM D.E. 205).

3. In the MSA. "Steady State" was characterized as the project's final stage, when the modernized welfare system was rolled out to every county statewide (MSA §3.2.1(1).

In a March 31, 2009 letter to FSSA Secretary Murphy, IBM pointed out that for nearly all of the issues singled out by Secretary Murphy in the Operational Verification and Validation (OV&V) report, there was either no performance standard or agreed-upon measure (i.e., no performance standard in effect) because the agreement made at the start of the contract was that performance standards would not be in effect until the project had reached "steady state" (IBM D.E. 75). More likely, as Murphy's email on July 2, 2009 (cited in full in Chapter 4) exposed, the State appeared to leverage a sham "audit" of performance on timeliness to set the desired termination in motion (PRIV-FSSA-00009589). In fact, the OV&V's monthly audit reports largely supported the narrative drawn from other performance data that significant progress was being made in the welfare modernization project, until Secretary Murphy assumed leadership of the FSSA at the start of 2009 and subsequently identified a plethora of new issues, as shown in Figure 5.2.

Although in its letter terminating the contract with IBM, the State suggested that progress toward modernization was not adequate or happening quickly enough, it was apparent that the State's use of performance monitoring in this case was antagonistic in nature and sought to sever the cords of cooperation in the PPP. In the dissolution of

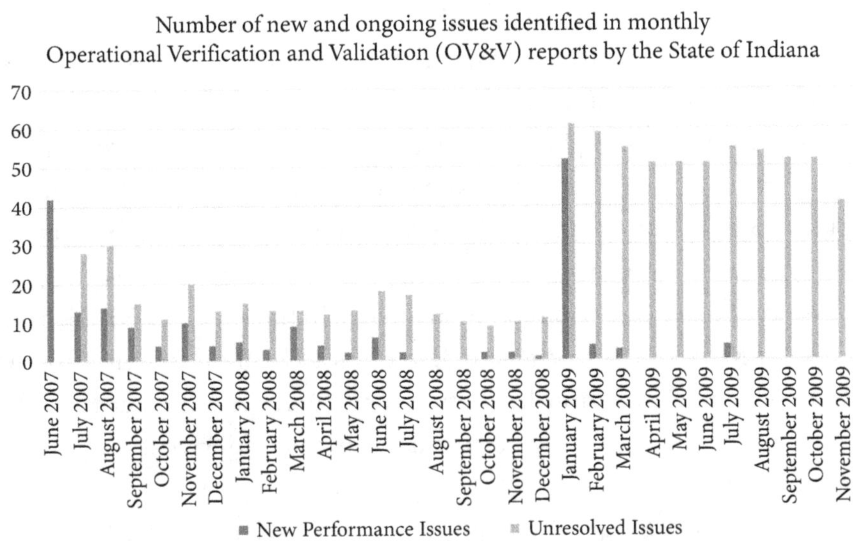

Figure 5.2 State of Indiana Monthly Performance Audit Reports Over Time

contractual relationships and PPPs, the underlying causes often extend beyond official explanations and are sometimes veiled within legal documents, as in the Indiana-IBM case.

The State's official justification for terminating the partnership with IBM, as stated in their filing with the Marion County Superior Court, was the alleged material breach of the MSA. However, a senior judge who was involved in the litigation of this case indicated in an interview that he was convinced the corrective action plan (CAP) imposed by the State was a "solution in search of breach" and that the State was unable to directly connect any problems to IBM's performance. Court filings, email exchanges among key stakeholders, and confidential discussions wove an intricate narrative involving both the formal and relational aspects of the government, prime contractor, and subcontractor relationships, as well as compounding external factors (including political influences) that exacerbated tensions among the partners and destabilized a PPP already deficient in trust, loyalty, reciprocity, and other elements vital to the success of any partnership.

Kirklees-KBOP: The use of performance information to support relational practice

The Indiana-IBM contract shows that sharing open performance information does not automatically unlock the positive effects theorized by Moynihan (2008). That contract was terminated despite performance improving against national benchmarks. The experience in the Kirklees-KBOP partnership corroborates this idea: it is not the sharing of performance information per se that is important, but how the parties respond to it via extant relational norms. In the Kirklees-KBOP case, the use of KPIs and performance data seem to be used to help support a more productive relationship between partners. This happened in the context of the project's early performance being underwhelming, as we described in Chapter 4.

Table 5.3 and Figure 5.3 highlight high-level performance information for the period up to September 2024, as reported by the

Table 5.3 Kirklees-KBOP Payment Trigger Targets and Actual Achievements

Payment trigger	Initial target	Working target	Actual achievement
Achieve a Stability and Well-being outcome	5450	5080	5112
Achieve an Accommodation outcome	3169	3241	3458
Achieve an Employment and Learning outcome	1173	1386	1817

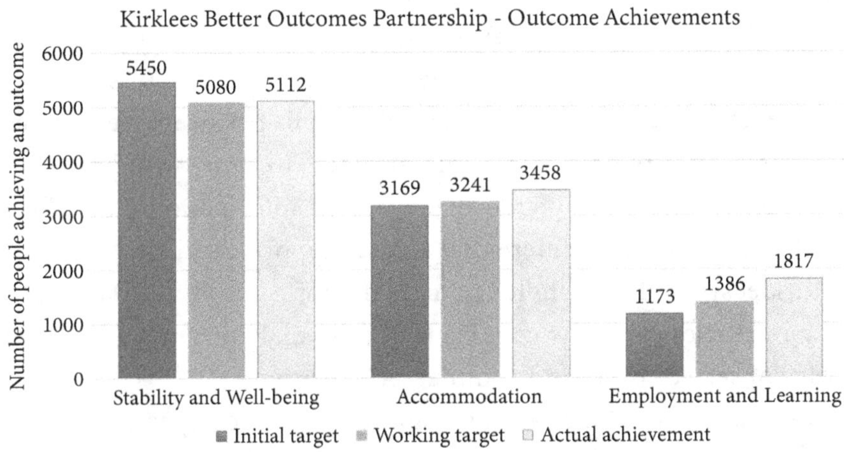

Figure 5.3 Kirklees Council-KBOP Outcome Achievements

Kirklees-KBOP project in February 2025. Reflecting the dynamic nature of the project, two target figures are displayed: the initial target, as reported at the start of the project, and the working targets by which the partners understood performance during delivery, based on the continual development of the project by its stakeholders.

The outcomes are reported across three broad categories: Stability and Well-being, Accommodation, and Employment and Learning. Each unit in the table represents an individual program participant who has successfully achieved a validated outcome. In the latter two categories, the working targets were higher than the initially reported targets, and each of these was exceeded (106% of Accommodation working target and

131% of Employment and Learning working target). As such, these represent an even greater success than initially expected. The Stability and Well-being target was lowered by 370 people, and this revised target was marginally exceeded (101%). The actual achievements represent 94% of the initial target; this, in itself, would be seen as strong performance given challenges to participants' well-being associated with the COVID-19 pandemic and cost-of-living crisis experienced in the UK during the service delivery period.

The performance information is hosted on a shared system, funded by the Council, called CDPSoft. This centralized data system is used by all of the partners, albeit with different levels of access. The Council and KBOP each have access to all data, with Council officers using it to monitor and validate outcome payments, and KBOP staff using data to manage participant referrals and compile performance information. The providers have more limited access to their own data, using the system to record key case management information (Rosenbach et al. 2023, 47–48). This differential access supports the different roles of the Kirklees-KBOP stakeholders, allowing for a coordinated approach that nevertheless remains cognizant of potential concerns around the privacy of service users and commercial sensitivity.

This open contract management approach has been particularly important in enabling the Council to trust that KBOP and the provider network act in the participants' best interests. Council contract managers are able to understand the overall performance and characteristics of the services, exploring features like outcome achievements, waiting lists, service response times, rejections from the service, and re-referrals. This allows an ongoing attentiveness not only to the contract's performance against specified outcomes, but also to a broader conception of public value. The system allows Council managers to audit evidence provided in support of outcomes payment, ensuring that service users are actually achieving the outcomes for which the KBOP prime contractor claims payments. Consideration of service performance beyond the directly payable outcomes allows public officials to scrutinize whether the higher-level goals of the contract—namely, serving vulnerable citizens' needs—are being met, helping to mitigate concerns around gaming practices on the part of contracted providers. This transparency of performance information also helps to mitigate Council staff's uneasiness about not having a sufficient platform for dialogue with subcontractors and the potential risks implied—specifically, losing important on-the-ground insight and erosion of long-term relationships with their local delivery ecosystem. It helps to alleviate concerns that operational issues might be hidden from the Council by collusion between the social prime and subcontractors, without the risks inherent in a subcontractor's direct liaison with the Council, which was a contributing factor in the downfall of Indiana-IBM.

Unlike the Indiana-IBM contract, the Kirklees-KBOP arrangement has not fixated on the minutiae of service delivery metrics. Instead, it affords considerable discretion and flexibility to delivery organizations who collaboratively developed the operational handbook that guides the nature and emphasis of frontline support. Frontline staff are allowed to come to agreement with each participant on the type of support they are to be offered, including whether it is virtual or face-to-face, the duration and location of sessions, and the frequency of support. A flexible and discretionary "personalization fund" enables frontline staff—in consultation with participants—to purchase items or services that augment and tailor the service. A board member for KBOP emphasized the ambition to devolve autonomy and professional decision-making to frontline staff:

> *"If there are things you think that would make this person's life a lot better, you have the authority to just go and do that. And come and tell us about it, if you think it worked really well, and other people will benefit from that."*

THE ROLE OF GOVERNANCE AND LEADERSHIP IN DETERMINING THE FATE OF CONTRACTUAL RELATIONSHIPS

Our two case-study PPPs both started off with extensive levels of measurement against a detailed roster of output and outcome information and intensive evidence requirements. But they subsequently followed very different trajectories in the management and use of performance information. The Indiana-IBM PPP adhered to the numerous, minor (process-oriented) KPIs throughout the partnership, and despite performing relatively well against the one outcome measure (work participation), they ended up before the Indiana Supreme Court. The Kirklees-KBOP PPP renegotiated the measures, treated them as an input for learning and adaptation, and have continued on positively in their collaboration. What contributed to each case's contrasting fate? Here, we further explore the differences in the way each has been governed and led.

It is clear from the amount of performance information collected and available for use that both Indiana-IBM and Kirklees-KBOP exemplify the data abundance that typifies the "information age" or "third industrial revolution" that took place in the late 20th century. Prior to this, leaders and decision-makers were forced to operate in a situation of information scarcity: there was less information, and it was much harder to find in a form that could be readily analyzed. To operate in this environment, governance tended to rely on centralizing information, where information was reported upward to a central authority. This authority, thus equipped with insights from a range of sources, would benefit from a more comprehensive view than each peripheral agent and be empowered to make decisions on behalf of all.

In a world where information is abundant and more widely accessible, centralization is less useful and may even be counterproductive to inclusive and instructive uses of performance information. In circumstances where the potential exists for a wide range of stakeholders to be given a comprehensive view and to be empowered to exercise their judgment, maintaining a hierarchical decision-making structure for its contemplation can undermine the benefits of purposeful performance information use. Moreover, it can lead to either the constant questioning of centralized decisions by peripheral agents or to the deliberate obstruction of information flow to maintain the legitimacy of centralized control, which drastically diminishes the potential for collective and delegated problem-solving.

Indiana-IBM: The perils of adopting conventional governance and leadership approaches

IBM's relationship with its subcontractors suggests that it struggled to retain legitimate centralized control in an information-rich environment. As the prime contractor, IBM had centralized oversight of subcontractors, but we saw in Chapter 4 how one of these—ACS—was unwilling to submit to this oversight from the start. ACS expressed early concerns *directly to the FSSA* about IBM's role as the prime contractor, despite the contractual requirement that "IBM is the sole point of contact with regard to contractual matters" (MSA § 14.6.2). A witness in the court case testified that an ACS employee, Richard Rhoad, maintained his office at the State with Anne Murphy's executive team and spent his time "going behind IBM's back to try to get IBM terminated." In proceedings before the Indiana Superior Court, ACS officials conceded that they breached their contract, and these covert communications also implied that the State violated its contract with IBM. As one reporter wrote, "It was no secret that the Daniels administration had conspired with the law firm of Barnes & Thornburg, which represented ACS, to concoct a plan to privatize the state's welfare services and steer the bulk of that work to the law firm's client" (Welsh 2012).

The State's approach to centralized control is also easily observable in the terms of the contract between the State of Indiana and IBM as prime contractor. In fact, Indiana-IBM could be described as an archetype of agency theory, which assumes that providers have an opposing goal to the contracting principal. For example, it is assumed that their goal is to maximize profit rather than increase quality or pass on cost savings. The theory therefore follows that the contracting principal should seek maximum control over the provider's activities. This is readily observable in the MSA contract. By design, it heralded the possibility of an early exit. The State not only reserved the right to terminate the agreement at its discretion (MSA, sec 16.3.2), but it could assume the role of prime contractor if it deemed an early termination advantageous. Furthermore, the State maintained the option to assume IBM's subcontractors under certain conditions (MSA, sec 14.8.1 [3]) and to purchase the computer equipment and other resources IBM had dedicated to the project (MSA, sec 16.6.6 [1], [3]). These provisions afforded the State of Indiana an easy exit option that Governor Daniels and FSSA Secretary Murphy chose to exercise in 2009, even as IBM continued to cooperate on a CAP. Moreover, after IBM was terminated, ACS was given a new eight-year contract worth more than $600 million to continue the project.

Such termination provisions are antithetical to a relational approach to managing the PPP. Did their existence indicate that premature termination was likely long foreseen as a possibility? Or were they simply boilerplate contract terms that IBM consented to as a condition of participating in public contract markets? One might question why a powerful corporation such as IBM would sign a contract that allowed unilateral termination without compensation, when the contract required them to make large, upfront asset-specific investments. But if such terms are standard in the market or the governance structure of PPPs, and competitors were subjected to similar terms, then a refusal on the part of IBM to agree to such terms would have placed them at a severe competitive disadvantage. It is possible that IBM considered the risk of financial losses associated with the termination rights across a portfolio of tens or hundreds of public contracts. The ensuing court cases and appeals recognized IBM's asset-specific investments (largely) in equipment, but the financial judgments associated with the failed project ultimately favored the State of Indiana.

Kirklees-KBOP: Using information as an asset

The contractual termination clauses are equally revealing in the case of the Kirklees-KBOP PPP. In direct contrast with Indiana-IBM, special termination clauses were negotiated that would ensure that the costs of early exit were shared between the Council and KBOP. Both parties would be required to cover the cost of any asset-specific investments made and not yet recouped at the time of termination. The existence of these nonstandard clauses, and the mutual consent to them by both parties prior to contract execution, signals a long-term commitment between the parties by intentionally erecting obstacles to easy dissolution.

Augmentation of the governance structures beyond what was already contractually stipulated (see Table 5.4) might be explained by the particular approach adopted by the new, permanent director who took leadership of KBOP in January 2020. This change in leadership marked a turning point for the project, as we described in the previous chapter. The new director moved the project away from a top-down performance management model. The collection and sharing of data became more transparent, as was the decision-making that it informed. The director described this approach in her own words:

> "It's very much working with each partner at their pace, understanding what they want to achieve and how we can get them there, while at the same time improving quality and impact or questioning as appropriate. Part of our role is gently challenging the way that people think, services or how systems operate to support ambitions for growth. We have conversations with them [service providers] when we identify opportunities: 'you're so strong in this area. Do you think this is an area where you would like to do more?' . . . What fundamentally underpins the management approach within KBOP is that relationship, collaboration, and trust. It is very much 'we are a partnership'. We may be . . . the contract holders within this, but KBOP is nothing without our partners . . ."
>
> (interview transcript, KBOP Managing Director)

Providers have described an informal feel to contract management meetings, based on honesty, supportiveness, and dialogue, even during phases of underperformance (Rosenbach et al. 2023).

This leadership style is consistent with recent advances in our understanding of modern leadership and how it is adapting to an abundance of information and complex, interwoven considerations that typify the modern operating context. Many leaders now regularly face "adaptive challenges," which—unlike technical problems that tend to have

Table 5.4 Regular Governance Forums in the Kirklees-KBOP PPP

Meeting	Key function	Main parties involved	Cadence
Strategic meetings			
KBOP Board	Accountability of KBOP to social investors	Social investment fund manager KBOP	Monthly
Council-KBOP meeting[a]	Accountability of KBOP to the Council	Council KBOP	Monthly
Operational meetings			
Individual provider performance review	Accountability of subcontractors to KBOP	KBOP Each provider in turn	Monthly (operational) Quarterly (strategic)
Collective provider performance review[b]	Accountability of sub-contractors to KBOP	KBOP All providers together	Quarterly

Operational change management	Sharing best practice and innovation and improving service delivery	KBOP All providers together	Monthly
Personalization working group	Advancing person-led service delivery	KBOP Mix of provider staff	Monthly
Co-production forum	Integration of people with lived experience in service design	KBOP People with lived experience from Kirklees services	Monthly

[a]Ultimately the KBOP Board and Council-KBOP meetings became integrated so that there was a shared agenda and joint attendance with only specific commercial items being scheduled for the KBOP Board exclusively.
[b]This collective performance review was not conducted in latter stages of the contract. In interviews in 2024, staff at provider organizations noted, with regret, the absence of these shared learning sessions.
Adapted from Rosenbach et al. 2023.

known solutions, no matter how complicated—will require "going beyond any authoritative expertise to mobilize discovery, shedding certain entrenched ways, tolerating losses and generating the capacity to thrive anew" (Heifetz et al. 2009). In this model, a leader must go beyond the boundary of their positional authority, build strong bonds of trust, and cultivate a wide network (often known as building "social capital").

The hands-on and open approach to governance that the formal contract seeded, and that the parties augmented relationally in practice under the new director, has proved essential in helping the stakeholders to jointly navigate what would otherwise have been a laborious monitoring regime, requiring the submission of monthly performance data and supplementary evidence. Continuous open communications between all the partners and a "no surprises" policy have forged trust. The partners have been able to embed learning and adaptation into the delivery of services and into the contractual relationships at all levels. Together, they work continuously toward better alignment of interests—from service users, through frontline workers, subcontractor management, prime contractor leadership, and the Council commissioners. In a continuous feedback loop, experiences at the frontline have informed both resource allocations for services delivery and the contracted performance measures; in turn, changes to these measures can be reflected on critically at the frontline. The contract is effectively a "living instrument" (van Lier et al. 2025). At the same time, some providers have found the inclusive and collaborative approach challenging, as it requires them to align their practices with peers in a single contract, rather than with other contracts within their own organization, and imposes KBOP's management culture on their staff (superseding their own) (Rosenbach et al. 2023).

The inclusive governance approach has also facilitated innovation. KBOP's Board members recognized that in seeking maximum achievement of payable outputs and outcomes, they would need to invest in ongoing innovation, and that the source of innovation was not in the boardroom, but close to the frontline of delivery. Indeed, ideas often emerge from a co-production forum set up by KBOP, which consists of service users and explicitly excludes any staff from delivery organizations who might close down productive discussion. At times, innovations have emerged from provider organizations coming together as a group, where they were all "all encouraged to come up with ideas" that could be advocated by the KBOP director and taken to the KBOP Board for decision. Providers have described "a willingness to work together, to listen to the experience from the frontline, and from the first line managers as to what actually is the real experience out there" (Rosenbach et al. 2023). Some of the innovations introduced to date include payment of tenancy deposits, which help participants to secure private accommodation by providing a guarantee to landlords, and training for frontline staff around motivational interviewing techniques to enable them to more effectively understand participants' ambitions.

CONCLUSION

We have shown in this chapter that the Kirklees-KBOP PPP has consistently adopted the tenets of formal-relational contracting in its use of performance information, while Indiana-IBM hewed to a more conventional, transactional approach that treated performance information as a tool of discipline and control. In Kirklees-KBOP, we observed that an intensive form of structured governance is used to manage the relationship between partners during delivery; the delivery model is continually adapted in the light of ongoing information; and contract terms are renegotiated in the context of an inclusive process of mutual reflection. Indiana-IBM, by contrast, adopted transactional, principal-agent models of governance typical of many PPPs, failed to meaningfully adapt its delivery model to changing circumstances, and resorted to termination over pursuing successful renegotiation. Table 5.5 presents a summary of the contrasting performance management approaches employed in the Indiana-IBM and Kirklees-KBOP PPPs, highlighting key differences that undoubtedly contributed to the divergent outcomes in these two complex, multiactor, and multilayered coalitions for public services delivery.

Table 5.5 Summary of Contrasting Approaches to Performance Management

Performance dimension	Indiana-IBM	Kirklees- KBOP
Performance measure use	Punitive	Learning
Performance measure evolution over time	Fixed	Flexible
Performance reporting/ Communication	KPI audits by 3rd party First Data	Rate card, collective stakeholder review, Council staff validate payable outcomes, followed by second Council team audit
Stakeholder integration	Limited stakeholder involvement	Multiple stakeholder involvement
Outcome vs. Process Measure	Focus primarily on process	Focus primarily on outcomes
Leadership/Governance	Antagonistic, lacking transparency	Collaborative, open

6

New Thinking for More Effective, Accountable, and Sustainable Public-Private Partnerships

In this concluding chapter, we highlight pivotal issues in contracting for public value and illuminate ongoing challenges with insights derived from both theory and our primary case studies. We anchor this discussion around four major themes: (1) championing public value: (2) rethinking public-private partnership (PPP) governance and centering relationship building: (3) fortifying PPPs with effective institutional and accountability mechanisms; and (4) envisaging systems change for long-term, public-private collaboration. We also elucidate their implications for practice and research to improve the future design and implementation of PPPs centered on public value.

THEME 1: CHAMPIONING PUBLIC VALUE

The overarching goal of any PPP, regardless of the scope of the project and structure of the partnership governance, should be to enhance public value. As discussed in Chapter 1, public value is broadly defined as "what is good for and valued by the public," and this needs to be centered

Contracting for Public Value. Carolyn J. Heinrich et al., Oxford University Press. © Oxford University Press (2026).
DOI: 10.1093/9780197763155.003.0006

and operationalized in both the formal and informal aspects of the PPP contract at the start of the relationship. In the context of the types of PPPs described in this book—involving complex, multiactor, and multilevel contractual relationships that deliver critical social services to vulnerable populations—concretely defining and measuring public value is a major undertaking in itself, and one that requires a substantial, upfront investment on the part of the partners and consideration of the interests (and values) of a broad range of public stakeholders.

Defining public value

Public value has too often been conceived of as "lowest cost," and in the context of public services, this frequently implies low-cost operations or eliminating process inefficiencies. This was evident in the key performance indicators (KPIs) included in the Indiana-IBM PPP contract. Nearly all of the numerous KPIs focused on increasing operational efficiencies, such as timely processing of applications, call response times, and website availability, or on specific deliverables such as a procedures manual. Although responsiveness to client contacts is clearly critical to service quality, a more holistic approach to public value would encompass more than process and financial metrics (see for example, Mazzucato 2018). In other words, while it is important to account for the fact that public and taxpayer dollars are at risk by monitoring efficiency, contracts should simultaneously focus attention on qualitative outcomes, such as citizen satisfaction, equity in access to services, and long-term community benefits. This broader definition emphasizes the importance of services that genuinely meet the needs and aspirations of the public, while ensuring responsible use of public funds, and requires engagement with the public to understand how to best deliver public value through the PPP. The experiences of some social service beneficiaries in Indiana suggested that values such as citizen satisfaction and equitable access were of lower priority in the project (see Box 6.1).

Box 6.1

Example of the Limited Conceptualization of Public Value in the Indiana-IBM PPP

The ordeal of Indiana resident Louise Cohoon and her mother, as reported in the *Los Angeles Times*, highlights the narrow conceptualization of public value, as realized in practice, in the Indiana-IBM PPP (Gold et al. 2011):

Louise Cohoon's 80-year-old mother was panic-stricken when she called in the Spring of 2011 from her home in Terre Haute, Indiana: without warning, the $97 monthly Medicaid payment that she relied on to supplement her $600-a-month income had been cut. Later, the state explained the reason: Her mother had failed to call into an eligibility hotline on a day in 2008 when she was hospitalized for congestive heart failure. Louise, 63-years old herself, said her mother was so upset she thought the news was going to kill her. Her cash-strapped family pulled together to help her get by until the state restored her benefits. Yet this took months and only happened because of pressure exerted by Legal Services attorneys.

The Kirklees-KBOP PPP incorporated public value into their formal contract through multiple mechanisms designed to prioritize meaningful social impact. Outcome-based measures focused on achieving long-term social outcomes, and performance was evaluated on indicators such as sustained accommodation, educational attainment, employment, mental health engagement, and reduced domestic violence. To ensure equity, the service design adjusted performance payments based on participant needs. Initially, the contract used cohorts for individuals with complex needs to provide targeted support for vulnerable populations but later shifted to prioritize individual participant goals without stratification. This prioritization of equity supports clients with varying experiences of disadvantage in receiving public resources proportionate to their level of need, holding the PPP accountable for both service delivery and financial responsibility. In addition, the contract is designed so that the magnitude of the outcome payments increases the longer an outcome is sustained (i.e., presumably generating positive returns to the public's investment over a longer period). In contrast, the Indiana-IBM contract lacked mechanisms for measuring client satisfaction, adapting to individual needs, achieving long-term social outcomes, and ensuring equitable service delivery. By treating public value as a financial efficiency proposition, the MSA neglected the holistic, person-centered approach exemplified by Kirklees-KBOP.

The Indiana-IBM and Kirklees-KBOP case studies also convey the importance of who is "brought to the table" as public value is defined and the formal and relational aspects of the contract are designed and developed. How the interests of these parties are respected—i.e., the degree of inclusivity and integrity—matters to the PPP configurations and outcomes. With minimal public input, Indiana determined that a principal aim of the PPP was to reduce the number of individuals reliant on welfare. Arguably, curtailing welfare dependency aligns with public objectives such as efficiency and fairness, yet achieving the pinnacle of public value also necessitates that such partnerships yield favorable socioeconomic outcomes, consistent with the broader goals of promoting social welfare and equity in opportunities. In fact, one of the overarching objectives articulated in the Indiana-IBM MSA states that the project will "assist and support clients through programs that foster personal responsibility, independence, social and economic self-sufficiency." Yet only one contract performance measure reflected this goal of enabling families to achieve a means of self-sufficiency, the family work participation rate. Moreover, the State did not offer arguments or evidence to suggest that privatizing welfare application processes and minimizing direct interpersonal interactions would facilitate this societal goal. The records of this PPP's formation provided no discernible indication that this initiative would enhance the socioeconomic conditions of welfare beneficiaries, and unlike in the Kirklees-KBOP partnership, the KPIs did not reflect this aspiration.

As the definition of public value inevitably varies across contexts, there is no single, most effective method for establishing consensus on public value. Moore (2014) highlights the need for a context-specific approach to defining public values,[1] emphasizing that any definition requires a thorough analysis of a community's unique needs, challenges, and priorities. This might include community engagement surveys, demographic and socioeconomic analyses, historical and cultural assessments, environmental evaluations, regulatory and policy framework reviews, and benchmarking against similar jurisdictions or projects. Nabatchi (2012) underscores the importance of public participation and deliberative processes in this endeavor. The process of engaging stakeholders and integrating their perspectives fosters a shared vision and lays the foundation for collaborative partnerships. Table 6.1 presents an overview of strategies for defining public value.

Delivering on public value

Indiana Governor Mitch Daniels had advocated for limited government and underscored privatization to reduce government waste in his campaign for governor, and he accordingly centralized anticipated cost efficiencies in the PPP accountability mechanisms. Although the efficient delivery of public services realizes tangible public benefits, the Master Services Agreement (MSA) featured efficiency as a cardinal policy aim, with the agreement delineating programmatic and administrative savings as two principal objectives. Correspondingly, the

1. While acknowledging that the terms have been used interchangeably in the literature, Fukumoto and Bozeman (2019, 635) distinguish "public value" from "public values." Public value was first defined by Mark Moore (1995) as simply value for the public, while alternative conceptualizations seek to normatively define, identify, and classify public values (Jørgensen and Bozeman 2007). Bozeman and Sarewitz (2011) define "public value" as the core public rationale for the endeavor. Rutgers (2008) suggests core values are "the most frequently referred to values" (p. 97).

Table 6.1 STRATEGIES FOR DEFINING PUBLIC VALUE

Defining public value for a specific jurisdiction and identifying the most relevant contract practices require a thorough analysis of the community's unique needs, challenges, and priorities (Moore 2014). Below is a list of strategies, accompanied by citations for additional information, guidance, and best practices on defining public value.

1. **Community Engagement and Surveys**: One of the most direct ways to understand what public value practices are relevant to a community is by engaging with community members (Nabatchi 2012; Stover et al. 2024).[a]

2. **Demographic and Socioeconomic Analysis**: Studying the demographic and socioeconomic profile of the community can provide insights into the kind of public value practices that could be most beneficial. For example, a community with a high addiction rate might benefit from rehabilitation services.[b]

3. **Historical and Cultural Assessment**: It's important to understand the community's history and culture and engage citizens in cultural mapping (Jeannotte 2016). The definition of public value and priorities may depend on historical issues the community has faced or cultural norms and values that are prominent.

4. **Environmental Assessment**: Environmental assessments help evaluate how projects and policies affect natural resources and public goods. They often assign monetary values to environmental impacts, which can be difficult because many environmental goods and services lack market prices. Methods like contingent valuation and choice modeling estimate these values to support policy decisions and resource management (Kahneman and Knetsch 1992; Litardi et al. 2020).

5. **Regulatory and Policy Framework**: Understanding local, regional, and national policies and regulations is essential when addressing public value issues. These frameworks highlight key concerns and guide efforts in the right direction (Kirkpatrick et al. 2004).

6. **Benchmarking**: Community benchmarking is a process where communities compare their performance, practices, or outcomes against similar communities or established standards to identify areas for improvement (Ellis 2006).

[a] *The Journal of Community Engagement and Scholarship* is dedicated to this topic. See https://jces.ua.edu/about.
[b] Visible Network Labs is an organization that provides guidance with community engagement activities. Their guide for how to get started is available at https://visiblenetworklabs.com/guides/community-engagement-101/#started. Public Participation Partners is another valuable resource. This women-owned and minority consulting firm provides tailored engagement plans and related services (e.g., stakeholder meetings, surveys, and demographic analyses). See https://publicparticipationpartners.com/what-we-do/data-collection/.

partners asserted (rather than engaging with nonprofit and community stakeholders involved in welfare services delivery to verify) that a technical solution to the welfare problem that featured a less expensive computer interface would be preferred to meeting in-person with a trained agent. From the start, they prioritized fewer visits by applicants to social service offices, or as Secretary Roob put it, "It's better for them and cheaper for us if they don't come into the office" (referring to Exhibit 90, 112 at 2, Judge Dryer's order of July 18, 2012, 6). In the absence of a more holistic construal of public value embedded in the contract and in the execution of project plans, the most vulnerable and disadvantaged groups who were either unable to use or uncomfortable with the technology, and who wanted above all to feel important and understood in their time of need (such as Louise Cahoon's mother), were marginalized in services delivery.

The Kirklees-KBOP contract sought to establish accountability mechanisms to ensure that clients with greater need and vulnerability would receive adequate attention and resources. The contract initially defined a "Complex Needs Cohort" of individuals with multifarious needs who would potentially be more difficult to serve, in order to incentivize providers to serve them equitably by aligning outcomes payments with the anticipated costs. Although this formal scheme for stratifying outcome payments based on need was subsequently eliminated, the partners shifted instead toward a relational approach that relied on frontline staff to discern program participants' needs and determine which outcome measures would serve as meaningful markers of change. The partnership board (attended by Council and KBOP staff) also considered the experiences of the KBOP service users in their performance reviews, and service providers were encouraged to present narrative accounts of participant journeys. Although this was at times perceived as pressure to surface "good news stories," it encouraged staff to reflect on the interaction between KPI measures and clients' lived experiences.

Additionally, specific contract clauses in the Kirklees-KBOP PPP called for coordination among the parties to facilitate an integrated approach to service delivery and a more holistic approach to understanding provider performance, such as encouraging attentiveness not only to performance on specific outcomes, but also equity in access to services, service integration, responsiveness, and enduring value for the public through the monitoring and rewarding longer-term outcomes. In contrast to the Indiana-IBM PPP, there was also broad participation in the auditing of performance evidence (e.g., by Council managers) to ensure that the higher-level goals of the contract—particularly serving vulnerable citizens' needs—were being prioritized and met. As discussed in Chapter 5, this shared approach to contract performance management aided Council contract managers in better understanding how various aspects of service characteristics and delivery were associated with outcome achievements and public value.

While formal contract provisions such as those in the Kirklees-KBOP PPP can foster public value, it is equally important to avoid or remove clauses that can undermine public value. Examples include compensation events, where governments are required to reimburse private contractors for revenue losses caused by policy changes, such as implementing new eligibility criteria for public health programs or expanding access to free services. Noncompete provisions may also prevent governments from introducing competing public programs, such as opening additional subsidized childcare centers or expanding public health clinics, to ensure the contractor's profitability. Clauses allowing contractors to challenge government actions, like changes in welfare policy or adjustments in service delivery standards, grant them quasi-governmental powers. These clauses constrain government flexibility, impose hidden costs on taxpayers, and prioritize private profits over public welfare and service delivery goals. To ensure that PPPs prioritize genuine public value creation rather than being driven by narrow financial or political interests, contract drafters can integrate public values into their agreements. Additionally, drafters can identify and remove clauses that detract from these objectives. Appendix 1 presents eight different types of clauses that should be judiciously considered in contract design in regard to how they balance the mitigation of private risks with the promotion of and accountability for public value.

Table 6.2 summarizes key aspects of the differing approaches of the Indiana-IBM and Kirklees-KBOP PPPs to contracting for public value.

The fact remains that government is positioned to do what no other actor can do—it has to be the ultimate champion of public value. Many of the challenges we aim to address with PPPs, the so-called "wicked problems," require coordinated effort across multiple levels of governance (formal and informal) and ongoing engagement with a wide range of constituencies and stakeholders. Thus, a broad vision and interests aligned with promoting public value is critical to the success of any PPP, and we argue that setting out to accomplish this through a formal contract alone is likely to divert the PPP away from a pathway to success. The actor who will be held most accountable for creating public value, the government, has to ensure a vision and approach focused on long-term goals and impacts, considering societal costs and benefits across constituencies, as well as the far-reaching consequences of not protecting the most vulnerable members of society (Mishra 1984). Our case analyses and the other research we draw on suggest that this requires a level of intentionality and collaboration that is more likely to be sustained in a PPP with some configuration of a formal-relational contract.

Table 6.2 Contrasting Approaches to Contracting for Public Value

Aspect	Indiana-IBM	Kirklees-KBOP
Philosophy/Values Emphasized	Process and efficiency outcomes	Social and cultural outcomes
Core Strategy	Data-driven decision-making for efficiency improvements	Emphasis on co-production and community engagement with distributed, data-led conversations to improve service effectiveness
Public Involvement	Limited direct public involvement, focus on outcomes	Promotes citizen participation in service design and delivery
Measurement of Success	Objective metrics such as cost savings and service delivery	A mix of subjective well-being and community outcomes and objective measures such as entry to employment
Innovation	Technology-driven innovation, including digital solutions	Collaborative spaces for service co-design and partnerships with local groups
Challenges	Overcoming bureaucratic inertia and funding constraints	Balancing diverse stakeholder interests and managing resources

THEME 2: PLACING RELATIONSHIP BUILDING AT THE CENTER OF PPP GOVERNANCE

In most PPPs, the choice of partners is a key first step in centering and building relationships in the public-private collaboration. Research suggests that PPPs may encounter difficulties when significant disparities exist in the partners' strategic orientations, technological frameworks, organizational cultures, risk assessments, and managerial approaches

(Das and Teng 1998, 2000). Moreover, conflicting interests among partners will inevitably pose significant challenges in aligning their long-term interests and facilitating cooperation (Kogut 1988). While both the Indiana-IBM and Kirklees-KBOP partners brought together diverse groups of partners, the Kirklees-KBOP emphasis on fostering cooperation and the relationships to sustain it was noticeably distinct from the Indiana-IBM PPP that started off with two partners, IBM and ACS, in direct competition and jockeying for the governor's attention. ACS likely perceived that there would be a payoff to its opportunistic behavior, and indeed, in the end, ACS ascended to replace IBM as the prime contractor. This subversive action could have been predicted based on existing knowledge that partnerships involving direct competitors tend to be fraught with contention and conflict (Kogut 1989), which inversely affects the level of trust among partners and is a detriment to promoting public value.

One approach to maintaining an emphasis on public value is to conceive of a PPP as part of an overall social contract, where the government and its partners solidify a commitment to social responsibility and effective governance and design the contract as an instrument of *enablement* instead of control. That is, rather than developing contracts with the primary intent to manage risk and allocate authority and control, a formal-relational contract is designed to provide the scaffolding for trust-based collaboration and to buttress the sustainability of the PPP and the attainment of its goals. This scaffolding consists of a formal articulation of the social norms or principles around joint working, maintaining a multilateral consensus, and supporting stakeholder engagement, such as inclusivity, loyalty, and fairness. Research finds that these relational norms and elements of social control are positively related to alliance performance (Aulakh et al. 1996).

As described in Chapter 2, the social exchange theory (SET) provides a guide as to how to center and cultivate trust in a PPP, with its emphasis on fair and equitable resource exchanges in relationships that anticipate a longer-term collaboration and implications for future exchanges. This orientation recognizes that circumstances will change, along with the parties' positioning in the PPP, but also that their interdependencies will necessitate cooperation to navigate these dynamics and stay on track to achieve the PPP goals and outcomes. In effect, facilitated by a strong relational orientation, the contract becomes a malleable, "living instrument" (van Lier et al. 2025), in which the experiences of all parties can inform changes in resource allocations and the contracted provisions. Alternatively, Box 6.2 provides an example of how the rigidity of the MSA and the lack of relational infrastructure in the Indiana-IBM PPP constrained the partners' ability to adapt to changing conditions.

Box 6.2

The Need for Flexibility and Adaptability in Formal-Relational Contracting

Accessing or pooling resources is often a key motivation for the formation of PPPs. Similarly, a diminishing level of resource interdependence or tapering need for the other partner's resources may pose a threat to the stability of alliances and precipitate the dissolution of relationships. This issue arose in the Indiana-IBM case, in which the contract required IBM to make substantial investments in hardware and software for welfare modernization. This interdependence was reinforced in that the system's customization for Indiana's welfare infrastructure necessitated a long-term partnership for IBM to recover the costs of its asset-specific investments. However, the alliance underwent a transformation as state employees and subcontractors (such as ACS) became more proficient with the system, lessening the exclusivity of IBM's expertise. The MSA included buyback options for IBM's equipment in the event of a premature contract termination, which were intended to mitigate IBM's risk and vulnerability. However, evolving dynamics altered the nature of the partners' interdependencies, shifting the balance of bargaining power toward the State and ACS. Because of the lack of flexibility in the PPP—in both the formal and relational elements undergirding it—the partners failed to adapt, which destabilized and brought about the demise of what was intended to be a long-term partnership (Malatesta and Smith 2014).

This accentuation of the relational aspects of a PPP does not negate, however, the importance of the formal written agreement. The literature recognizes the need for both contract rigidity (for clarity, protection, and enforceability) and flexibility (to adapt to change and unforeseen events) in contracts. Formal contracts should specify the rights and responsibilities of the parties, as clear and unambiguous guidelines foster accountability. Yet a degree of flexibility also allows adjustments to be made as circumstances change without bringing on formal renegotiations. The merits of this approach were borne out in the Kirklees-KBOP partnership, where measures used to understand the performance of services were actively critiqued and revised without need for formal contract renegotiation.

The idea of the formal-relational contract changes our conceptualization of the core role of the formal agreement, from one that intends to be as prescriptive and complete as possible to one that establishes a framework for fostering the relationships necessary to sustain the PPP as the state of the world changes. This shift also implies that governments and their partners need to let go of the inclination to uncritically incorporate standard boilerplate language into PPP agreements, such as the MSA in the Indiana-IBM case, as it is more likely to have the effect of undermining rather than fostering relational norms.

Indeed, the Indiana-IBM case demonstrates that prescriptive clauses and provisions can erode trust and destabilize contract relationships, such as the personnel provision in the Indiana-IBM MSA that accorded the State the unilateral right to interview and approve any project manager and key subcontractors of IBM (10.5.1). The MSA was replete with other one-sided clauses, which provided the State with remedies in the event of IBM's nonperformance, for example, specifying penalties, liquated damages, and corrective action plans (CAPs) (15.2, 15.7). Although the clauses aimed to protect the State and taxpayers, *in the absence of a strong relational foundation to the PPP*, they increased the risks that the parties would adopt defensive postures, fearing that open acknowledgment of issues could trigger the clauses.

On the whole, such one-way clauses lack reciprocity and can dampen team morale, create conflict of interest concerns, complicate future negotiations, and provoke legal disputes. For a fruitful contractual relationship, parties should exercise these types of clauses judiciously (taking into consideration principles of fairness or equal treatment), maintain open communications through relational mechanisms, and periodically reassess the relevance of any such stipulations. More generally, the parties to a PPP should be wary of contract clauses and provisions that introduce a transactional tone to the relationship instead of focusing attention on shared objectives, joint problem-solving, and mutual benefits. In the Kirklees-KBOP PPP, trust, reciprocity, and shared decision-making played a central role in navigating the PPP challenges, whereas in the Indiana-IBM case, the absence of these mechanisms led to adversarial relationships.

THEME 3: FORTIFYING PPPS WITH EFFECTIVE INSTITUTIONAL AND ACCOUNTABILITY MECHANISMS

The success of PPPs hinges not only on the intricacies of the formal contract and relational norms and infrastructure, but also on the robustness of institutional mechanisms that enable their effective and collaborative functioning and accountability to the public. Institutional mechanisms, including laws and policies related to Requests for Proposals (RFPs) and contract bidding, are intended to ensure that contracts are awarded and executed fairly, considering both public and private interests. Pragmatic policies mandate the transparency of contracts and their availability for public scrutiny, alongside legal requisites for declaring lobbying efforts and potential conflicts of interest, and thereby elevate ethical standards during the contracting process. In effect, transparency, accountability, and ethics are key principles of governance that underlie the social contract scaffolding a PPP.

Transparency ideally should include not only financial transparency about budgets and expenditures, but also transparency about conflicts of interest, performance shortcomings, and challenges as the project unfolds. The potential for corruption or too-cozy relationships have been factors of public concern in the turn toward relational contracting, although they are also a peril in more formalized arrangements (see Box 6.3). Importantly, the relational aspects of the contract need to be made as transparent as the formal ones. The legal enforceability of the guiding principles of a social or relational contract, or a general "doctrine of good faith," are increasingly recognized in courts of law, as long as the principles underlying "good faith" are articulated explicitly in the partnership (contract) infrastructure.

Box 6.3

Safeguarding Public Value and Mitigating Against Self-interest over Public Interest

A frequent driver of corruption-related inefficiencies associated with PPPs is the quest for private enrichment among political insiders, which may, in turn, compromise efforts toward achieving cost savings for the public (Kaufmann 2005). Suggestive evidence of this practice is commonplace: an analysis of £2.3 trillion worth of US government contracts awarded between 2001–2012 showed that politically connected firms bid 5.4% lower than unconnected ones on average and were three times as likely to successfully renegotiate (Brogaard et al. 2021). The Indiana-IBM case evidence suggests individuals and entities with close ties to Indiana Governor Daniels may have realized considerable financial benefits at the expense of the public. Notably, prior to Governor Daniels's authorization of the privatization plan, the Lucas Group, a consulting firm, was granted a contract to draft the specifications for the bidding process of the system's management. The nearly $4 million contract, approved by FSSA Secretary Roob, divulged the firm's connections to a former local government official who had previously served as a senior consultant for the Lucas Group. This, in turn, exposed an intricate web of affiliations and potential conflicts of interest that diminished the integrity of the Indiana-IBM PPP and raised critical questions about the governance and oversight mechanisms in place to safeguard public value. As Doug Masson observed, "The myth is that

Continued

Continued

privatization will create cheaper government. All too often, PPPs create a profit center for well-connected friends and well-wishers of the people making the privatization decisions" (2010, https://www.masson.us/blog/?s=mitch+roob).

Diffuse accountability is a core challenge that PPPs navigate, as decision-making and oversight are shared among multiple stakeholders. The involvement of multiple principals and agents in networked relationships adds complexity and makes it more difficult to attribute responsibility, although this is also where relational infrastructure can be key to reinforcing cooperation over conflict. When power imbalances arise, a more relational approach can preclude influential stakeholders from dominating decision-making and marginalizing the voices of less influential or advantaged groups. This is also where the front-end work of relational consensus building can support a clear strategic direction (centered on public value) for the PPP, which is critical as decision-making processes involving multiple actors and diverse interests can become fragmented over time, especially in the face of unanticipated events and risks.

Once again, the Indiana-IBM case illuminates the shortcomings of a PPP where the "front-end" relational work was neglected and a 160-page formal contract (MSA) with numerous schedules, exhibits, and appendices did little to facilitate transparency and accountability for the public or ethical exchanges among the partners. The State of Indiana, for example, failed to provide the public with critical information or opportunities for input from service users and other stakeholders at the project start, and there were numerous potential conflicts of interest among the parties that were not disclosed to the public (such as the close professional and personal connections between senior government officials and the main subcontractor, ACS). Furthermore, the communication failures evident at the project inception continued as the project progressed. Transparency was largely a facade as the PPP lacked a formal communication and engagement plan and other institutional mechanisms for enabling feedback from program beneficiaries, community leaders, and other stakeholders to inform programmatic and service adjustments. As the project unfolded, reports to the public were misleading and aimed at delivering the right political message, rather than accurate performance information or the true state of affairs, particularly as challenges arose. As a result, the mixed messages on performance also hindered accountability. A straightforward search on the Indiana Department of Administration website even now yields inconsistent and incomplete results, showcasing the lack of transparency in regard to contract specifics and performance data. These shortcomings were highlighted by organizations like the Center of Public Integrity and Global Integrity, which in 2015, gave Indiana a dismal accountability score of 62, the equivalent of a D-. Indiana earned an F in the categories of public access to information and political financing, ethics, entities, and civil service oversight.[2]

We hence turn to the Kirklees-KBOP case for insights into institutional mechanisms that exhibit promise for increased transparency, accountability, and ethical execution of social services delivery in PPPs. Like the Indiana-IBM PPP, the Kirklees-KBOP partnership includes a substantial performance monitoring regime that requires monthly submissions of performance data from partnering providers. Some delivery providers have struggled with the burden of reporting and validating outcomes achievement data. Yet rather than becoming a compliance-oriented exercise in public accountability, the KBOP's open and collaborative approach to governance has been critical to cultivating an honest, trust-based, and supportive dialogue among the partners, even when performance results may be below expectations. The Kirklees-KBOP partners have also ensured that the governance structures are inclusive and provide opportunities for meetings and communications that go beyond day-to-day operations and performance issues and attend to the longer-term goals that require more forward-looking and strategic thinking about the contract and collaboration. For example, the

2. See reports available at https://publicaccountability.org/.

contract includes specific mechanisms, such as a change procedure that invites discussions "in good faith" among the partners about anything that might increase their chances of achieving the PPP goals. This, in turn, increases the transparency of the partners' efforts to make changes intended to improve the project outcomes.

The special termination clause negotiated to ensure that any costs of an early termination would be shared between the partners also reflected this "good faith" approach. In other words, the informal processes of communication, sharing of critical information, and negotiation of "friendly terms" and cooperative strategies are formalized in the contract, creating pivotal feedback channels for continuous improvement. Transparency and open articulation of the Kirklees-KBOP partnership to the public could nonetheless be enhanced. In the UK, only limited contract details tend to be available in the public domain, and at the time of writing only limited performance information has been shared in the public domain, as the result of a national government-funded evaluation[3]. There is concern regarding the apocryphal unsuccessful third party—i.e., a bidder who was not awarded the contract—who may act in bad faith to discredit contract award or decision-making.

This discussion of the contrasting approaches to public accountability in our two cases underscores that a focus on procedural compliance is unlikely to be the guarantor of ethical standards in service delivery that some might assume it would be. In reality, relational mechanisms, rather than increasing collusion opportunities, may make it harder to collude by thickening the web of social connections governing a contract, collaboratively monitoring the PPP's progress, and elevating ethical standards. With limited relational governance, the Indiana-IBM case exemplified a traditional, punitive accountability model characterized by rigid, rules-based mechanisms that emphasized process compliance and detailed KPIs. Performance metrics were weaponized for blame allocation rather than constructive improvement. In stark contrast, the Kirklees-KBOP partnership prioritized relationship building, flexibility, and mutual understanding in a collaborative, learning-oriented

3. See https://golab.bsg.ox.ac.uk/knowledge-bank/indigo/impact-bond-dataset-v2/INDIGO-POJ-0175/#results. More data are expected to be released through various evaluation streams later in 2025.

accountability approach. Performance evaluation was not about strict compliance, but about generating insights, sharing knowledge, and continuously improving service delivery. At their best, the accountability mechanisms were horizontal and participatory, encouraging open dialogue and transparent information sharing, compared with hierarchical authority structures in the Indiana-IBM PPP that contributed to power confrontations when misalignments or misinterpretations arose between formal and real authority.

The fundamental differences between these two approaches to accountability can also be linked to variations in communication style, power distribution, organizational culture, and leadership orientation. The Indiana-IBM model relied on formal audits and unilateral performance assessment, whereas the Kirklees-KBOP PPP created accountability frameworks that were adaptable, inclusive, and focused on collective problem-solving. In Appendix 2, we summarize guidance for incorporating provisions into PPP contracts that translate public values into practice effectively. For example, transparency provisions should include information disclosure requirements, public reporting of performance metrics, and clear procedures for citizen access to documents. Accountability mechanisms should enable citizen feedback, independent audits, and transparent reporting on service outcomes. Cost and efficiency clauses should mandate cost comparisons, periodic evaluations, and detailed justifications for overruns. Stakeholder engagement provisions could ensure community input through surveys, co-production forums, and diverse representation. Lastly, ethical implementation should address societal challenges by defining social impact goals, reducing economic inequality, and upholding democratic values through measurable metrics.

THEME 4: ENVISAGING SYSTEMS CHANGE FOR LONG-TERM, PUBLIC-PRIVATE COLLABORATION

Peter Senge argued that "systems thinking is a discipline for seeing wholes . . . a framework for seeing interrelationships rather than things . . ." (1990: 59). The partners to a PPP and the contracts and relational scaffolding at the center of these partnerships are developed and executed in the context of a wider ecosystem with other public stakeholders and authorities (e.g., legislative, judicial). And just as there are multiple levels of governance in the broader ecosystem of PPPs that affect their resilience, there are often multilevel governance challenges within PPPs (e.g., subcontracted relationships or even a supply chain extending beyond the direct contractual relationships, stakeholders that are not party to the PPP), which complicate the working relationships and their nurturing and sustainability.

Yet the contracting literature largely frames public-private relationships in the context of bilateral contracts and the formal, legal structures that govern their execution. We need a shift in systemic thinking and a recognition of the multiparty architecture and infrastructure that is essential for governing and problem-solving. This includes clear, multilateral communications structures and processes for realizing consensus in decision-making, as well as mechanisms such as "bench-learning," which brings together data that are often highly fragmented (i.e., spread across multiple partners, stakeholders, and the external environment) to better understand how things are working, progress toward the collective PPP goals, and what could be improved. Elements of this "bench-learning" approach were apparent in the early stages of KBOP's "under new management" era. The alliance of KBOP delivery organizations convened regularly to understand collective performance and to share solutions and best practices. Yet this has proved challenging to sustain, and as the end of the PPP approaches, these practices are being sidelined as providers focus on operational realities. Recognizing that the practice of bench-learning is demanding, we argue that dedicated resources and periodic reviews and calls for renewal should be encouraged to promote its sustainability.

In calling for new thinking about systems change, we also consider the types of systems-level change that could augment opportunities for formal-relational contracting and its success in PPPs. For example, our case analyses, along with recent empirical research (Domingos et al. 2025), suggests that allowing governments discretion to start the contracting process on a relational footing can potentially improve cooperation among the parties and facilitate less costly adaptations to challenging circumstances, that is, by encouraging a more collaborative approach to problem-solving or a favorable orientation toward any renegotiations. In some systems, this might require substantive changes to public procurement rules, such as those that emphasize "lowest price" criteria at the contract award stage. For example, the new UK Procurement Act emphasizes that contracts should be awarded to the Most Advantageous Tender, revising and broadening the previous requirement to award the contract to the Most *Economically* Advantageous Tender (Procurement Act 2023). In other systems where the flexibility for setting off on a relational foot already exists, cultural change among procurement professionals (and allied professions such as public law) may be expedient (e.g., through training) to encourage a relational start. David Frydlinger has suggested that governments should begin by issuing a request for *partners* to start the contracting process, in contrast to soliciting *bids* for public procurement.[4] In other words, the focus of the discussions would be on what the bidder brings to the table to support the success of the partnership, rather than on evaluating the monetary value or costs of the bids and what they comprise.

More generally, we might reimagine the role of government in PPPs, from the conventional principal-agent relationship to one that can be likened to that of a coxswain on a rowing crew. In encouraging more private involvement in public services delivery, David Osborne and Ted Gaebler argued, "The job of government is to steer, not to row the boat. Delivering services is rowing, and government is not good at rowing" (1992). At the risk of straining the metaphor, the job of the coxswain is not *just* to steer, it's to chart a course, set the pace, avoid obstacles, and encourage the crew. In this envisaged role, government is not only a partner, but also a leader. The interest in advancing broader public value, and the consequences of not doing so, ultimately land with

4. David Frydlinger made this suggestion at the Social Outcomes Conference hosted by the Government Outcomes Lab, Blavatnik School of Government, Oxford, UK, in September 2023.

governments, not contractors. The government, like a coxswain, executes the critical functions of steering and coordinating the collaborative efforts among the partners as they undertake the following types of responsibilities:

1. *Partnership development*: The government initiates and fosters the partnership between the public and private sectors, starting with selecting the most suitable partners (versus bid) at the start. This involves first identifying potential partners, conducting reviews and feasibility assessments, and then forming relationships to establish a strong foundation for collaboration.
2. *Strategic planning*: In conjunction with the identified partners, the government articulates and codevelops the strategic direction and goals of the PPP. Together, the partners ensure alignment between the objectives of the public sector and interests of the private partner(s), while also considering the broader public interest and the value proposition of the partnership.
3. *Contract negotiation and management*: Recognizing that ongoing negotiations can be a beneficial component of collaboration (versus a one-time event or precipitated by negative events), the government facilitates discussions and any resulting restructuring of the PPP contractual arrangements. The partners cooperate to ensure that the contract revisions reflect agreed-upon terms; safeguard the public's interests; elucidate the roles, responsibilities, and performance expectations of all parties; and allow for fair-minded monitoring and oversight.
4. *Risk management*: With the foremost responsibility for guaranteeing public value, the government leads in assessing and managing risks associated with the PPP. This includes identifying potential risks, collaborating with partners to design risk mitigation strategies, and monitoring risk factors throughout the partnership's duration. The government also

verifies that appropriate mechanisms are in place to address and resolve any risks that materialize over the course of the relationship.

5. *Stakeholder engagement*: The government holds the important responsibility of ensuring the public interest is represented among the various stakeholders brought to the table, including government agencies, private partners, community organizations, and the general public. The government fosters collaboration and transparency by clearly communicating the purpose, benefits, and progress of the PPP and addressing concerns or issues raised by stakeholders throughout the partnership.
6. *Performance monitoring and evaluation*: A "bench-learning" approach to performance management is facilitated and funded by the government to track the PPP progress with the partners against established goals and performance indicators. They collaborate in collecting and analyzing performance data and in holding performance review sessions to discuss how the data can inform improvements in outcomes and the PPP's effectiveness, as well as to ensure transparency in reporting outcomes to the public.
7. *Public interest safeguarding*: Throughout the PPP, the government upholds the public interest, ensuring that the partnership delivers public value and aligns with legal and regulatory requirements, maintains transparency and accountability, and serves the broader public welfare.

The positioning of government as project and PPP leader is supported by research that emphasizes the distinctions in both the motivations of public servants (Perry 2000) and the institutions that guide the values and actions of those who work in the public sector. The leaders of organizations have a specific role to play in how they shape and are shaped by logic structures, enabling varying power positions and social identities. Institutional logics are the socially constructed patterns, practices, assumptions, values, beliefs, and rules that individuals use to produce and reproduce their material subsistence, organize time and space, and make sense of their social reality (Friedland and Alford 1991). The concept of institutional logic suggests that organizations have unique organizing principles, reference frames, and scripts for behaviors and legitimacy standards. The government, as "coxswain," can enable, facilitate, and guide collaboration in the PPP.

Another significant systems change that has been envisioned to advance the adoption of formal-relational contracting models is greater recognition by the courts of the legal enforceability of relational infrastructure, such as the guiding principles that underlie "good faith," particularly when these are explicitly stated in the contract. In fact, the landmark court cases discussed in Chapter 2 collectively suggest that parties engaged in PPPs can enhance the enforceability of good faith by integrating explicit and precise language into their formal contractual agreements. Courts in the UK increasingly emphasize the fundamental purpose of agreements, recognizing that contracts are dynamic instruments requiring flexible and contextual interpretation. Recent cases such as *Amey v. Birmingham City Council* [2018] EWCA Civ 264, *Bates v. Post Office Ltd.* [2019] EWHC 606, and *Compound Photonics Group Ltd; Faulkner v. Vollin Holdings Ltd* [2022] EWCA Civ 1371 illustrate this shift, prioritizing cooperative intent and discouraging opportunism that technically complies with terms while undermining core objectives. Judges consider relational dynamics, commercial realities, and long-term sustainability, encouraging clearer agreements with robust renegotiation and dispute resolution mechanisms. This shift moves contract law from rigid formalism to a principle-based approach, valuing reasonableness, good faith, and commercial relationships.

Meanwhile, although the US Supreme Court has not recently ruled on the "duty of good faith," the principle remains central to contract law in the US. The Uniform Commercial Code (UCC) mandates good faith in contract performance and enforcement, as stated in UCC Section 1–203. Lower courts continue to interpret this obligation, shaping modern understandings of contractual good faith, as demonstrated in cases like *Centex Corp. v. United States*, 395 F.3d 1283, 1304 (Fed. Cir. 2005) and

Metcalf Constr. Co. v. United States, 742 F.3d 984 (Fed. Cir. 2014). Each of these cases has contributed to the evolving framework of good faith in contractual performance and enforcement.

In Appendix 3, we draw out specific contract language from these court cases that illustrates how contracting parties can tailor the language to crystallize the duty of good faith and enhance the enforceability of relational norms within the contract. For example, "good faith" language or clauses embedded in the formal contracts include the following:

- "Notwithstanding the detailed terms herein, the parties recognize an implied duty of good faith in the execution and interpretation of this contract, committing to act honestly, fairly, and in a manner that upholds the spirit and broader purpose of the agreement." *Amey v. Birmingham City Council [2018] EWCA Civ 264*
- "Both parties agree to perform their obligations under this contract in good faith. No clause in this contract shall be interpreted in a way that prevents the implication of a duty of good faith in the execution of contractual responsibilities." *Bates v. Post Office Ltd., [2019] EWHC 606*
- "Both parties hereby acknowledge and agree to uphold a broad obligation of good faith throughout the duration of this partnership. This obligation entails a commitment to act with integrity, fairness, and in a spirit of cooperation, consistent with the venture's long-term objectives and spirit." *Al Nehayan v. Kent [2018] EWHC 333 (Comm) (22 February 2018)*

One of the cases also incorporated a provision that explicitly recognizes the risks of overly prescriptive formal contract language: "The parties recognize that overly strict and narrow drafting of terms may be counterproductive. Therefore, this contract is designed to allow flexibility and adaptability, ensuring practicality and reasonableness in its application over the long term." Other terms and clauses in the contracts stipulate the commitment to a long-term partnership and that "not every aspect of this collaboration can or will be detailed" in the contract. Language in the clauses and terms also articulate the principles by which the parties will abide in their interactions, such as integrity, mutual trust and confidence, honesty, and "fair dealing." These principles are, in turn, reflected in language that accentuates their pledge to act in a "spirit of cooperation" and collaborate throughout the partnership, e.g., "The parties shall collaborate closely in the performance of this contract, sharing information, resources, and expertise to achieve the common goals outlined herein."

CONCLUSION

We have drawn on two in-depth case analyses of complex, multiactor PPPs based in the US and UK, decades of research on public-private contracting, and recent insights from leading thinkers to consider how PPPs can be better designed and managed to produce more value for the public in social services delivery. The application of formal-relational contracting to the pursuit of public value is emergent, and there is much work still to be done in both research and practice, which we elaborate on below. Yet we believe there are important theoretical and practical insights to highlight, each of which prompts additional questions for researchers and practitioners about how to enhance the foundations for more effective, accountable, and sustainable approaches to public sector contracting.

Novel theoretical and empirical insights that inform practice

In Chapter 4, we used process tracing to identify and test key propositions that emerged from our PPP cases. Following Aghion and Tirole (1997), we distinguished formal authority (the contractual right to make decisions) from real authority (actual control over decisions) and found strong support for the tenet that the allocation of authority is not merely an administrative or contractual exercise but a critical mechanism for shaping organizational behavior and effectiveness. The Indiana-IBM and Kirklees-KBOP cases provide rich evidence showing how written agreements can either be aligned or fundamentally disconnected from real decision-making dynamics, and how real authority can systematically and strategically undermine formal authority structures. Communication channels emerge not as neutral information conduits, but as sophisticated tools for power redistribution, revealing that authority allocation is far more dynamic and continuously negotiated than previous theoretical models suggested. Moreover, the way authority is distributed directly influences information-sharing strategies, decision-making processes, trust development, performance motivation, and accountability mechanisms. The Indiana-IBM case serves as a cautionary tale of how misaligned authority can rapidly erode organizational effectiveness, while the Kirklees-KBOP model offers a blueprint for more dynamic, responsive governance structures.

These two cases also illuminate new theoretical and practical implications of Aghion and Tirole's insights about strategic information sharing. In the Indiana-IBM case, communication became a tool for strategic manipulation, with subcontractors like ACS strategically communicating in ways that undermined the prime contractor. Our research extends the original theory by showing how communication can be used not only to share information, but also to actively reshape authority structures. Additionally, the Indiana-IBM case, with its network of twelve subcontractors, reveals how authority allocation becomes exponentially more complex in networked environments, adding depth to the original theoretical conception.

Our case analysis also contributes to and expands existing theoretical perspectives on organizational dynamics, offering a nuanced reimagining of how authority, governance, and interorganizational relationships operate in practice. The observations from these cases align with public management literature recognizing the governance complexities inherent in multiactor partnerships that defy standardized frameworks (e.g., Agranoff 2007; McGuire and Agranoff 2011; Emerson et al. 2012). The cases expose principal-agent models as inadequate for capturing the intricate ways organizational actors strategically reinterpret and manipulate contractual boundaries. Relatedly, the case evidence contributes to public governance theory by showing the inadequacy of traditional top-down governance models and presenting compelling evidence for user-centered and adaptive service delivery approaches. The case evidence further reveals that communication strategies may matter more than rigid formal rules, as power relationships are continuously negotiated rather than statically determined. By demonstrating how external environments continuously reshape organizational dynamics, these cases advance a more sophisticated understanding of interorganizational relationships.

In regard to our second proposition about the role of relational mechanisms vis-à-vis formal contractual structures, our process tracing analysis lends robust empirical validation to the importance of trust, communication, and other relational mechanisms that may even override formal contractual provisions (Bertelli and Smith 2010). The findings also align closely with prior research that promotes relationship-centered approaches to managing uncertainty and fostering trust to achieve long-term success in partnerships (Macneil 1978; Frydlinger et al. 2021; Frydlinger and Hart 2024; Vitasek and Frydlinger 2021). The ongoing success of the Kirklees-KBOP partnership reflects how the cultivation of trust, shared governance, and mutual respect enabled the parties to adapt to unforeseen challenges and focus on shared objectives. In the Indiana-IBM PPP, alternatively, the over-reliance on rigid formal provisions, such as detailed KPIs and process-based measures, thwarted collaboration and adaptability, and the lack of relational governance contributed to the ensuing breakdown of trust and adversarial use of formal mechanisms. The paths to these contrasting outcomes reflect a lesson articulated by the acclaimed college basketball coach, John Wooden, who recounted how he had to continuously adapt to succeed: *"Failure isn't fatal, but failure to change might be"* (White 2013).

While Frydlinger and Hart (2024) provide a compelling theoretical argument for relational contracting, and Brown et al. (2013) generate convincing insights into collaborative governance, the findings from our in-depth case analyses contribute concrete, comparative evidence to support and refine their claims. For example, the smoking gun test in the Kirklees-KBOP case provides evidence of how relational mechanisms (e.g., shared governance) contributed to successful outcomes; this is typically assumed yet not empirically demonstrated as it is here. In addition, the hoop test in the Indiana-IBM case confirms that relational breakdowns, rather than formal provisions, were the primary drivers of failure. This empirical validation strengthens the argument that relational mechanisms are critical, even in partnerships governed by robust formal contracts. Our case analyses also show how formal and relational elements interact, and may complement one another, rather than serving as competing approaches. The Kirklees-KBOP case demonstrates how formal provisions can actively enable and reinforce relational mechanisms when designed thoughtfully, for example, through simplified performance metrics and shared governance forums that facilitate trust building. Conversely, the Indiana-IBM case evidence reveals how rigid formal provisions can actively undermine relational dynamics, as seen in how performance metrics became weapons in an increasingly adversarial relationship.

In addition, the cases contribute a dynamic, temporal perspective that is lacking in prior research, providing empirical evidence of possible causal pathways through which relational mechanisms influence PPP outcomes. The temporal analysis identified alternative causal paths and intervening variables not fully explored in existing theoretical work, particularly the crucial roles of leadership, institutional support, and external pressures in shaping how relational mechanisms operate in practice. In addition, the analysis revealed how relational mechanisms evolve and interact with changing contexts. For example, the Kirklees-KBOP case shows how trust and reciprocity can be progressively strengthened through iterative problem-solving and shared governance, while Indiana-IBM illustrates how early relational breakdowns can cascade into broader conflicts if not addressed. This temporal dimension helps explain why similar formal structures can lead to vastly different outcomes depending on the evolution of relational dynamics.

Practical implications for more effective, accountable, and sustainable PPPs

We now return to our heuristic model (Figures 2.1–2.3) of how public and private partners can come together in the context of precarious contracting circumstances to navigate dynamically onto a pathway toward sustained collaboration and PPP success. Utilizing this framing, we collate some key insights and understandings and their practical implications, along with outstanding questions that this work has uncovered. We focus on three key themes: the potential for greater relationality in PPPs, the role of government in safeguarding public value, and the need for an adaptive approach that navigates between an emphasis on formality and relationality as conditions dictate.

First, our work suggests that PPPs are unlikely to move out of difficult contracting circumstances simply by layering on more rules, clauses, schedules, and other formal provisions to steer the partners. As both the Indiana-IBM and Kirklees-KBOP cases illustrated, the inherent challenges and complexities of social services delivery to vulnerable populations and the unpredictability of environmental factors (natural, economic, political, and social) ensure that interruptions to the "best-laid" plans will be the norm rather than the exception, particularly in longer-term contractual relationships. Provided that it is inclusive and centered on a broad conception of public value, relational infrastructure cultivated in a PPP—guiding principles and norms, plans developed on the basis of a shared vision of goals, forums for communication and "bench learning," etc.—is more likely to support a collaborative and flexible approach to problem-solving and adaptation. To be clear, we are not suggesting that relational mechanisms should displace formal arrangements, but rather that the partners work together to find an appropriate balance between formal and relational over time and as dynamic situations require. And as manifested in the Kirklees-KBOP case, this does not imply that all problems will be readily resolved, but it makes it more likely that cooperation will triumph over opportunism and self-interest and that the partners will make necessary adjustments to sustain the

PPP. We accordingly pose the following questions for both practitioners and academics to consider in advancing a formal-relational model for contracting in PPPs.

- What types of capacities do we need to strengthen among public managers and partner leaders for cultivating productive and inclusive partner relationships?
- What formal and relational contract mechanisms are most effective in incentivizing upfront investments and cooperation in the partnership at the outset of a PPP?
- Recognizing that the pathway to sustained collaboration and success will not be direct or linear, what types of mechanisms or provisions can be used to enhance and support learning over time and apprise the partners when they are leaning too heavily on the formal or relational elements (to avoid going off course)?
- What types of changes in public funding of PPPs are needed—such as tiered, evidence-based grantmaking with payouts tied to milestones in the generation of public value (versus one-off contracts)—to support the longevity of PPPs?

Second, our work suggests that the government plays a critical role in ensuring contractual mechanisms for measuring and monitoring PPP performance and upholding accountability to the public for outcomes and public value creation. This includes the responsibilities that it may pass on to private contractors for generating public value in social services delivery. We argue that to do this effectively requires going beyond traditional short-term, procedural, and financial metrics and encompassing broader, longer-term measures of societal impact and well-being that the partners agree are central to their shared project goals. Moreover, our case analyses suggest that accountability to the public is more robust when the partners develop collaborative mechanisms for data sharing and facilitating honest, transparent, and supportive dialogue about performance results, as well as forward-looking strategies for addressing performance shortcomings that leverage the partners' collective capabilities and fairly distribute risks. Efforts to increase transparency to the public also need to recognize, however, that elected officials are attuned to political cycles, and public expectations for evidence of performance may run counter to a longer-term orientation toward public value generation. In addition, political landscapes can shift over time and undermine both deftly cultivated relationships and formal contractual arrangements, knocking the partners off course on the path to sustained collaboration and success. These challenges again point to the importance of developing "good faith" principles and contractual language that enhance the role and enforceability of relational norms in the daily work of PPPs, which, in turn, can allow for flexibility and adjustments to performance regimes over time and responsiveness to external factors. We offer the following questions for further consideration by practitioners and academics as they strive to strengthen accountability for public value creation in PPPs.

- What types of systems changes would encourage a shift away from public accountability practices that emphasize auditing short-term metrics or KPIs that are not anchored in public value over assessing progress toward longer-term public goals and societal impacts?
- What types of institutional or management changes would bolster fairness and transparency in the allocation of authority and responsibility among PPP partners for performance outcomes and enhance the scrutiny of public value creation?
- Are there contractual or legal provisions that could release PPPs from restrictions that allow parties and subcontractors to circumvent transparency (e.g., those protecting commercial sensitivity or proprietary interests or that obscure the presence of conflicts of interests)?
- Recognizing the potential for the judiciary to enter into the interpretation of a PPP contract or a contested outcome of a PPP (as in the Indiana-IBM case), what factors should guide the determination of contractual language at the outset of a partnership (e.g., the balance between looser, relational

language versus tighter formal provisions pertaining to public accountability)?

Lastly, we reiterate the inference that there is no prevailing prescription or model for incorporating particular degrees of formalism or relationalism to ensure the effective functioning and success of complex, social welfare–focused PPPs. Although more experience with and evidence on formal-relational contracting practices in PPPs is needed to understand how partners may best balance formal and relational mechanisms in contract design and implementation, we expect that the equilibrium in any given PPP will inevitably evolve as relationships mature and the PPP work progresses in the context of a dynamic environment. That is, the partners may need to shift between an emphasis on greater formalization versus greater relationality along the formal-relational spectrum as time and circumstances require. If the partnership is working effectively, there should be considerable learning over time that the partners can leverage to facilitate continuous improvement of outcomes and value for the public.

APPENDIX 1

Clauses Potentially Undermining Public Value

1. **Noncompete Clauses**: These clauses restrict governments' provision of similar services. For example, suppose a private company is contracted to run a publicly funded homeless shelter under a PPP arrangement. A noncompete clause in the contract might stipulate that the government cannot establish or fund additional shelters within a certain geographic radius or expand public housing services that could reduce reliance on the private facility.
2. **Compensation Clauses for Adverse Actions**: These provisions require governments to compensate private operators for policy decisions that might reduce project revenues, such as implementing environmental regulations or changes in toll rates. This undermines the government's ability to prioritize public welfare or respond to changing needs without incurring financial penalties.
3. **Long-term Contract Duration**: Contracts that span decades (e.g., 30 to 99 years) lock governments into terms that may no longer align with public interests as circumstances evolve. The lengthy commitment reduces governments' capacity to adapt to changes in technology, demographics, or policy priorities.
4. **Revenue Guarantees**: Clauses guaranteeing minimum revenue for private operators shift financial risks from the private sector to taxpayers. For example, in contracts for privately operated prisons governments often agree to clauses that require a minimum occupancy rate, such as 90% or higher, for the

duration of the contract. If the prison population falls below this threshold, the government is required to compensate the private operator for the unused capacity.

5. **Misalignment of Interests**: Clauses may create a misalignment between public interest and private profit. For example, the public interest lies in reducing incarceration rates through effective social programs, rehabilitation, or policy reform, while a PPP for the management of a prison may rely on a financial model that maintains or increases inmate populations.
6. **Restrictions on Public Oversight**: Some PPPs limit government oversight or public access to operational and financial data, reducing transparency and accountability. This can lead to inefficiencies, cost overruns, or poor service quality, with little recourse for public authorities.
7. **Broad Definitions of Force Majeure**: Contracts sometimes include expansive force majeure clauses that allow private organizations to claim relief or compensation for events beyond their control. When these clauses are overly broad, they can lead to disputes or unjustified costs for governments.
8. **High Termination Penalties**: PPP agreements often include substantial financial penalties for terminating contracts prematurely, even if the project is failing to meet public needs. These penalties can discourage governments from intervening in underperforming projects, perpetuating poor outcomes.[1]

1. Paul Verkuil's *Why Privatization of Government Functions Threatens Democracy and What We Can Do About It* (2007) examines the increasing reliance of governments on private contractors to perform core (inherently) governmental functions such as public welfare. Verkuil argues that this trend raises significant concerns about accountability and democratic governance.

APPENDIX 2

Translating Public Values to PPP Contract Design and Practice

Transparency Provisions

- Require information disclosure
- Mandate public reporting of performance metrics
- Limit claims of "commercial sensitivity"
- Specify which documents are publicly accessible
- Specify practices and procedures for citizen access to documents.

Accountability Mechanisms

- Create mechanisms for citizen feedback
- Include provisions for independent performance audits
- Require transparent reporting on services delivery outcomes
- Establish regular public stakeholder review forums

Cost and Efficiency Provisions

- Mandate initial and ongoing cost comparisons with alternative services delivery methods
- Include provisions for periodic cost-efficiency evaluations
- Require detailed justification for any cost overruns
- Require detailed cost breakdowns

Stakeholder Engagement

- Mandate periodic community engagement surveys
- Create mechanisms for incorporating stakeholder input
- Establish co-production forums

- Include diverse demographic representation in contract governance

Ethical Implementation Provisions

- Explicitly state commitment to addressing societal challenges
- Define specific social impact goals
- Include metrics for reducing economic inequality
- Outline mechanisms for upholding democratic values

APPENDIX 3

Translating Judicial Insights into Language for PPP Contracts

By adhering to the principles established by the judiciary, contracting parties can foster a cooperative relationship ensuring that the services delivered meet the intended goals and safeguard public interest more effectively.

Purpose	Example Clause	Legal Basis
UK Cases		
Integrity Clause	The parties commit to perform their roles with the utmost integrity, adhering to the highest standards of ethical conduct and professional practice throughout the duration of this contract.	*Bates v. Post Office Ltd.*, [2019] EWHC 606
Mutual Commitment and Cooperation Clause	The parties commit to extensive cooperation and communication throughout the duration of this contract, acknowledging that the success of the project depends on a collaborative and adaptive partnership.	*Amey v. Birmingham City Council*, [2018] EWCA Civ 264

Continued

Continued

Purpose	Example Clause	Legal Basis
Honesty as Core Obligation	At a minimum, the duty of good faith under this agreement encompasses an obligation to act honestly in all dealings related to this partnership. This includes, but is not limited to, truthful communication, accurate representation of facts, and sincerity in fulfilling contractual responsibilities.	Compound Photonics Group Ltd., [2021] EWHC 787 *Faulkner v. Vollin Holdings Ltd.*, [2022] EWCA Civ 1371
US Cases		
Noninterference	The parties acknowledge that fair dealing includes refraining from interfering with another party's performance or from acting to destroy another party's reasonable expectations regarding the fruits of the contract.	*Centex Corp. v. United States*, 395 F.3d 1283, 1304 (Fed.Cir.2005)
Duty of Good Faith and Fair Dealing	The parties agree to perform their respective obligations in good faith and with fair dealing. Each party shall refrain from any action that prevents or hinders the other party's performance. The parties further agree to engage in reasonable efforts to communicate and resolve disputes in a timely manner.	*Metcalf Constr. Co. v. United States*, 742 F.3d 984 (Fed. Cir. 2014)

REFERENCES

CHAPTER 1

Afzal, Kamran Ali, and Mark Considine. 2014. *Democratic Accountability and International Human Development: Regimes, Institutions and Resources*. Taylor & Francis Group.

Alford, John, and Janine O'Flynn. 2009. "Making Sense of Public Value: Concepts, Critiques, and Emergent Meanings." *International Journal of Public Administration* 32 (3–4): 171–91.

Ariño, Africa, and José de la Torre. 1998. "Learning from Failure: Towards an Evolutionary Model of Collaborative Ventures." *Organization Science* 9 (3): 306–25.

Ashoka. 2013. "'Conscious Capitalism': Q&A with Whole Foods CEO John Mackey." *Fortune*, March 1, 2013. https://www.forbes.com/sites/ashoka/2013/03/01/qa-with-whole-foods-ceo-john-mackey-about-conscious-capitalism/.

Bakker, Marjan, Chris H. J. Hartgerink, Jelte M. Wicherts, and Han L. J. van der Maas. 2016. "Researchers' Intuitions About Power in Psychological Research." *Psychological Science* 27 (8): 1069–77.

Barr, Donald A. 2007. "A Research Protocol to Evaluate the Effectiveness of Public–Private Partnerships as a Means to Improve Health and Welfare Systems Worldwide." *American Journal of Public Health* 97 (1): 19–25.

Benington, John, and Mark H. Moore. 2011. "Public Value in Complex and Changing Times." In *Public Value: Theory and Practice*, edited by John Benington and Mark H. Moore, 1–30. Palgrave Macmillan.

Blavot, Oceane, Rodolfo Bejarano, and Mae Buenaventur. 2022. *History RePPPeated II: Why Public-Private Partnerships Are Not the Solution*. Eurodad.

Böll Stiftung, Heinrich. 2018. *History RePPPeated - How Public Private Partnerships Are Failing*. Heinrich Böll Foundation, Germany.

Boyer, Eric J., David M. Van Slyke, and Juan D. Rogers. 2016. "An Empirical Examination of Public Involvement in Public–Private Partnerships: Qualifying the Benefits of Public Involvement in PPPs." *Journal of Public Administration Research and Theory* 26 (1): 45–61.

Boyer, Eric J., Juan D. Rogers, and David M. Van Slyke. 2018. "Analysing Managerial Perceptions of When and How to Structure Public Involvement in Public–Private Partnerships." *Local Government Studies* 44 (4): 443–64.

Bozeman, Barry. 2007. *Public Values and Public Interest: Counterbalancing Economic Individualism.* Georgetown University Press.

Brown, Trevor L., Matthew Potoski, and David M. Van Slyke. 2013. *Complex Contracting.* Cambridge University Press.

Bryson, John M., Barbara C. Crosby, and Melissa Middleton Stone. 2015. "Designing and Implementing Cross-Sector Collaborations: Needed and Challenging." *Public Administration Review* 75 (5): 647–63. https://doi.org/10.1111/puar.12432.

Brown, Trevor L., Matthew Potoski, and David M. Van Slyke. 2018. "Complex Contracting: Management Challenges and Solutions." *Public Administration Review* 78 (5): 739–47.

Bryson, John M., Barbara C. Crosby, and Laura Bloomberg. 2014. "Public Value Governance: Moving Beyond Traditional Public Administration and the New Public Management." *Public Administration Review* 74: 445–56.

Chen, Cheng, Michael Hubbard, and Chun-Sung Liao. 2013. "When Public–Private Partnerships Fail: Analysing Citizen Engagement in Public–Private Partnerships—Cases from Taiwan and China." *Public Management Review* 15 (6): 839–57.

Chiapello, Ève, and Lisa Knoll. 2020. "The Welfare Conventions Approach: A Comparative Perspective on Social Impact Bonds." *Journal of Comparative Policy Analysis* 22 (2): 100–15.

Cooper, Christine, Carol Graham, and Darlene Himick. 2016. "Social Impact Bonds: The Securitization of the Homeless." *Accounting, Organizations and Society* 55: 63–82. https://doi.org/10.1016/j.aos.2016.10.003.

Dannin, Ellen. 2011. "Crumbling Infrastructure, Crumbling Democracy: Infrastructure Privatization Contracts and Their Effects on State and Local Governance." *Northwestern Journal of Law and Social Policy* 6: 47–86.

Das, T. K., and Bing-Sheng Teng. 2000. "A Resource-Based Theory of Strategic Alliances." *Journal of Management* 26 (1): 31–61. https://doi.org/10.1177/014920630002600105.

Dubnick, Melvin J., and H. George Frederickson. 2010. "Accountable Agents: Federal Performance Measurement and Third-Party Government." *Journal of Public Administration Research and Theory* 20 (Supplement 1)): i143–59.

Dyer, Jeffrey H., and Harbir Singh. 1998a. "The Relational View: Cooperative Strategy and Sources of Interorganizational Competitive Advantage." *Academy of Management Review* 23 (4): 660–79.

Dyer, Jeffrey H., and Harbir Singh. 1998b. "Cooperative Strategies and Sources of Interorganizational Competitive Advantage: The Role of Relational Rent." *Strategic Management Journal* 19 (4): 293–317.

Frydlinger, David, Kate Vitasek, Jim Bergman, and Tim Cummins. 2021. *Contracting in the New Economy: Using Relational Contracts to Boost Trust and Collaboration in Strategic Business Relationships.* Palgrave Macmillan.

Frydlinger, David, and Oliver Hart. 2023. "Overcoming Contractual Incompleteness: The Role of Guiding Principles." *The Journal of Law, Economics, and Organization*. https://doi.org/10.1093/jleo/ewac027.

Frydlinger, David. 2024. *Rules of the Game for Sustainable Business: Laws, Contracts and Morality*. Kluwer Law International.

Gilo, David, and Ariel Porat. 2006. "The Hidden Roles of Boilerplate and Standard-Form Contracts: Strategic Imposition of Transaction Costs, Segmentation of Consumers, and Anticompetitive Effects." *Michigan Law Review* 104: 983.

Heinrich, Carolyn J., and Yung Chun Choi. 2007. "Performance-Based Contracting in Social Welfare Programs." *The American Review of Public Administration* 37(4): 409–35.

Hodge, Graeme A., and Carsten Greve. 2007. "Public–Private Partnerships: An International Performance Review." *Public Administration Review* 67: 545–68.

Hodge, Graeme A., and Carsten Greve. 2016. "On Public–Private Partnership Performance: A Contemporary Review." *Public Works Management & Policy* 22(1): 55–78. https://doi.org/10.1177/1087724X16657830.

Hodge, Graeme A., Carsten Greve, and Anthony E. Boardman, eds. 2010. *International Handbook on Public-Private Partnership*. Edward Elgar Publishing.

Janik, Laura L. 2014. "From the Bench to the Bush: The Children's Vaccine Initiative and Troubled Public-Private Partnerships for Health." *Global Health Governance* 8(1): 96–116.

Kroll, Alexander, and Donald P. Moynihan. 2015. "Creating Public Value Using Performance Information." In *Public Value and Public Administration*, edited by John M. Bryson, Barbara C. Crosby, and Laura Bloomberg, 189–206. Georgetown University Press.

Macneil, Ian R. 1963. "Time of Acceptance: Too Many Problems for a Single Rule." *University of Pennsylvania Law Review* 112: 947–1005.

Moore, Mark H. 2013. *Recognizing Public Value*. Harvard University Press.

Osborne, Stephen P., ed. 2000. *Public–Private Partnerships: Theory and Practice in International Perspective*. Routledge.

Rybnicek, Robert, Julia Plakolm, and Lisa Baumgartner. 2020. "Risks in Public–Private Partnerships: A Systematic Literature Review of Risk Factors, Their Impact and Risk Mitigation Strategies." *Public Performance & Management Review* 43(5): 1174–208. https://doi.org/10.1080/15309576.2020.1741406.

Thomas, P., S. A. G. Schyvers, H. van den Berg, and B. S. van der Wouden. 2015. "Public–Private Partnerships, Management Capacity and Public Service Efficiency." *Policy & Politics* 43(2): 269–88.

Warner, Mildred E. 2013. "Private Finance for Public Goods: Social Impact Bonds." *Journal of Economic Policy Reform* 16(4): 303–19. https://doi.org/10.1080/17487870.2013.835727.

Williams, Ian, and Helen Shearer. 2011. "Appraising Public Value: Past, Present and Futures." *Public Administration* 89: 1367–84.

CHAPTER 2

Albertson, Kevin, Chris Fox, Chris O'Leary, and Gary Painter. 2020. "Towards a Theoretical Framework for Social Impact Bonds." *Nonprofit Policy Forum* 11 (2): 1–10.

Ball, Nigel, and Michael Gibson. 2022. *Partnerships with Principles: Putting Relationships at the Heart of Public Contracts for Better Social Outcomes*. Government Outcomes Lab, Blavatnik School of Government, University of Oxford.

Frydlinger, David, Kate Vitasek, Jim Bergman, and Tim Cummins. 2021. "The Psychology of Contracting." In *Contracting in the New Economy: Using Relational Contracts to Boost Trust and Collaboration in Strategic Business Relationships*, 71–87. Palgrave Macmillan.

Freeman, R. Edward. 2000. *Strategic Management: A Stakeholder Approach*. Cambridge University Press.

Freeman, R. Edward. 2006. *Managing for Stakeholders: Survival, Reputation, and Success*. Yale University Press.

Gerring, John. 2004. "What Is a Case Study and What Is It Good For?" *American Political Science Review* 98 (2): 341–54.

Gilson, Ronald J., Charles F. Sabel, and Robert E. Scott. 2010. "Braiding: The Interaction of Formal and Informal Contracting in Theory, Practice, and Doctrine." Stanford Law and Economics Olin Working Paper No. 389, Columbia Law and Economics Working Paper No. 367. https://dx.doi.org/10.2139/ssrn.1535575.

Hart, Oliver D., and Bengt Holmström. 1986. "The Theory of Contracts." Presented at The World Congress of the Econometrics Society. https://dspace.mit.edu/bitstream/handle/1721.1/64265/theoryofcontract00hart.pdf. Accessed March 1, 2023.

Hart, Oliver D., and John Moore. 1990. "Property Rights and the Nature of the Firm." *Journal of Political Economy* 98: 1119–58.

Hart, Oliver D., Andrei Shleifer, and Robert W. Vishny. 1997. "The Proper Scope of Government: Theory and an Application to Prisons." *Quarterly Journal of Economics* 112 (4): 1127–61.

Heinrich, Carolyn J., and Youseok Choi. 2007. "Performance-Based Contracting in Social Welfare Programs." *The American Review of Public Administration* 37 (4): 409–35.

Hobbes, Thomas. (1651) 2002. The Leviathan. Full Text EBook. Project Gutenberg. Release Date: July 2, 2002 [eBook #3207]. Most recently updated: March 27, 2021. Accessed March 14, 2023.

Klein, Benjamin, Robert A. Crawford, and Armen A. Alchian. 1978. "Vertical Integration, Appropriable Rents, and the Competitive Contracting Process." *Journal of Law and Economics* 21: 297–326.

Macaulay, Stewart. 1963. "Non-Contractual Relations in Business: A Preliminary Study." *American Sociological Review* 28 (1): 55–67.

Macaulay, Stewart. 2003. "The Real and the Paper Deal: Empirical Pictures of Relationships, Complexity and the Urge for Transparent Simple Rules." *Modern Law Review* 66 (1): 44–79.

Macneil, Ian R. 1960. "Review of Law in Society: An Introduction to Freedom of Contract, by H. Shepherd and B. D. Sher." *Cornell Law Quarterly* 46: 176–79.

Macneil, Ian R. 1974. "The Many Futures of Contracts." *Southern California Law Review* 47: 691–816.

Macneil, Ian R. 1969. "Whither Contracts?" *Journal of Legal Education* 21: 403–18.

Osborne, Stephen P. 2006. "The New Public Governance?" *Public Management Review* 8 (3): 377–87.

Pongsiri, Nutavoot. 2002. "Regulation and Public-Private Partnerships." *International Journal of Public Sector Management* 15 (6): 487–95. https://doi.org/10.1108/09513550210439634.

Sandfort, Jodi. 1999. "The Structural Impediments to Human Service Collaboration: Examining Welfare Reform at the Front Lines." *Social Service Review* 73 (3): 314–39. https://doi.org/10.1086/514426.

Sappington, David E. M. 1991. "Incentives in Principal-Agent Relationships." *Journal of Economic Perspectives* 5 (2): 45–66.

Savas, E. S. 2000. *Privatisation and Public-Private Partnerships.* Chatham House Publishers.

Schilke, Oliver, and Fabrice Lumineau. 2018. "The Double-Edged Effect of Contracts on Alliance Performance." *Journal of Management* 44 (7): 2827–58.

Weber, Libby, and Kyle Mayer. 2014. "Transaction Cost Economics and the Cognitive Perspective: Investigating the Sources and Governance of Interpretative Uncertainty." *Academy of Management Review* 39 (3): 344–63. https://doi.org/10.5465/amr.2011.0463.

Williamson, Oliver E. 1975. *Markets and Hierarchies: Analysis and Antitrust Implications.* The Free Press.

Williamson, Oliver E. 1979. "Transaction-Cost Economics: The Governance of Contractual Relations." *Journal of Law and Economics* 22 (2): 233–61.

Williamson, Oliver E. 1981. "The Economics of Organization: The Transaction Cost Approach." *American Journal of Sociology* 87 (3): 548–77.

Williamson, Oliver E. 1985. *The Economic Institutions of Capitalism: Firms, Markets, Relational Contracting.* Free Press.

Williamson, Oliver E. 1993. "The Evolving Science of Organization." *Journal of Institutional and Theoretical Economics* 149 (1): 36–63.

CHAPTER 3

Barzelay, Michael. 2007. "Learning from Second-Hand Experience: Methodology for Extrapolation-Oriented Case Research." *Governance* 20 (3): 521–43.

Beach, Derek. 2020. *Process Tracing Methods.* Springer Fachmedien.

Beach, Derek, and Rasmus Brun Pedersen. 2013. *Process-Tracing Methods: Foundations and Guidelines.* University of Michigan Press.

Bennett, Andrew, and Jeffrey T. Checkel. 2015. *Process Tracing: From Metaphor to Analytic Tool.* Cambridge University Press.

Bennett, Andrew, and Jeffrey T. Checkel, eds. 2016. *Process Tracing.* Cambridge University Press.

Carter, Eleanor, Clare FitzGerald, Ruth Dixon, Charles Economy, Tijen Hameed, and Mara Airoldi. 2018. *Building the Tools for Public Services to Secure Better Outcomes: Collaboration, Prevention, Innovation*. Government Outcomes Lab, Blavatnik School of Government, University of Oxford. https://golab.bsg.ox.ac.uk/documents/176/BSG-GOLab-EvidenceReport.pdf.

Collier, David. 2011. "Understanding Process Tracing." *PS: Political Science & Politics* 44 (4): 823–30.

Dryer, David. 2012. Findings of Fact, Conclusions of Law, and Judgment for IBM. Marion Superior Court, Civil Division 10, Cause No. 49D10-1005-PL-021451. State of Indiana, County of Marion, acting on behalf of the Indiana Family & Social Services Administration.

Frydlinger, David, and Oliver Hart. 2023. "Overcoming Contractual Incompleteness: The Role of Guiding Principles." *The Journal of Law, Economics, and Organization*. https://doi.org/10.1093/jleo/ewac027.

Flyvbjerg, Bent. 2006. "Five Misunderstandings About Case-Study Research." *Qualitative Inquiry* 12 (2): 219–45.

George, Alexander L., and Andrew Bennett. 2005. *Case Studies and Theory Development in the Social Sciences*. MIT Press.

Goldsmith, Stephen, and Tim Burke. 2009. "Moving from Core Functions to Core Values." In *Unlocking the Power of Networks: Keys to High-Performance Government*, edited by Stephen Goldsmith and Donald F. Kettl, ch. 5. Brookings Institution Press.

Hart, Oliver, and John Moore. 2008. "Contracts as Reference Points." *The Quarterly Journal of Economics* 123 (1): 1–48.

Indiana Legislative Services Agency. 2004. FSSA Evaluation Committee Issues Relating to the Organizational Structure of the Office of the Secretary of Family and Social Services.

Jarrett, Tim. 2012. The Supporting People Programme (No. 12/40). House of Commons Library. http://researchbriefings.files.parliament.uk/documents/RP12-40/RP12-40.pdf.

Kirklees Better Outcomes Partnership. 2020. About Us. KBOP. https://www.kirkleesbetteroutcomespartnership.org.

Mahoney, James. 2012. "The Logic of Process Tracing Tests in the Social Sciences." *Sociological Methods & Research* 41(4): 570–97.

Mahoney, James, and Gary Goertz. 2006. "A Tale of Two Cultures: Contrasting Quantitative and Qualitative Research." *Political Analysis* 14 (3): 227–49.

National Audit Office (NAO). 2015. Outcome-Based Payment Schemes: Government's Use of Payment by Results. https://www.nao.org.uk/wp-content/uploads/2015/06/Outcome-based-payment-schemes-governments-use-of-payment-by-results.pdf.

O'Connor, Alice. 2001. *Poverty Knowledge: Social Science, Social Policy, and the Poor in Twentieth-Century U.S. History*. Princeton University Press.

Office of the Deputy Prime Minister (ODPM) Committee. 2004. Supporting Vulnerable and Older People: The Supporting People Programme, Tenth Report of Session 2003-04, Vol. 1: Report, Together with Formal Minutes, Oral and Written

Evidence. House of Commons. https://publications.parliament.uk/pa/cm200304/cmselect/cmodpm/504/504.pdf.

Overby, Stephanie. 2012. "IBM Beats Indiana in Outsourcing Case No One 'Deserves to Win.'" *CIO* (July 26). https://www.cio.com/article/286833/legal-ibm-beats-indiana-in-outsourcing-case-no-one-deserves-to-win.html cio.com

Pollitt, Christopher. "The Evolving Narratives of Public Management Reform: 40 Years of Reform White Papers in the UK." *Public Management Review* 15(6): 899–922. https://doi.org/10.1080/14719037.2012.725761.

Ragin, Charles C. 2009. "Reflections on Casing and Case-Oriented Research." In *The SAGE Handbook of Case-Based Methods*, edited by David Byrne and Charles C. Ragin, 522–34. SAGE.

Rosenbach, Franziska, and Eleanor Carter. 2021. Kirklees Integrated Support Service and Better Outcomes Partnership: The First Report from a Longitudinal Evaluation of a Life Chances Fund Impact Bond. HM Government. https://assets.publishing.service.gov.uk/government/uploads/system/uploads/attachment_data/file/1003288/Kirklees_Integrated_Support_Service_report.pdf.

Seawright, Jason, and John Gerring. 2008. "Case Selection Techniques in Case Study Research: A Menu of Qualitative and Quantitative Options." *Political Research Quarterly* 61 (2): 294–308.

Senge, Peter M. 1990. *The Fifth Discipline*. Doubleday Business.

Schillemans, Thomas, and Mark A. P. Bovens. 2015. "The Challenge of Multiple Accountability: Does Redundancy Lead to Overload?" In *Accountable Governance: Problems and Promises*, edited by Mark J. Dubnick and H. George Frederickson, 3–21. M. E. Sharpe.

Soss, Joe. 2021. "On Casing a Study versus Studying a Case." In *Rethinking Comparison: Innovative Methods for Qualitative Political Inquiry*, 84–106. Cambridge University Press.

CHAPTER 4

Baraki, B., and J. Phagoora. 2022. *Evaluating the Person-Led, Transitional and Strength Based (PTS) Response.* New Economics Foundation and Mayday Trust. https://maydaytrust.org.uk/wp-content/uploads/2022/02/Evaluating-the-PTS-Model_Final-Report_23Feb2022_final.pdf.

Baker, George P. 2002. "Distortion and Risk in Optimal Incentive Contracts." *Journal of Human Resources* 37: 728–51.

Beamish, Paul W. 1987. "Joint Ventures in LDCs: Partner Selection and Performance." *Management International Review* 27: 23–37.

Bevan, Gwyn, and Christopher Hood. 2006. "What's Measured Is What Matters: Targets and Gaming in the English Public Health Care System." *Public Administration* 84: 517–38.

Brown, Trevor L., and Matthew Potoski. 2003. "Transaction Costs and Institutional Explanations for Government Service Production Decisions." *Journal of Public Administration Research and Theory* 13 (4): 441–68.

Brown, Trevor L., Matthew Potoski, and David M. Van Slyke. "Managing Complex Contracts: A Theoretical Approach." *Journal of Public Administration Research and Theory* 26 (2): 294–308.

Brown, Trevor L., Matthew Potoski, and David M. Van Slyke. 2018. "Complex Contracting: Management Challenges and Solutions." *Public Administration Review* 78 (5): 739–47.

Brunjes, Benjamin M. 2020. "Competition and Federal Contractor Performance." *Journal of Public Administration Research and Theory* 30 (2): 202–19.

Covey, Stephen R., and Rebecca R. Merrill. 2006. *The Speed of Trust: The One Thing That Changes Everything*. Simon & Schuster.

Das, Taposh K., and Bing-Sheng Teng. 2003. "Partner Analysis and Alliance Performance." *Scandinavian Journal of Management* 19 (3): 279–308.

Domingos, Fernando Deodato, Carolyn Heinrich, Stéphane Saussier, and M. Shiva. "The Interplay of Discretion and Complexity in Public Contracting." *Journal of Public Administration Research and Theory* 35(2) (April): 148–63.

Doz, Yves L. 1996. "The Evolution of Cooperation in Strategic Alliances: Initial Conditions or Learning Processes?" *Strategic Management Journal* 17 (Summer Special Issue): 55–83.

Ebrahim, Alnoor. 2019. *Measuring Social Change: Performance and Accountability in a Complex World*. Stanford University Press.

Goldsmith, Stephen, and Donald F. Kettl. 2009. *Unlocking the Power of Networks: Keys to High-Performance Government*. Brookings Institution.

Granovetter, Mark. "The Strength of Weak Ties." *American Journal of Sociology* 78 (6): 1360–80.

Gulati, Ranjay. 1995. "Does Familiarity Breed Trust? The Implications of Repeated Ties for Contractual Choice in Alliances." *Academy of Management Journal* 38 (1): 85–112. https://doi.org/10.2307/256729.

Hadfield, Gillian K., and Iva Bozovic. 2016. "Scaffolding: Using Formal Contracts to Support Informal Relations in Support of Innovation." *Wisconsin Law Review* 5: 981–1032.

Hart, Oliver, and John Moore. 1988. "Incomplete Contracts and Renegotiation." *Econometrica* 56: 755–86.

Hefetz, Amir, and Mildred Warner. 2004. "Privatization and Its Reverse: Explaining the Dynamics of the Government Contracting Process." *Journal of Public Administration Research and Theory* 14 (2): 171–90.

Heinrich, Carolyn J., and Gerald Marschke. 2010. "Incentives and Their Dynamics in Public Sector Performance Management Systems." *Journal of Policy Analysis and Management* 29 (1): 183–208.

Heinrich, Carolyn J., and Sarah E. Kabourek. 2019. "Pay-for-Success Development in the United States: Feasible or Failing to Launch?" *Public Administration Review* 79 (6): 867–79.

Huxham, Chris, and Siv Vangen. 2013. *Managing to Collaborate: The Theory and Practice of Collaborative Advantage*. Routledge.

Joskow, Paul L. 1987. "Contract Duration and Relationship-Specific Investments: Empirical Evidence from Coal Markets." *The American Economic Review* 77 (1): 168–85.

Kogut, Bruce. 1989. "The Stability of Joint Ventures: Reciprocity and Competitive Rivalry." *Journal of Industrial Economics* 38 (2): 183–98.

Lazzarini, Sérgio. 2022. *The Right Privatization: Why Private Firms in Public Initiatives Need Capable Governments.* Cambridge University Press.

Luo, Yadong. 1997. "Partner Selection and Venturing Success: The Case of Joint Ventures with Firms in the People's Republic of China." *Organization Science* 8: 648–62.

Macneil, Ian R. 1980. *The New Social Contract: An Inquiry into Modern Contractual Relations.* Yale University Press.

Macneil, Ian R., and David Campbell. 2001. *The Relational Theory of Contract: Selected Works of Ian Macneil.* Sweet & Maxwell.

Mannix, Mary R., Cary LaCheen, Henry A. Freedman, and Marc Cohan.2008. "Public Benefits Privatization and Modernization: Recent Developments and Advocacy." *Clearinghouse Review* 42: 4.

Marlow, Andrew. "Kirklees Council 'Will Not Go Bust,' Says Chief Financial Officer as Meeting Hears Its Financial Position Is Looking Up." Dewsbury Reporter, December 8, 2023.

Milward, H. Brinton, and Keith G. Provan. 2000. "Governing the Hollow State." *Journal of Public Administration Research and Theory* 10 (2): 359–79.

Rainey, Hal G., Sergio Fernandez, and Deanna Malatesta. 2021. *Understanding and Managing Public Organizations.* Wiley Publishing.

Ring, Peter S., and Andrew H. Van de Ven. 1994. "Developmental Processes of Cooperative Interorganizational Relationships." *Academy of Management Review* 19 (1): 90–118. https://doi.org/10.2307/258836.

Rogerson, William P. 1992. "Contractual Solutions to the Hold-Up Problem." *The Review of Economic Studies* 59 (4) (September): 777–93. https://doi.org/10.2307/2297997.

Rosenbach, Franziska, and Eleanor Carter. 2020. *Kirklees Integrated Support Service and Better Outcomes Partnership: The First Report from a Longitudinal Evaluation of a Life Chances Fund Impact Bond.* Government Outcomes Lab, Blavatnik School of Government, University of Oxford.

Rosenbach, Franziska, Floor A. van Lier, Francisco Domingos, and Eleanor Carter. 2023. *The Kirklees Better Outcomes Partnership: The Second Report of a Longitudinal Evaluation of a Life Chances Fund Impact Bond.* Government Outcomes Lab, Blavatnik School of Government, University of Oxford.

Rosenbach, Franziska, Eleanor Carter, Floor-Anne van Lier, and Marina Patouna. 2025. *The Kirklees Better Outcomes Partnership: The Final Qualitative Process Evaluation Report of the Kirklees Better Outcomes Partnership, a Life Chances Fund Impact Bond.* Government Outcomes Lab, Blavatnik School of Government, University of Oxford.

Timmins, Nicholas. 2016. *Universal Credit: From Disaster to Recovery*. Institute for Government.

van Lier, Floor-Anne, Mark Gibson, Eleanor Carter, Franziska Rosenbach, and Francisco Domingos. Forthcoming. The Contract as a Living Instrument: Formal and Informal-Relational Practice in a Complex Public Service Delivery Contract.

Williamson, Oliver. 1981. "The Economics of Organization: The Transaction Cost Approach." *American Journal of Sociology* 87 (3): 548–77.

CHAPTER 5

Brown, Trevor and Matthew Potoski.2004. "Managing the Public Service Market." *Public Administration Review* 64 (6): 656–68.

Carter, Eleanor and Adam Whitworth. 2015. "Creaming and Parking in Quasi-Marketised Welfare-to-Work Schemes: Designed Out Of or Designed In to the UK Work Programme?" *Journal of Social Policy* 44 (2): 277–96.

Feiock, Richard, James Clingermayer, and Carl Dasse. 2003. "Sector Choices for Public Service Delivery: The Transaction Cost Implications of Executive Turnover." *Public Management Review* 5 (2): 163–76.

Hatry, Harry P. 1999. *Performance Measurement: Getting Results*. The Urban Institute Press.

Heifetz, Ronald, Alexander Grashow, and Marty Linsky. 2009. *The Practice of Adaptive Leadership*. Harvard Business Press.

Helper, Susan, and David I. Levine. 1992. "Long-Term Supplier Relations and Product-Market Structure." *The Journal of Law, Economics, and Organization* 8 (3): 561–81.

Hevenstone, Debra, Alec Fraser, Lukas Hobi, and Gemma Geuke. 2023. "Why Is Impact Measurement Abandoned in Practice? Evidence Use in Evaluation and Contracting for Five European Social Impact Bonds." *Evaluation* 29 (1): 91–109.

Koning, Pierre, and Carolyn J. Heinrich. 2013. "Cream-Skimming, Parking and Other Intended and Unintended Effects of High-Powered, Performance-Based Contracts." *Journal of Policy Analysis and Management* 32 (3): 461–83.

Moynihan, Donald P. 2008. *The Dynamics of Performance Management: Constructing Information and Reform*. Georgetown University Press.

Ostrom, Elinor, and James Walker, eds. 2003. *Trust and Reciprocity: Interdisciplinary Lessons from Experimental Research*. Russell Sage Foundation.

Romzek, Barbara S.1998. "Where the Buck Stops: Accountability in Reformed Public Organizations." In *Transforming Government: Lessons from the Reinvention Labs*, edited by Patricia W. Ingraham, James R. Thompson, and Ronald P. Sanders, 145–58. San Francisco: Jossey-Bass.

Rosenbach, F., Felix van Lier, Fernando Domingos, and Eleanor Carter. 2023. *The Kirklees Better Outcomes Partnership: The Second Report of a Longitudinal Evaluation of a Life Chances Fund Impact Bond*. HM Government.

Turner, J. R. 2004. "Farsighted Project Contract Management: Incomplete in Its Entirety." *Construction Management and Economics* 22 (1): 75–83.

van Lier, Floor-Anne, Mark Gibson, Eleanor Carter, Franziska Rosenbach, and Francisco Domingos. 2025. The Contract as a Living Instrument: Formal and Informal-Relational Practice in a Complex Public Service Delivery Contract. Working paper, University of Oxford.

Welsh, G. 2012. "Advance Indiana: State Paid Barnes & Thornburg $9.6 Million For Losing Case Against IBM." *Advance Indiana*, July 19, 2012. https://advanceindiana.blogspot.com/2012/07/state-paid-barnes-thornburg-96-million.html

Williamson, Oliver E. 1985. *The Economic Institutions of Capitalism: Firms, Markets, Relational Contracting*. Free Press.

Zhu, Pearl. 2017. *Performance Master: Take a Holistic Approach to Unlock Digital Performance*. Lulu.com. Ebook.

CHAPTER 6

Aghion, Philippe, and Jean Tirole. 1997. "Formal and Real Authority in Organizations." *Journal of Political Economy* 105 (1): 1–29.

Agranoff, Robert. 2007. *Managing within Networks: Adding Value to Public Organizations*. Georgetown University Press.

Aulakh, Preet S., Masaaki Kotabe, and Arvind Sahay. 1996. "Trust and Performance in Cross-Border Marketing Partnerships: A Behavioral Approach." *Journal of International Business Studies* 27: 1005–32.

Bertelli, Anthony Michael, and Craig R. Smith. 2010. "Relational Contracting and Network Management." *Journal of Public Administration Research and Theory* 20 (suppl. 1): 21–40.

Bozeman, Barry, and Daniel Sarewitz. 2011. "Public Value Mapping and Science Policy Evaluation." *Minerva* 49 (1): 1–23. https://doi.org/10.1007/s11024-011-9161-7.

Brogaard, Jonathan, Matthew Denes, and Ran Duchin. 2021. "Political Influence and the Renegotiation of Government Contracts." *The Review of Financial Studies* 34 (6): 3095–137.

Brown, Trevor L., Matthew Potoski, and David M. Van Slyke. 2013. *Complex Contracting*. Cambridge University Press.

Das, T. K., and Bing-Sheng Teng. 1998. "Resource and Risk Management in the Strategic Alliance Making Process." *Journal of Management* 24 (1): 21–42.

Domingos, Fernando Deodato, Carolyn Heinrich, Stéphane Saussier, and M. Shiva. 2025. "The Interplay of Discretion and Complexity in Public Contracting." *Journal of Public Administration Research and Theory* 35 (2) (April): 148–63. https://doi.org/10.1093/jopart/muaf004.

Ellis, Judith. 2006. "All Inclusive Benchmarking." *Journal of Nursing Management* 14 (5): 377–83. https://doi.org/10.1111/j.1365-2934.2006.00596.x.

Friedland, Roger, and Robert R. Alford. 1991. "Bringing Society Back In: Symbols, Practices, and Institutional Contradictions." In *The New Institutionalism in Organizational Analysis*, edited by Walter W. Powell and Paul J. DiMaggio, 232–66. University of Chicago Press.

Frydlinger, David, Kate Vitasek, Jim Bergman, and Tim Cummins. 2021. *Contracting in the New Economy: Using Relational Contracts to Boost Trust and Collaboration in Strategic Business Relationships*. Palgrave Macmillan.

Frydlinger, David, and Oliver Hart. 2024. "Overcoming Contractual Incompleteness: The Role of Guiding Principles." *The Journal of Law, Economics, and Organization* 40 (3): 625–47.

Frydlinger, David, Oliver Hart, and Kate Vitasek. 2019. "A New Approach to Contracts: How to Build Better Long-Term Strategic Partnerships." *Harvard Business Review* 97 (5): 116–26.

Fukumoto, Emiko, and Barry Bozeman. 2019. "Public Values Theory: What Is Missing?" *The American Review of Public Administration* 49 (6): 635–48.

Gold, Matea, Melanie Mason, and Tom Hamburger. 2011. "Indiana's Bumpy Road to Privatization." *Los Angeles Times*, June 24, 2011. https://www.latimes.com/archives/la-xpm-2011-jun-24-la-na-indiana-privatize-20110624-story.html.

Jeannotte, M. Sharon. 2016. "Story-Telling about Place: Engaging Citizens in Cultural Mapping." *City, Culture and Society* 7 (1): 35–41.

Jørgensen, Torben Beck, and Barry Bozeman. 2007. "Public Values: An Inventory." *Administration & Society* 39 (3): 354–81.

Kahneman, Daniel, and Jack L. Knetsch. 1992. "Valuing Public Goods: The Purchase of Moral Satisfaction." *Journal of Environmental Economics and Management* 22 (1): 57–70.

Kaufmann, Daniel. 2005. "Six Questions on the Cost of Corruption with World Bank Institute Global Governance Director Daniel Kaufmann." News-The World Bank, Washington, D.C.

Kirkpatrick, Colin, David Parker, and Yin-Fang Zhang. 2004. "Regulatory Impact Assessment in Developing and Transition Economies: A Survey of Current Practice." *Public Money & Management* 24 (5): 291–96. https://doi.org/10.1111/j.1467-9302.2004.00436.x.

Kogut, Bruce. 1988. "Joint Ventures: Theoretical and Empirical Perspectives." *Strategic Management Journal* 9: 319–32.

Litardi, Irene, Gloria Fiorani, and Daniele Alimonti. 2020. "The State of the Art of Green Public Procurement in Europe: Documental Analysis of European Practices." In *Accountability, Ethics and Sustainability of Organizations: New Theories, Strategies and Tools for Survival and Growth*, 175–92.

Malatesta, Deanna, and Craig R. Smith. 2014. "Designing Contracts for Complex Services." *Public Administration* 92 (3): 531–48.

Masson, Doug. 2010. "Advance Indiana, Moldthan, Roob and FSSA Privatization." Mason's Blog: A Citizen's Guide to Indiana, July 13, 2010. https://www.masson.us/blog/advance-indiana-moldthan-roob-and-fssa-privatization/.

Mazzucato, Mariana. 2018. *The Value of Everything: Making and Taking in the Global Economy*. Penguin.

Macneil, Ian Roderick. 1978. "Contracts: Adjustment of Long-Term Economic Relations under Classical, Neoclassical, and Relational Contract Law." *Northwestern University Law Review* 72 (6): 854–905.

Mishra, Ramesh. 1984. *The Welfare State in Crisis.* Wheatsheaf.

McGuire, Michael, and Robert Agranoff. 2011. "The Limitations of Public Management Networks." *Public Administration* 89 (2): 265–84.

Moore, Mark H. 1995. *Creating Public Value: Strategic Management in Government.* Harvard University Press.

Moore, Mark H. 2014. "Public Value Accounting: Establishing the Philosophical Basis." *Public Administration Review* 74 (4): 465–77.

Nabatchi, Tina. 2012. "Putting the 'Public' Back in Public Values Research: Designing Participation to Identify and Respond to Values." *Public Administration Review* 72 (5): 699–708.

Perry, James L. 2000. "Bringing Society In: Toward a Theory of Public Service Motivation." *Journal of Public Administration Research and Theory* 10 (2): 471–88.

Rutgers, Mark R. 2008. "Sorting Out Public Values? On the Contingency of Value Classification in Public Administration." *Administrative Theory & Praxis* 30: 92–113.

Stover, Jesse, Laxmisupriya Avadhanula, and Suruchi Sood. 2024. "A Review of Strategies and Levels of Community Engagement in Strengths-Based and Needs-Based Health Communication Interventions." *Frontiers in Public Health* 12: 1231827.

van Lier, Floor-Anne, Mark Gibson, Eleanor Carter, Franziska Rosenbach, and Francisco Domingos. 2025. *The Contract as a Living Instrument: Formal and Informal Relational Practice in a Complex Public Service Delivery Contract.* Working paper, University of Oxford.

Verkuil, Paul R. 2007. *Outsourcing Sovereignty: Why Privatization of Government Functions Threatens Democracy and What We Can Do About It.* Cambridge University Press.

Vitasek, Kate, and David Frydlinger. 2021. "Contracting in the New Economy: What Is New? Why the Need to Change? And a Suggested Approach for Creating Strategic Contracts." *University of Pacific Law Review* 53:583–618.

White, Miles D. 2013. "The Reinvention Imperative." *Harvard Business Review*, November, https://hbr.org/2013/11/the-reinvention-imperative.

INDEX

For the benefit of digital users, indexed terms that span two pages (e.g., 52–53) may, on occasion, appear on only one of those pages.

Tables, figures, and boxes are indicated by an italic *t*, *f*, and *b* following the page number.

www.ingramcontent.com/pod-product-compliance
Lightning Source LLC
Chambersburg PA
CBHW070228270426
43912CB00028B/157/J
* 9 7 8 0 1 9 7 7 6 3 1 2 4 *